Canon EOS-1

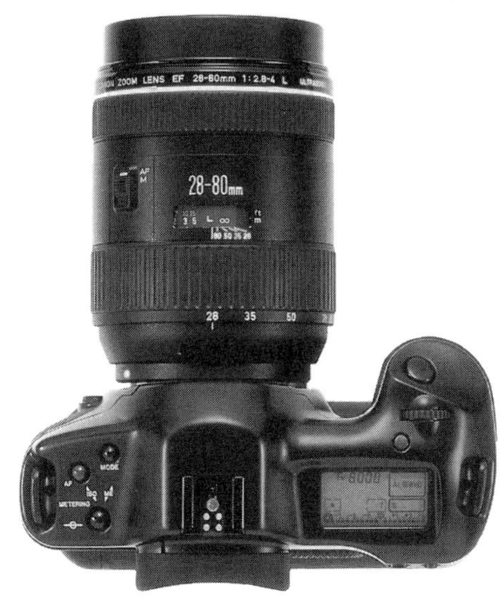

Günter Spitzing

HOVE~FOUNTAIN BOOKS

Canon EOS-1

First English Edition July 1990
English Translation: Liselotte Sperl
Translation Editor: Georgina Fuller
Technical Editor: George Wakefield
Sub-editing & Design: Shirley Kilpatrick
Typeset by Icon Publications Limited, Kelso, Scotland
Printed in Germany by Kösel GmbH, Kempten

ISBN 0-86343-225-5
USA ISBN 0-906447-64-X

Published by
HOVE~FOUNTAIN BOOKS
the joint imprint of

Fountain Press Ltd
Queensborough House
Claremont Road, Surbiton
Surrey KT6 4QU

&

Hove Foto Books
34 Church Road, Hove
Sussex BN3 2GJ

UK Trade Distribution by
Fountain Press Ltd

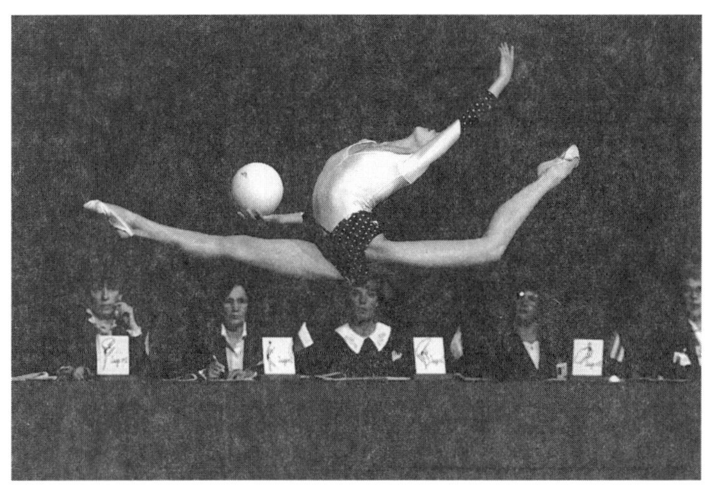

The world's top sports photograph of 1990, above,
was photographed by **Gérard Vandystadt** *of Vandystadt/Allsport,*
the Paris-based agency, using Canon equipment.
His picture, taken using Elinchrom studio electronic flash
and a super-fast telephoto lens on ISO 50 film, won 1st Sport Award of
the World Press Photo 1990. It shows China's Wang Xiuyun at the
Tournoi international 1989 de Gymnastique Rythmique et Sportive de
Corbeil.

Contents

Part V

Special Features of the EOS-1 95

Part VI

Artificial Light and Flash 108

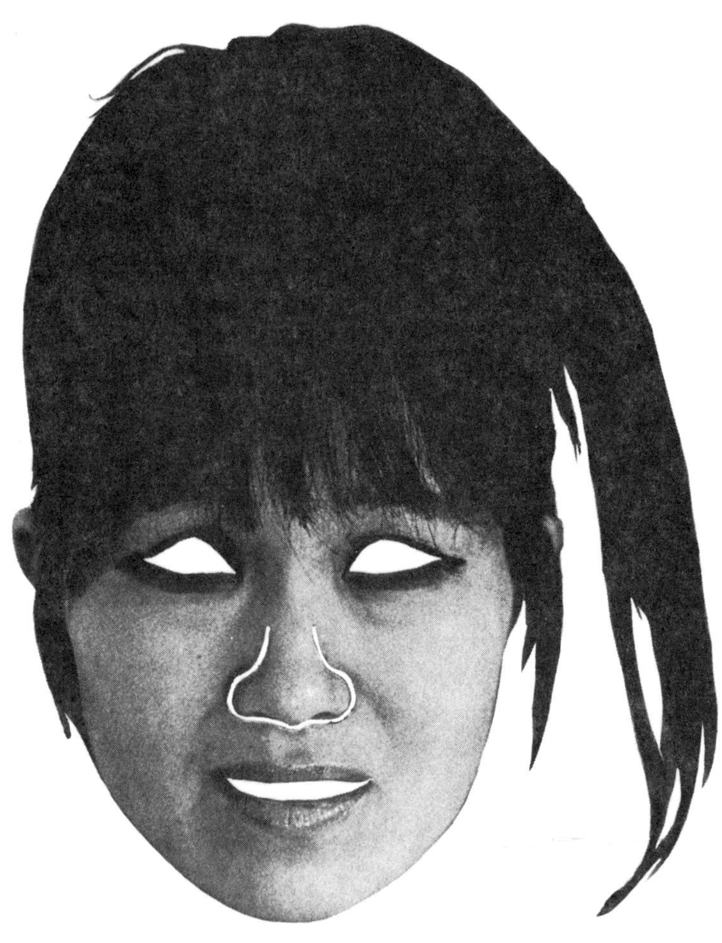

Portrait mask: This mask was cut out from a black-and-white portrait, the result was then photographed.

Foreword

EOS Number ONE – the EOS for the Discerning

The Professional EOS

Each model of the EOS system has its own characteristics, advantages and limitations.

The EOS-1 is a fantastic camera. Personally I took to it straight away – not only does it feel comfortable in your hands, but its design and performance are superb.

The design of the EOS-1 within the framework of the EOS System
• Design of the EOS-System: cameras within this system offer many more facilities, serving the photographer's creative intentions towards better pictures, while at the same time reducing the number of operating controls (buttons and dials). This was achieved by arranging the necessary steps for the individual settings (e.g. manual setting of aperture and shutter speed, selection of aperture or shutter speed priority modes, etc.) in two stages: pressing one of the buttons (some seldom-used function buttons are hidden away under a cover) activates the particular function without actually changing any value. The selected function or value is then changed by turning the main dial, conveniently placed near the release button, either to the right or left to increase or decrease it by the required amount.   *• Design of the EOS-1: the EOS cameras models 600(630), 620, 650, etc. can be used either as automatic cameras – or, set to the appropriate shooting mode, as highly sophisticated photographic tools with a variety of finely attuned functions. The fully automatic operation is made even easier, the access to special functions, such as exposure compensation, is made a little more difficult. The idea behind this reasoning was to prevent unintentional operation of a button in the automatic shooting mode. However, used as a professional tool, the EOS-1 accommodates the expert's every wish, allowing choice of all special functions. It is still possible to photograph quite simply but the special functions are now readily accessible. It is possible to use the EOS-1 quickly making the basic settings and, say, dialling-in an exposure compensation, or to shift the automatically-controlled aperture/shutter speed combination, to change the metering angle or the autofocus operation.*

I have the highest praise for the EOS-1, it deserves its place as "Number 1". The fact that I have bought it myself speaks louder than any words. After a short trial I was convinced not only of its excellent range of functions but also of its robustness.

Versatile and reliable: the professional EOS-1

It is true, there are other EOS models, mainly the 600 and the 620, that are perfectly suited for professional use. However, the number ONE in the EOS system has the additional advantage of being much less sensitive to atmospheric conditions. The aluminium core of the body is embedded in fibreglass-re-enforced plastic that is highly impact- and shatter-proof. The operating and display elements are embedded in the body which makes the whole camera reasonably impervious to rain, spray and dust. Important electronic connections are duplicated to ensure reliability even under harsh climatic conditions. I know how important this is, particularly as I often go on photographic explorations in the Far East or on long hiking tours in the Greek mountains. A camera has to withstand a variety of stresses on excursions like these. However, should the worst come to the worst and the EOS-1 malfunctions, take it to your nearest EOS dealer who can subject it to a computer analysis which should identify the fault straight away. Apart from its great physical toughness, the EOS-1 is particularly versatile in its exposure functions and shooting modes. Compared with the 600 (630) and 620 it offers the amazingly fast shutter speed of 1/8000th sec. and, a facility which I find particularly interesting and important, genuine spot metering. The autofocus has also been considerably improved – it is now possible to focus on structures with either horizontal or vertical lines. Moreover, focusing is even faster and functions perfectly down to an even lower lighting level. Another important detail is the dioptric adjustment of eyesight correction between +3 to –1 dioptres. A further difference between the EOS-1 and other models is that less emphasis has been placed on safeguarding the fully automatic program mode against inadvertent manipulations. The basic thinking was that this camera would be used mainly by professionals or dedicated amateur photographers who would wish to have easy access to the special functions in program mode. A brief summary of the camera follows.

Short Description of the EOS-1

Type: *35mm single lens reflex camera with focal plane shutter, interchangeable lenses with bayonet fitting.*

Lenses: *0.72-times magnification of the subject with a 50mm lens focused on infinity. Focusing on a closer subject, particularly with longer focal lengths, produces pictures with greater magnification. With 50mm lens, viewfinder shows nearly 100% of image recorded by the film.*

Dioptric adjustment: *adjustable by turning knob under the eyepiece cover between –3 and +1 dioptres.*

Shutter: *vertical travelling metal focal plane type; all speeds between 1/8000th and 30 sec. electronically controlled plus long exposures (bulb). Flash synchronization up to 1/250th sec., shutter speeds manually adjustable in 1/3rd step increments.*

AF System: *TTL-CT-SIR (Cross Type Secondary Image Registration) phase detection. 2 shooting modes: ONE SHOT (AF lock) and AI SERVO with Focus Prediction.*

Autofocus Working Range: *exposure values from EV-1 to 18 at ISO 100/21°.*

Autofocus Auxiliary Light: *specified Canon Speedlites automatically project light via an ultra-bright LED, peak emission in the near infrared range (700nm).*

Exposure control: *four metering modes:*

1. *Evaluative metering across the whole frame*
2. *Partial metering (5.8% of the picture area)*
3. *Spot metering (2.3%)*
4. *Centre-weighted average metering.*

Metering Range: *EV0 - EV20 with ƒ1.4 lens and ISO 100/21° film or equivalent conditions*

Exposure modes:

1. ***P*** *intelligent program mode with variable shift function*
2. ***Av*** *aperture priority mode*
3. ***Tv*** *shutter speed priority mode*
4. ***M*** *manual operation*
5. ***Bulb*** *long exposure time*
6. *Flash* ***A-TTL*** *and* ***TTL*** *control with EOS system flashguns*
7. ***DEPTH*** *mode, automatic depth-of-field control.*

Exposure compensation: *+/– 3 ƒ-stops in 1/3rd steps*

Depth of field preview: *by pressing depth of field check button*

Film speed setting: *manually from ISO 6 to 6400, automatically by DX-code from ISO 25 to 5000.*

Film loading: *automatic*

Film rewinding: *automatic*

Film transport: *automatic; single mode (S) or continuous (C).*

Power source: *6V lithium battery 2CR5 in removable handgrip (or 8 1.5V AA-size batteries or same size rechargeable batteries in optional attachable booster).*

Battery test: *press button for appropriate display. Just before batteries become exhausted the display changes to a "battery low" warning (bc).*

Battery capacity: *under ideal circumstances 40 films with 36 exposures at +20° C; 7 at –20° C.*

Battery for Databack (special accessory): *CR1220, 5 year useful life, exchanged at a minimum charge by Canon.*

Special Functions: *eight (CF) functions, either for permanent or short-term operation, programmable by the user.*

Two flash contacts:

1. Centre contact in hotshoe, suitable for flashguns with contact shoe, transfer of all special functions to EOS system flash units (automatic flash ready, exposure control, auxiliary IR flash for AF control in poor lighting).

2. PC terminal for connection via standard cable (no transfer of special functions).

Remote Control Socket: *lower right side of camera.*
Data Display: in the viewfinder and LCD panel

Multiple exposures: *up to nine exposures can be preset (by employing a little trick an unlimited number of exposures are possible)*

Auto Exposure bracketing: *+/–3 stops in 1/3rd step increments. Three exposures are made in sequence.*

Self-timer: *electronically controlled with a 2 or 10 sec. delay. Red light on the front of camera counts down the sequence.*

Weight: *850g without battery, 890g with battery.*

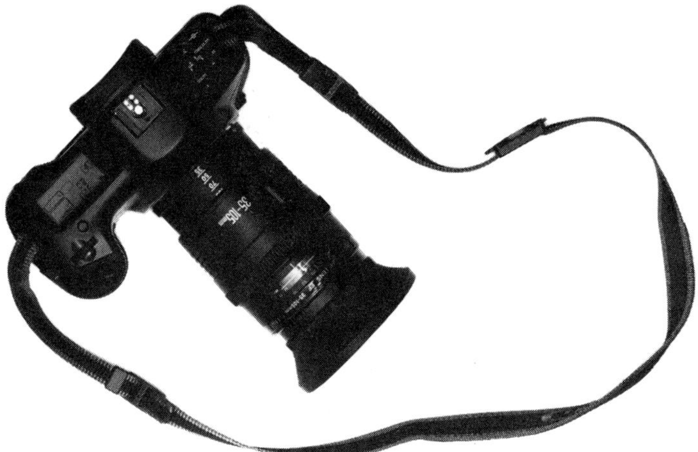

Books should be read

Some books are read from cover to cover, others from back to front. Informative literature is seldom read in this way. The reader usually seeks certain information which he picks out as and when he needs it. I have therefore included a guide as to how this book was organised to help you find your way around:

- Part I contains a short introduction to basic photographic principles. I considered leaving this part out but thought better of it; it may be that a less experienced photographer reaches for this sophisticated camera and he will find it essential to learn a little about creative means in photography. Naturally, I am aware that most users of the EOS-1 are experienced photographers and this gave me the opportunity to delve a little deeper into the subject, to discuss also the reasons why we might take pictures.
- Part II discusses how the camera is prepared to take pictures – loading film and batteries as well as the choice of film material.
- Part III describes, in a clear and logical way, the automatic operation of the EOS-1 in daylight and with flash. It may also serve as a refresher course in case you have not used your EOS-1 for a while.
- Part IV considers the special characteristics of the various operational modes of the EOS-1.
- Part V shows how the many integrated facilities may be used in practice.
- Part VI describes in some depth flash and artificial light photography.
- Part VII is devoted to lenses and how they may be employed for objective and subjective image creation.
- Part VIII describes various accessories and how and when they are useful.
- Part IX covers the EOS system lenses and a guide to the camera.

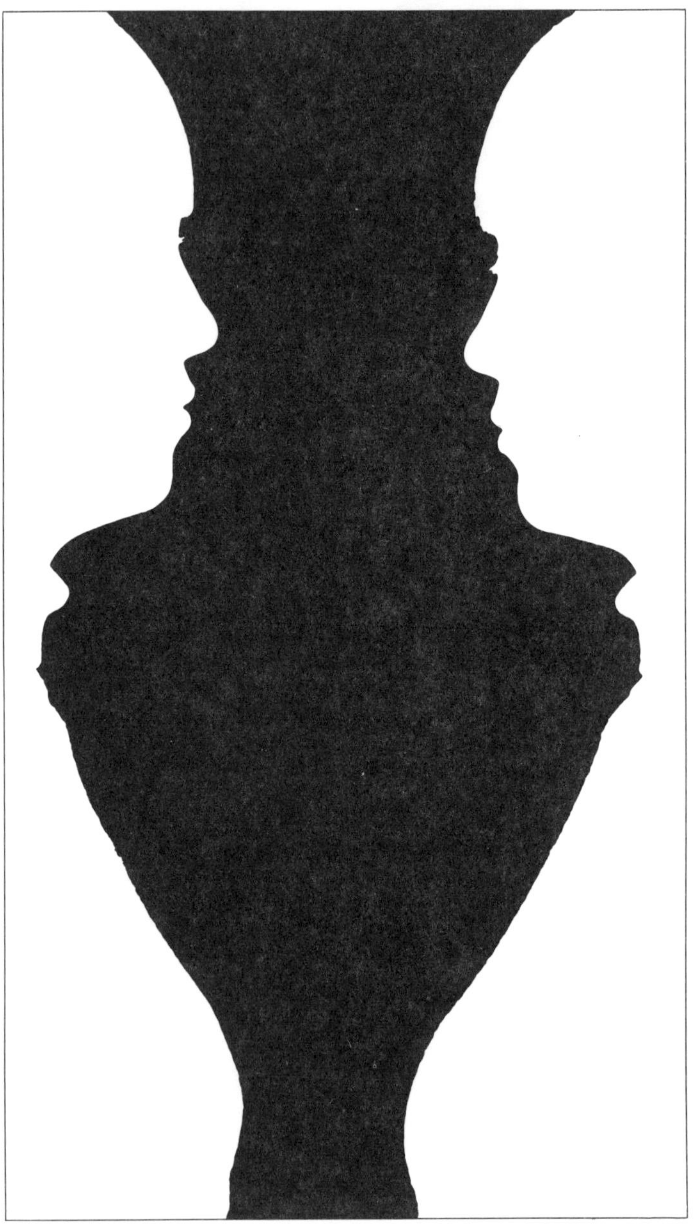

PART 1

Capturing Time and Space – A Short Introduction

Photographic Conquest of Space

Extending the sharpness zone

Your camera – every camera – is a machine capable of capturing an event in time and space. Whenever you photograph you capture an image occurring at a certain time and in a certain space as a permanent picture. How this is done, how the subject is placed within the time-space dimension, is the important factor in picture creation.

The lens focal length determines the framing and how sharp the image will be, which also depends on the distance between the lens and the subject and the relative arrangement of foreground and background. The extension of sharply depicted subject depth depends on the focal length of the lens and the aperture setting.

Greatest possible Depth of Field	*Least Depth of Field*
stopped down aperture	*wide open aperture*
great distance to subject	*subject close to camera*
short focal length lens	*long focal length lens*

The focal length of the lens and the distance of the subject to the camera determine the reproduction scale of the subject. The depth-of-field is greater the smaller the reproduction scale, provided the aperture setting is kept constant. Keeping the reproduction scale constant, the depth-of-field depends on the size of the aperture. In photography the aperture is always an important consideration.

The aperture is a ring of moveable metal blades forming a hole of variable size. But the size of the aperture is only the means, the important thing is how it affects the final picture by the amount of light that is allowed to pass through the hole.

A large depth-of-field will capture a subject in its entirety from front to back sharply in the picture. Any remaining foreground and background depicted more or less sharply, will be incidental – it remains unemphasised – as these areas are not clearly defined. Unsharpness is therefore also important in image creation as it provides a meaningful

The silhouette of a vase? Look more closely. This is a negative print of two silhouettes, the "vase" being merely the space between the two human figures.

contrast to the sharply defined main subject. The main subject is emphasised by the blurred surroundings; in contrast to the unsharp areas the sharp subject detail obtains a surprising tangibility. A large depth-of-field shows the spatial extent of the subject, a narrow depth of field lends the sharp subject detail an almost bodily presence.

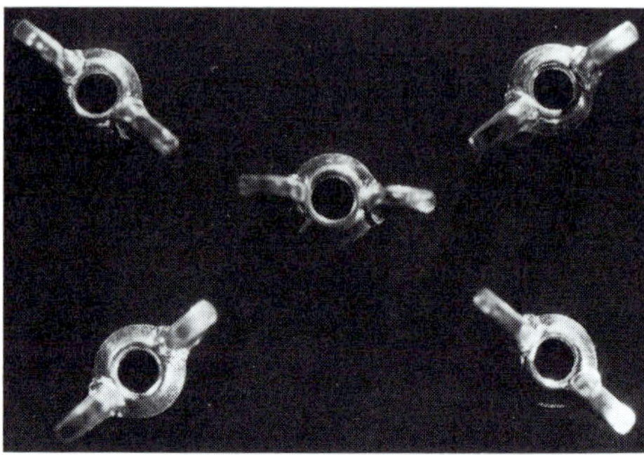

Picture of wing nuts illuminated by several spotlights. If the focusing plane is selected to coincide exactly with the brilliant reflections they appear sharp in the picture

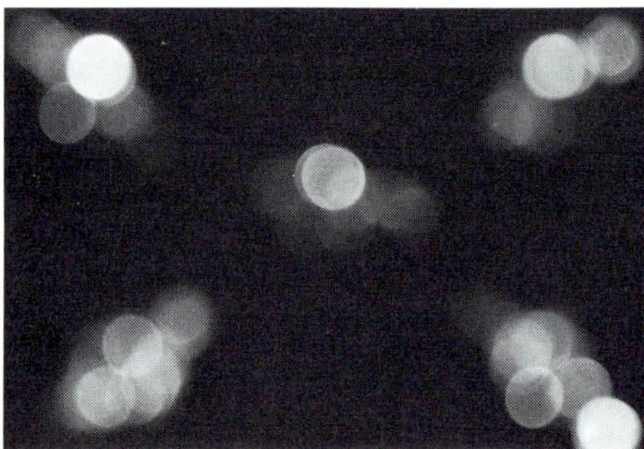

The same subject. Now the focusing plane has been brought forward. The reflections are now shown as circles of light. If I had selected the focusing plane further back the result would have been similar. In both instances the aperture was *f*11.

Lens apertures:
lenses with maximum apertures between f1 and f2 are considered particularly fast. Maximum apertures of f1, f1.1 and f1.2 are found only with standard lenses and medium telephoto lenses up to 85mm – the so-called portrait lenses. Because the maximum aperture value (f-number) is defined as the ratio between the largest aperture opening and focal length of the lens, the speed of longer lenses is restricted. A 400mm lens with a speed of f1 would be impossibly heavy.

Aperture value	Intermediate aperture value	Exposure time in seconds	Remarks
1 (1.0)		**1/8000**	*If we take a situation where a shutter speed of 1/8000th sec. and an aperture value of ƒ1 produce the correct exposure the shutter speeds will vary with increasingly smaller apertures as shown here. The aperture values in bold numbers (for example ƒ11 and ƒ8) in the first column indicate full aperture stops, the size is always reduced by half from one full stop to the next. Two full aperture stops difference means only a quarter of the light is allowed to enter through the aperture opening. The aperture values and shutter speeds of the EOS-1 are particularly accurately adjustable, in one-third stops.*
	1.1	1/6400	
	1.2	1/5000	
1.4		**1/4000**	
	1.6	1/3200	
	1.8	1/2500	
2		**1/2000**	
	2.2	1/1600	
	2.5	1/1250	
2.8		**1/1000**	
	3.2	1/800	
	3.5	1/640	
4		**1/500**	
	4.5	1/400	
5.6		**1/250**	
	6.3	1/200	
	7.1	1/160	
8		**1/125**	
	9	1/100	
	10	1/80	
11		**1/60**	
	13	1/50	
	14	1/40	
16		**1/30**	
	18	1/25	
	20	1/20	
22		**1/15**	
	25	1/13	
	29	1/10	
32		**1/8**	

The size of the aperture determines how much light can enter. However, it is not the only factor. There are other parameters such as the number of elements in the lens construction. Zoom lenses allow less light to pass through than fixed focal length lenses. If, for example, you attach the compact macro EF 50mm, ƒ2.5 to your EOS-1 the program mode may set for the given circumstances ƒ8 and 1/250th sec; under the same conditions but using the EF 35-105mm, ƒ3.5-4.5 zoom at 50mm, the settings would be ƒ8 and 1/180th sec.

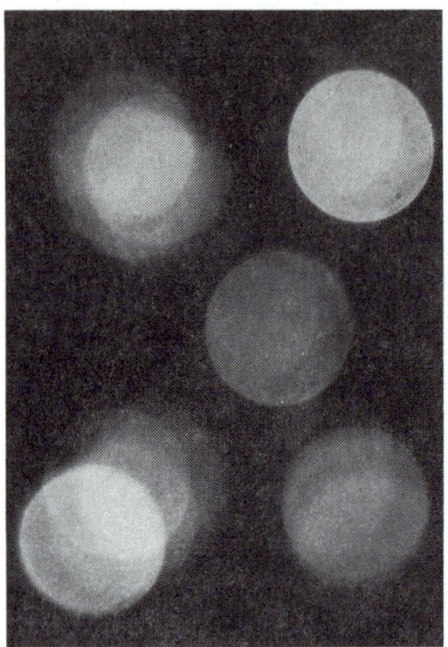

Opening the aperture to *f*4 makes the circles appear even larger and they begin to overlap. A similar effect can be achieved by moving the focusing plane even further away in either direction.

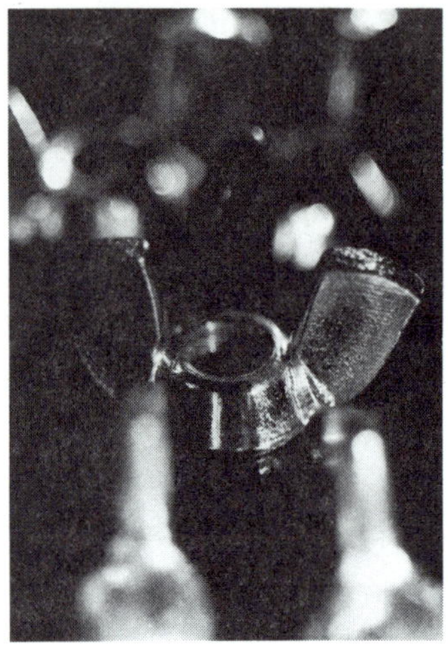

Again the same subject. This time from an oblique angle bringing some of the reflections into sharp focus while others are already outside the depth of field. The light circles become larger with increasing distance from the focusing plane.

Location of sharpness within the subject space

Once you have decided to show your subject in a narrow depth of field you then have to decide where this narrow band of sharpness is to be positioned – in the foreground, in the background or somewhere in between.

Sharpness in the foreground in front of an unsharp background:

A sharply-depicted subject in the foreground against a blurred background is the normal way a small depth of field is used. The character of the foreground subject changes with the degree of

The use of a 300mm lens sets the glowing red ball of the sun impressively into the picture. Every 100mm focal length means an increase of 1mm diameter. Sunsets and sunrises should be slightly under-exposed. Best to use centre-weighted integral metering, applying an exposure compensation of about -1 stop, or use selective metering without applying any compensations. To use spot-metering mode on the relatively large area of the sun would produce an incorrect, too short, exposure. Did you notice that I used another trick in these pictures? I used Ektachrome 160 tungsten film. This is the reason why the surrounding sky turned out such a deep blue. With ordinary daylight film the sky would have had a distinct yellow-reddish bias.

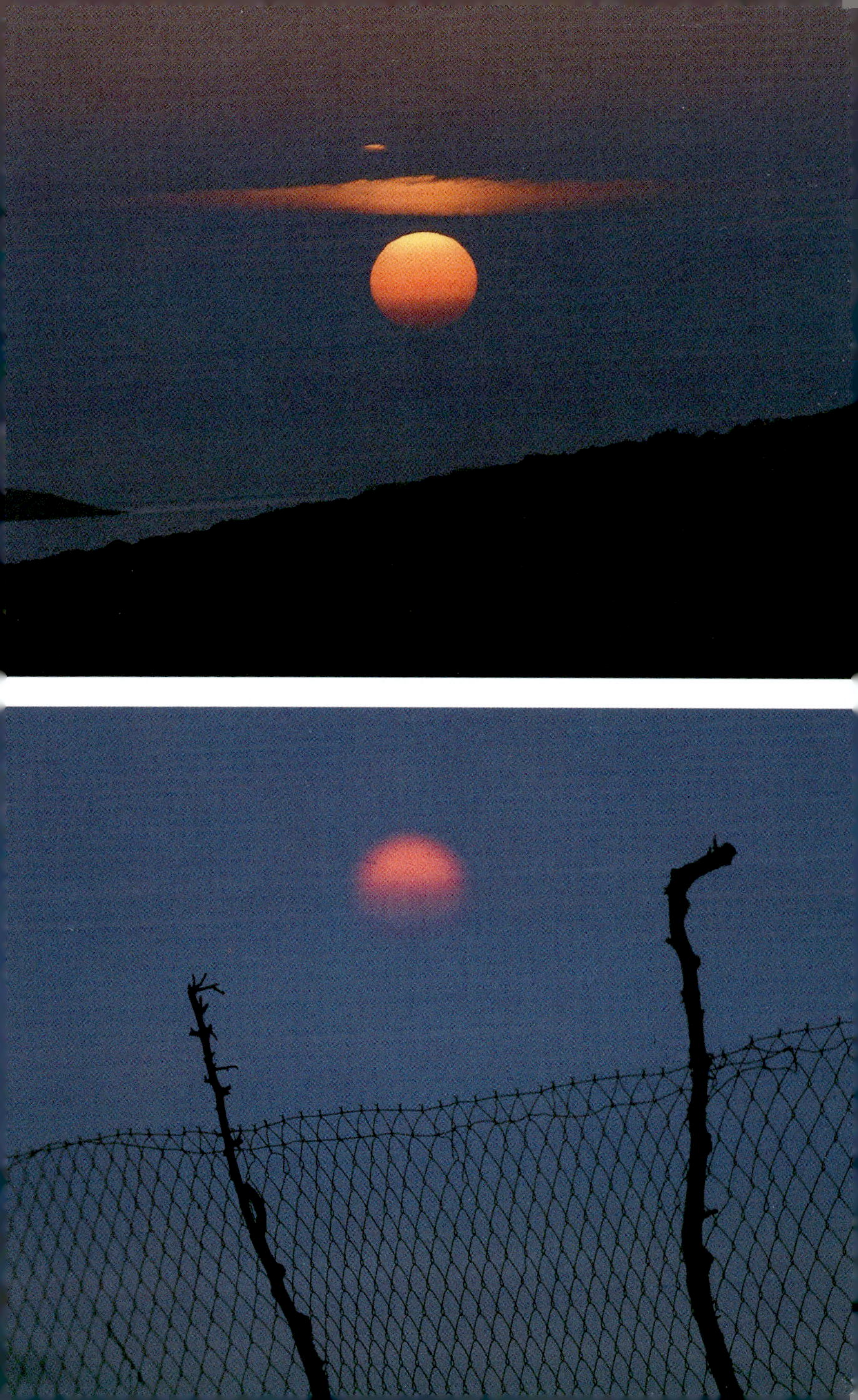

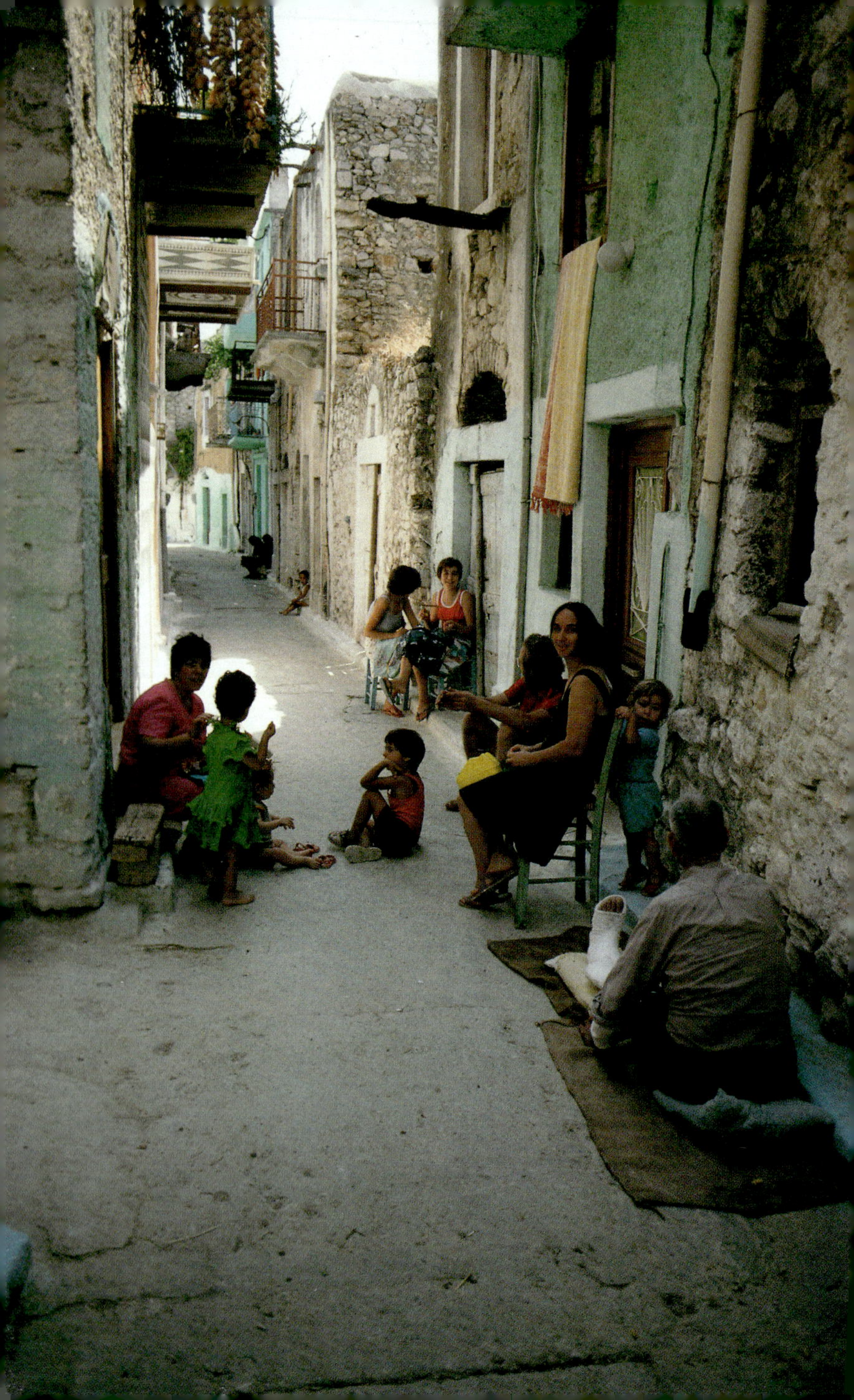

unsharpness of the background. The way the background is presented creates the desired impression for the foreground. A subject can be presented in quite a different way.

Let's assume you take a picture of one of your friends in front of the Acropolis in Athens. If the background is included sharply in the picture we see the result as a form of documentary. It is a witness of time and space as it can be identified as having been taken in a particular era by the fashions and the place is obvious too.

But if the background is shown slightly blurred, although still recognisable as the Acropolis, then the sharply-defined foreground will emphasise the important factor of your friend with the ruins providing the spatial and temporal environment.

If the background is shown even more blurred so that the Acropolis is no longer recognisable then it has lost all its importance. The blurred outlines could be anywhere in the Mediterranean and it could be any time of year. The factual information is totally lost and the background then becomes incidental.

Dedicated portrait photographers who like to use sophisticated methods, use a strong colour in the unsharpness zone – say a bright red – which contains a similar high attention value as the sharply depicted face. In this way the blurred but bright colour provides an effective counterpoint to the sharply-rendered main subject.

Sharpness in the background behind an unsharp foreground:
Compositions like this are usually most attractive because of the tension conveyed by the sharp background trying to break forth from the unsharp details in the foreground. In particular unsharp "windows" in the foreground attract the eye to the information contained in the background. Moreover the spatial effect is emphasised. For example, an unsharp tree trunk in the foreground compels the viewer's gaze further into the landscape beyond to look for the unobstructed view in the background.

Photographic tasks require a variety of, sometimes diametrically opposite, solutions. Often it is necessary to represent a main subject, as mentioned above, by separating it spatially from any incidental objects in front and behind. Then there is the case when an object is deliberately confusing – perhaps because it appears too banal in isolated simplicity. This is usually done by hiding the object in question behind an unsharp foreground.

In this way we may create pictures that owe their effect to the poster-like quality of their colours while others appeal to the viewer by posing riddles that he is invited to solve.

Snapshot with a wide-angle lens: a typical street scene in a Greek village. I managed to release the shutter at exactly the right moment. The picture has a certain tension and charm because most of the "players' are not aware of the camera.

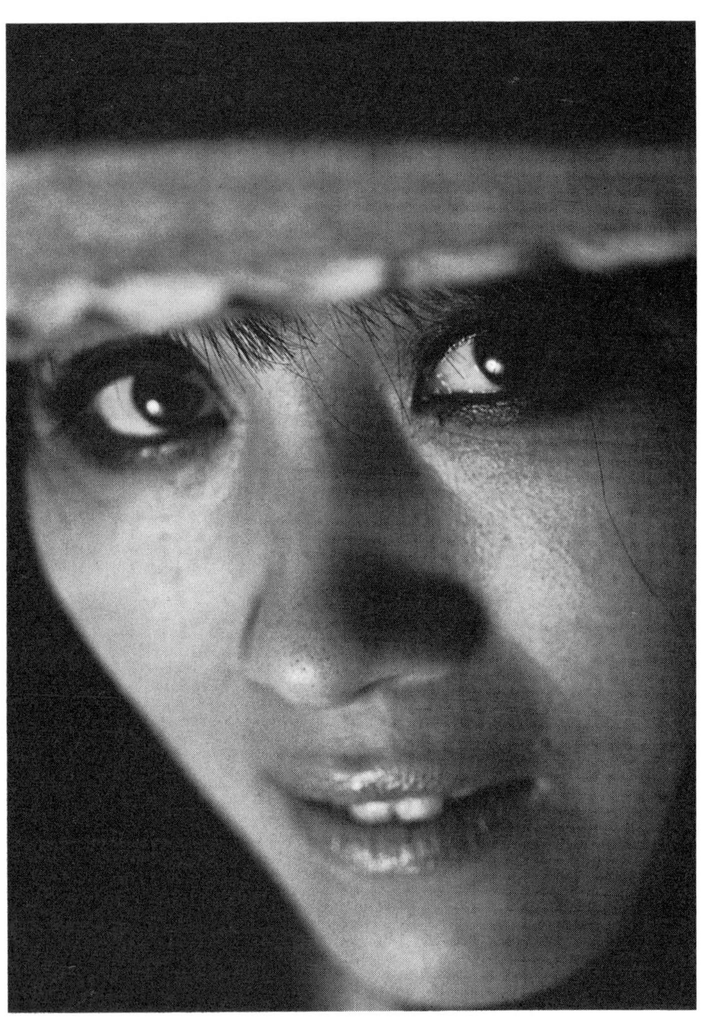

In this case the focus was set for the eyes and the hat brim in the foreground is unsharp.

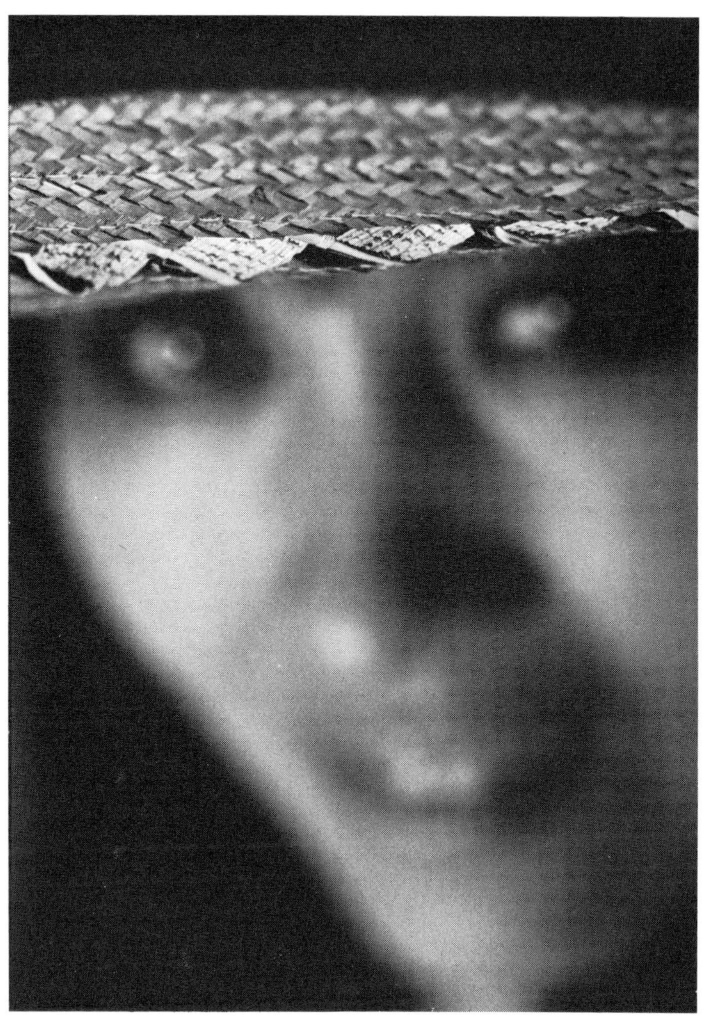

The same subject, but now the face is blurred with only the brim of the hat in sharp focus.

The unsharpness overlapping the sharp background intrudes on the reality of time and space. The images are no longer documentations of a particular place at a particular time but they gain a timeless quality.

Sharp details embedded in undefined clouds in the foreground and background:

Subjects that extend into space, especially well-constructed, detailed ones are particularly suitable for this type of treatment. In this case it is probably best to use a long lens then shift the focusing plane through the subject and to observe the effect in the viewfinder. Often you will find that there are several creative possibilities offered by such subjects. The sharply-depicted detail has a particularly strong spatial effect within its unsharp surroundings although it seems to float in an undefined space.

This makes me think of classical Chinese landscape paintings and sculptures – there too clouds were used to relate individual items within the composition.

Relationship of different objects at different distances

Regardless of whether the entire subject space is to be shown in sharp focus, or if parts should be more or less unsharp, it is important to establish a relationship between the individual components within the composition. Sometimes this arrangement of details could be taken quite literally as, for example, is often the case with close-ups. Let's say I wish to photograph a rose in a vase; I would arrange a suitable background to enhance the impact of the composition. In the case of landscapes the photographer has to move around to find the most suitable shooting position so as to set a suitable foreground detail against the most effective view of the landscape. Moving around in this way means that the space around the camera is turned and changed accordingly.

I like to watch other photographers as they work. Some like spontaneously to catch a subject as it presents itself. Others will walk for miles, climb up hills, ladders, stools, kneel or crouch down to get exactly the right framing to suit their intentions and to obtain the correct shooting position to master the photographic space.

I am not against spontaneous snapshots. Many interesting pictures have been taken this way – an opportunity presents itself and has to be taken without hesitation – but snapshots that are also good pictures are the exception rather than the rule. It may be a good idea to shoot away quickly if the subject seems to be of the fleeting kind but often it may be advantageous to follow the quick shot with some further, more carefully considered exposures. This effort for the correct shooting position may involve as little as a slight shift of the body or it might means a strenuous climb up a hill.

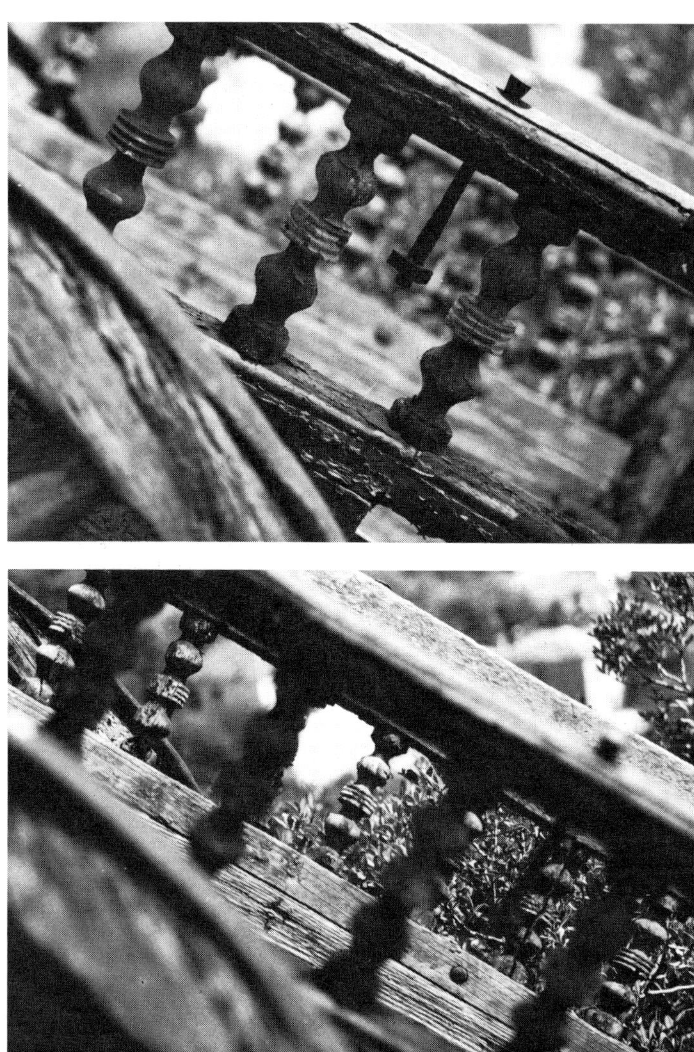

Two shots of an old hand cart. In one picture the sharpness was reduced to the columns in the foreground, in the other to those in the background.

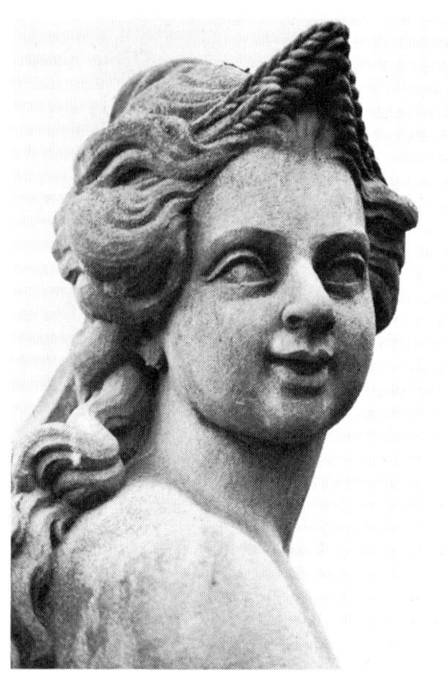

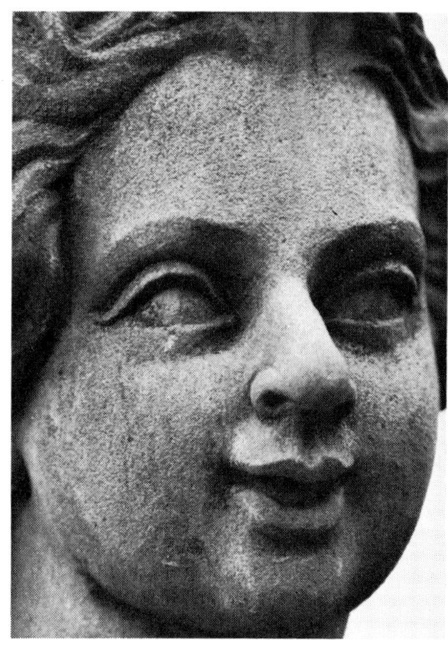

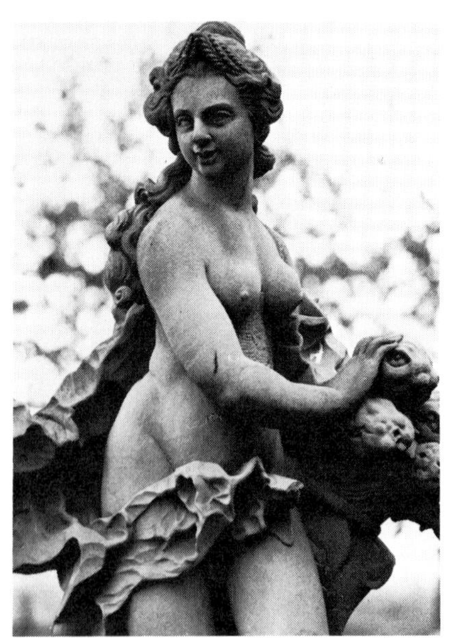

The coquettish statue of Aphrodite in the rose gardens in Bamberg. I circled around the figure with my 70-210mm zoom taking various shots with different focal length settings. The apparent change in the expression of this rigid figure is quite surprising. Please note also how the background changes. In the first two shots we have a relatively dark figure against a bright background. The last picture shows a bright statue against a relatively dark, undefined background formed by the unsharply-rendered foliage of the trees

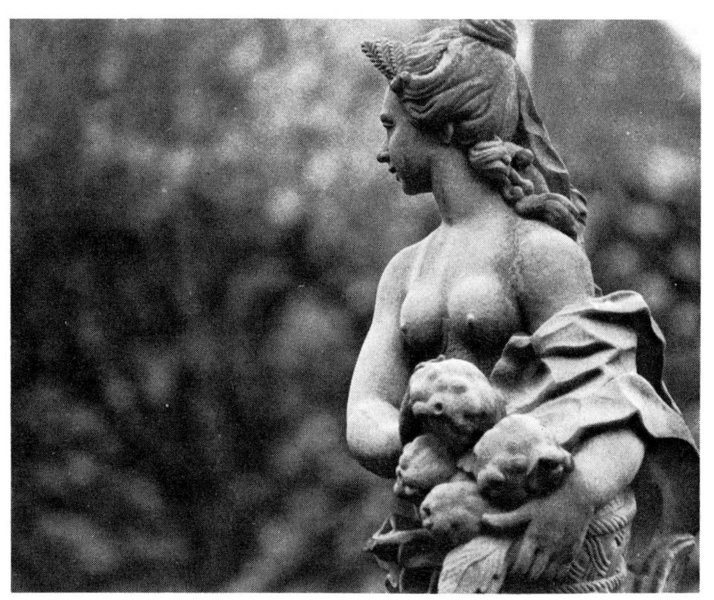

Photographic Conquest of Time

Freezing the subject with a fast shutter speed

The shutter is designed to master this aspect. The shutter excludes the light. Its effect depends on the brief time when it opens to allow the light through so it is strange that it is called "shutter" and not "opener"! The size of the hole formed by the aperture and the length of time the shutter is open to allow the light through it are the elements that form the picture. If there were no aperture or shutter there would be only brightness. The EOS-1 represents the pinnacle of the brief time: its shutter can slice an instant measuring a mere 1/8000th sec. from the flow of time but you are only likely to be able to use it with a really fast film in the brightest sunshine.

Although a welcome by-product of this fast shutter of the EOS-1 is the shortest possible flash synchronization time of only 1/250th sec. The duration of an electronic flash is even shorter – it projects its powerful light for about 1/1000th to 1/10,000th sec. The flash synchronization time of any SLR camera is the time when both shutter blinds – the one that uncovers the film and the one that follows to cover it – are open to allow the film emulsion to be exposed.

These really short exposure times ensure that fast movements, which even the eye cannot capture as clear, unblurred images, are rendered as completely sharp.

Part II

Getting the EOS-1 Ready for Action

Energy from a Lithium Battery

Two batteries – one in the camera and one in reserve

The energy source of the EOS-1 is the 2CR5 lithium battery. This satisfies the entire power requirements for your EOS-1, the displays in LCD panel and viewfinder, the autofocus, the shutter speed and aperture settings and also the motorised film transport. Lithium batteries are not cheap but the demands made on them are considerable and the price is reasonable in comparison. According to Canon you should be able to expose up to 75, 24-exposure films in summer temperatures. In cold conditions, temperatures down to – 20 ° C, this output drops down to 12 rolls of film. Personally I prefer to take the rather cautious estimate and allow one battery for every 30 films, keeping one in reserve, just in case. To compare this with the EOS 600 and the EOS 620, one battery will easily expose 40 films. The EOS-1 is heavier in its construction, heavier components have to be moved, all this costs extra battery power. If I am travelling I always make sure I take at least one more battery than I think I'll need; better to be safe than sorry!

One word of caution though; the official specifications and my own guidelines can be taken as a very rough indication only. After all the power consumption depends largely on how frequently you make use of the many special functions incorporated in the EOS-1. If you keep on playing with a long telephoto lens or a macro lens, continuously trying out various focus settings, or if you use the fast shooting sequence then you should not be surprised if the battery shows early signs of exhaustion. One thing I can state with certainty: you will be lucky to expose more than 20 films with your first two batteries. The temptation to experiment with your new EOS-1 is too strong but this is inevitable to start with. After all it is important that you become completely familiar with your camera. It is advisable to remove the battery from the camera if it is not going to be used for some time, e.g. three weeks or more.

Inserting or replacing the battery

The steps to follow are:

- loosen the screw at the bottom right of the camera body with a coin and remove the handgrip,
- if there is an exhausted battery in the compartment immediately above the housing bottom, hold the grip in the palm of your right

hand and with your left index finger press down on the top of the battery and prise it out,

- insert a new battery by sliding it in at an angle and then push it home. The convex side of the battery must point inwards and the contacts downwards,
- replace the handgrip and secure the screw.

Enough power? – bc – battery check

The lithium battery – or the 8 AA-size batteries in the booster (see next section) are not exhausted – at least not totally – as long as the basic displays are still visible in the LCD panel. These are:

- when the camera is switched off with film loaded – the frame number and the film symbol, together with a line of dashes,
- when the camera is switched on – one of the exposure mode symbols, the type of metering symbol, one of the shooting modes, and the exposure compensation scale,
- if the release is pressed half-way, activating exposure metering and AF function, the automatically-selected aperture value and shutter speed.

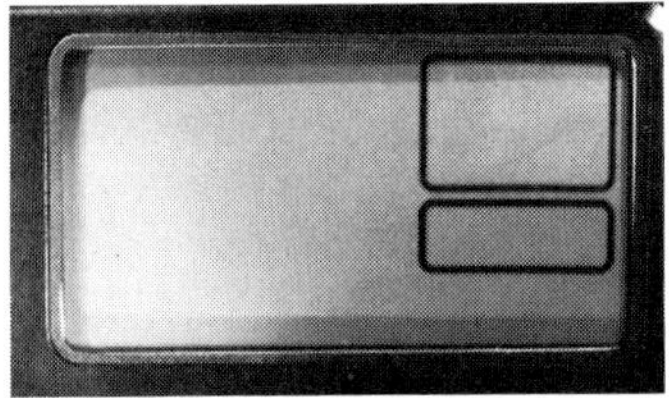

LCD Panel

If there is no battery in the camera or if the battery is exhausted. The same display also appears if a fully charged battery, but no film, is loaded into the EOS and it is switched off.

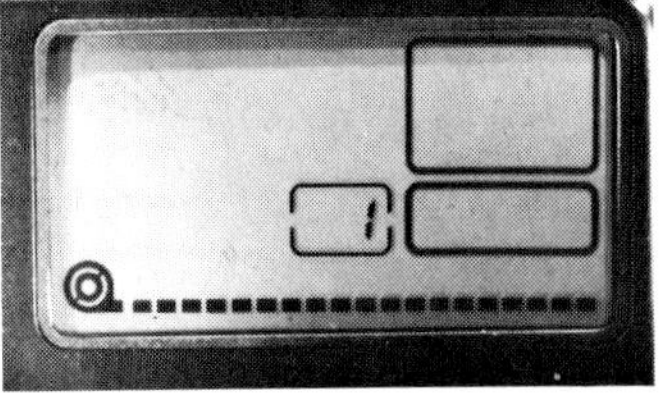

With a charged, or partially charged, battery and the film loaded but the camera switched off.

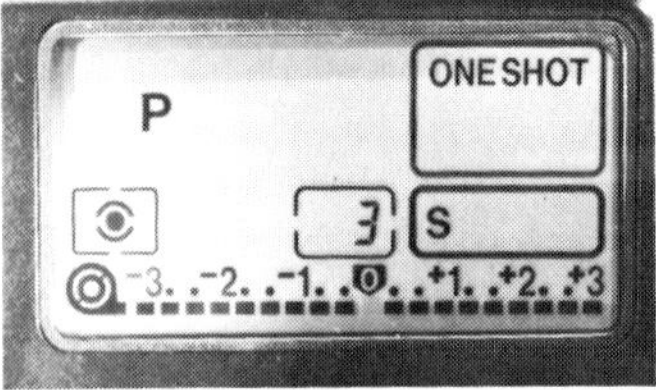

Camera switched on and film loaded, release not pressed.

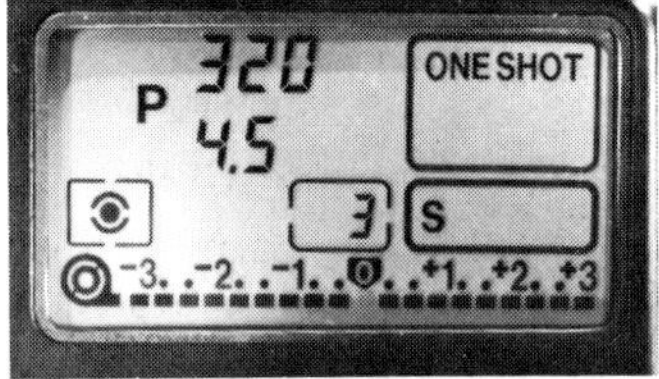

Camera switched on, film loaded, release pressed half-way.

The shutter can definitely be released as long as these basic displays are visible but they do not inform you of the actual state of the battery, i.e. how much energy is in reserve. It could be that a nearly-exhausted lithium battery has insufficient reserves to rewind an exposed film, although the shutter can still be released. It is therefore a good idea to check, perhaps after every 2 or 3 films, how far close the battery is to exhaustion.

- Switch EOS-1 on – turn the lever at the rear of the camera from L(ock) to A, or to audible in-focus position.
- Open the palm door on the right side of the camera body and press the black raised button (second from the top). As long as this button is kept pressed, the display in the LCD panel will show the letters bc and, depending on the state of the battery, 1, 2 or 3 bars.

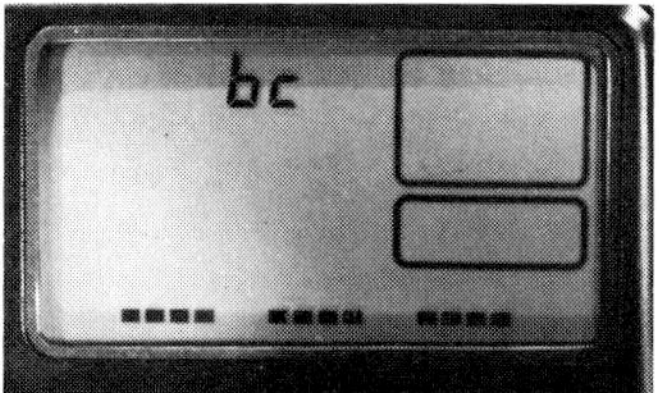

Battery Check
(2CR5 or 8 AA size batteries in the booster)

3 bars: battery fresh, no energy problems. Still, it is wise to have a spare battery at home.

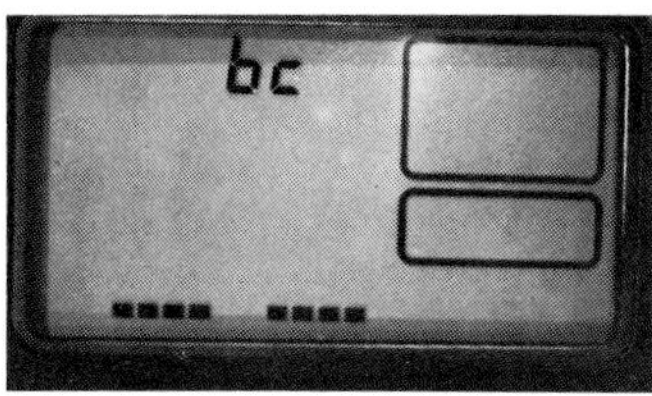

2 bars: the battery is partly exhausted. There should be sufficient energy for 3 or 4 more films, either with lithium battery or AA-size batteries, but it is time to buy a spare battery.

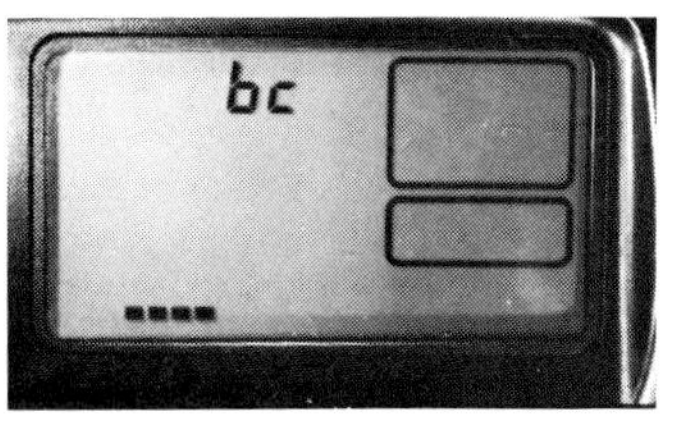

1 bar: possibly flashing or no bar at all. The battery is nearly exhausted. A new one is urgently required. Immediately before the battery dies the LCD panel automatically changes to display a battery-low warning – the letters bc flash.

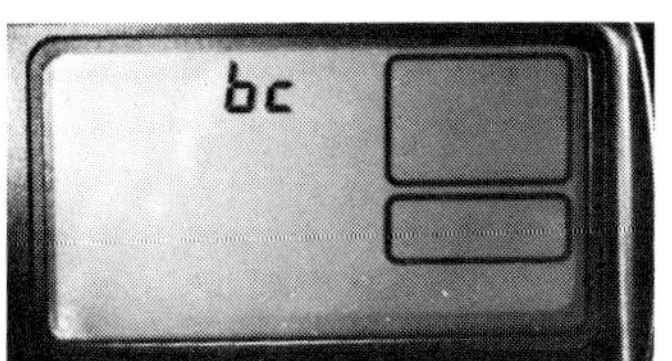

If the battery is totally exhausted then there is no display at all – neither in the panel nor in the viewfinder.

The EOS-1 – driven by 8 AA-size alkaline or re-chargeable batteries in the booster

This booster is a special handgrip with a large bottom plate. To attach, remove the normal handgrip and the motor drive coupler cover, and fix securely with the knurled screw to the tripod thread of the camera. Now the EOS-1 is powered by 8 1.5V AA-size batteries loaded in the booster. To load new batteries, the booster need not be removed from the camera. On its left side is a lever; fold out and turn counter-clockwise to open the drawer containing the battery compartment.

What can this booster do?

- The film through-put is increased by 25% in warm weather, i.e. 40 films of 36 exposures each. In low temperatures, –20 ° C, the output will be only about 4 to 5 36 exp. films.
- The frame frequency in fast shooting mode (c), which is about 2.5 frames per second without the booster, can be increased to 5.5 frames per second (ch) with the booster.
- Instead of the alkaline batteries, you can use rechargeable batteries. These are environmentally friendly and cheaper in the long run.

Apart from having its own central on/off switch, it has also a separate shutter release and AE-Lock button which are designed to facilitate shooting in upright format.

Limitless Choice of Films

Film loading – an automatic experience

The EOS-1 can be opened even if the booster is attached. To open, push down the cover latch while pressing the back cover lock button.

If you are not sure whether a film is loaded, check the film window at the rear of the camera. Most manufacturers provide film data in this position. Only if you are using a data back with your EOS-1 (see page 157, Command Back E1) will this extra safety feature not be available.

A new feature has been introduced with the EOS-1 whereby you can always check in the viewfinder whether a film is loaded. On the right below the scale for exposure compensation an “F” is displayed whenever a film is loaded and the camera is switched on. This letter is replaced with the number of frames still available at the last two frames. As soon as all frames are exposed “0” appears.

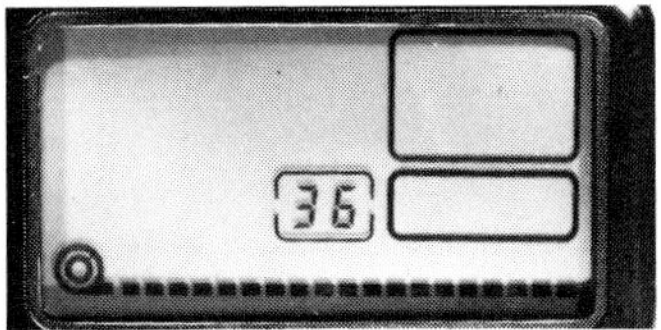

Film symbol with line made up of a long row of dashes at the lower edge of the LCD panel: film loaded – do not open the back cover!

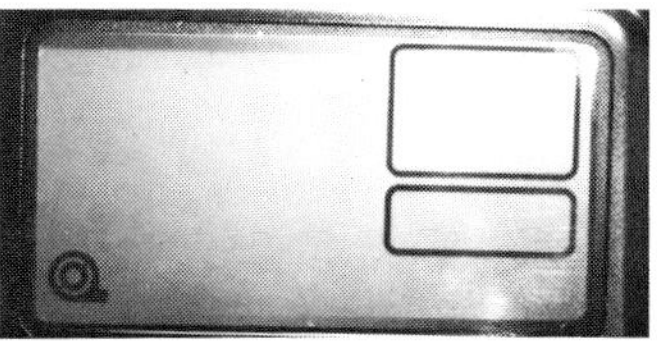

Film symbol displayed or blinks with EOS-1 switched on: film in the camera has been completely exposed and has been rewound. Open the back cover, remove the film and load a new one.

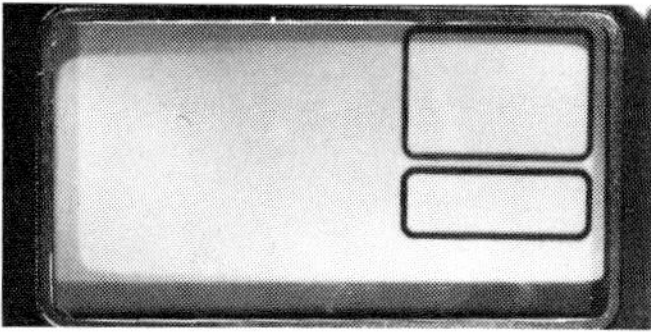

No display (2 empty boxes). Careful! This could mean:
1. Camera switched off. No film loaded
2. Battery totally exhausted or no battery inserted (in this case the panel stays blank even if the camera is switched on) but a film could be loaded.

To load a film:

- open the camera back and insert the upper, flat end of the film cassette into the film chamber and press down. Pull the film leader across the shutter blinds until the end is aligned with the orange marker and at least one or two of the teeth of the sprocket wheel engage in the film perforations. Two points to watch – make sure that you do not touch the shutter blinds and the film leader must not get creased or badly bent, otherwise the film will not load properly,
- close back cover and switch camera on. The film will automatically be advanced to the first frame. In the LCD panel 1 will appear in the frame counter. If the film is loaded properly, and it is DX-coded, the speed will be automatically read-in.

Now the camera is ready to take the first pictures. After each exposure the film is automatically wound to the next frame. After the last exposure the film is automatically rewound into the cassette. The whole process is extremely fast and simple.

The widest range of film materials – with or without DX coding!

There is a wide range of film material (known as 24x36mm, 35mm or 135mm film) available for the EOS-1 which is particularly economical, widely available and easily obtainable and is offered in a particularly wide variety of types and specifications. Film in cassettes is offered in different lengths – typically 12, 20, 24 and 36 exposures. Of these, the 36 exposure film (135-36) will most probably be the most sensible choice for the professional and dedicated amateur photographer.

The format of the individual frames is 24x36mm. The actual size of the final picture is slightly smaller. In the EOS the actual size of the nominal format is almost totally utilised.

Different Types of Colour Film

Colour Print FIlm

is processed to produce colour negatives which are then enlarged and printed up on colour paper. It is also possible to print black-and-white enlargements or colour, or black-and-white slides from a colour negative. This type of film material is capable of accommodating a wide subject contrast. Subjects with little contrast, on the other hand, appear rather flat. Colour negative film is mainly offered for shooting in daylight. This type of film, used in artificial lighting without a filter, will produce a heavily yellow-reddish colour bias. This can be partly compensated for by using the appropriate filtration during printing. However, the prints may have to be sent to a special lab.

Colour Slide Film

is a reversal film and is processed and mounted in frames. Usually you send them to a processing lab and they are returned framed and boxed. Photographic labs can also make colour prints from colour slides. However, the best results are achieved if you can do it yourself and this is not too difficult. Very contrasty subjects are usually most impressive as projected slides. Paper prints of contrasty slides have the disadvantage that they lack detail in both the dark and the light areas. Rather flat subjects tend to gain in impact in slides. There is a variety of types of colour slide material available for different applications:

Daylight Colour Slide Film

is balanced for shooting in daylight or with electronic flash. This is the most commonly-used type of film and is considered the standard film – at least for the amateur photographer. Pictures taken in daylight or in fluorescent light, on a daylight film generally have a rather pronounced bluish or green cast. This can be corrected by using the appropriate filter, but usually it is simpler to accept the colour cast. Another possibility is to fill-in important subject details by using flash. Colour pictures taken with daylight print film in tungsten light show a strong yellowish-red bias. In the majority of cases this is quite unacceptable, and a bluish conversion filter should be used on the lens.

Tungsten Colour Slide Film

is suitable for shooting in tungsten light and halogen or photographic lamps. The domestic light bulbs emit a greater proportion of yellow and red light than daylight and the sensitivity of the emulsion to the blue component of the light is increased in this type of film material. Using this film in ordinary daylight produces a slide with a strong blue bias. I like to use tungsten film in my small studio for portraits and still-life and sometimes in daylight for special effect shots.

Special Colour Slide Film

first the well-known false colour infrared film: Ektachrome Infrared 35mm ISO 200/24°. Of further interest are the special films for slide copying. However, these films are also quite suitable for ordinary photography, particularly if you are faced with a subject with extremely high contrast.

Types of Black-and White Film

Black-and-White Print Film

the most usual is the negative print film. However, it is also possible to produce slides from this type of film material. Most amateur photographers these days prefer colour material but black-and-white material is still very popular for the professional photographer, not only because it is used often for subsequent publication as black-and-white print, but it also has a very particular charm and graphic quality. Then there is the group of dedicated amateur photographers who will develop and print their own negatives. These days it is quite simple to produce very good black-and-white prints in a home darkroom.

Black-and-White Slide Film

is processed into black-and-white slides. For this purpose you can buy Agfa Dia-Direct Film ISO12/12°.

Black-and-White Special Films

Apart from the black-and-white infrared film, Kodak High Speed Infrared 35mm ISO 50/18°, I must mention mainly the high contrast document films for reproduction and graphic effects – Afgaortho 25 Professional ISO 25/15° and Kodak Technical Pan 2415. These films are particularly useful for experimentation in graphic image making.

The most interesting and important characteristic of any film is its speed:

- films with low speed require a lot of light, are very fine grained and bear a low number to identify their low speed rating.
- films of high speed require less light, possess larger grain and therefore the pictures appear not so sharp, and are identified by a high number.

ISO Film Speeds			
Slow	***Average***	***Fast***	***Very fast***
*[**6**/9°]*	***80**/20°*	***250**/25°*	***1250**/32°*
*[**8**/10°]*	***100**/21°*	***320**/26°*	***1600**/33°*
*[**10**/11°]*	***125**/22°*	***400**/27°*	***2000**/34°*
*[**12**/12°]*	***160**/23°*	***500**/28°*	***2500**/35°*
*[**16**/13°]*	***200**/24°*	***640**/29°*	***3200**/36°*
*[**20**/14°]*		***800**/30°*	***4000**/37°*
***25**/15°*		***1000**/31°*	***5000**/38°*
***32**/16°*			*[**6400**/39°]*
***40**/17°*			
***50**/18°*			
***64**/19°*			

The listed speeds are those that can be programmed into the EOS-1. The notations printed in brackets can only be programmed by hand, the other speeds are read-in automatically or can be entered by hand. For reasons of space, the LCD panel always shows only the arithmetical speed number. This is printed in bold in the table – e.g. ISO 400 instead of ISO 400/27°.

These numbers are the ISO values which are made up of two parts. The first part is the same as the old ASA speed, and doubling the number means doubling the film speed. The second part corresponds to the old German DIN numbers. In the DIN notation an increase of 3 units corresponds to a doubling of the film speed. Whenever space demands, manufacturers leave off the oblique stroke and the second part of the notation, using the arithmetical speed number only.

The film speed range that can be programmed into the EOS is in fact larger than the actual speeds generally offered. The slowest films that are used these days are ISO 25/15° slide film (Kodachrome 25) and colour print film (Ektar 25). Both of these films are very fine grained and slower films are not available.

The fastest film available is the black-and-white negative film Kodak T-Max 3200. Generally you get better results if you overexpose this film

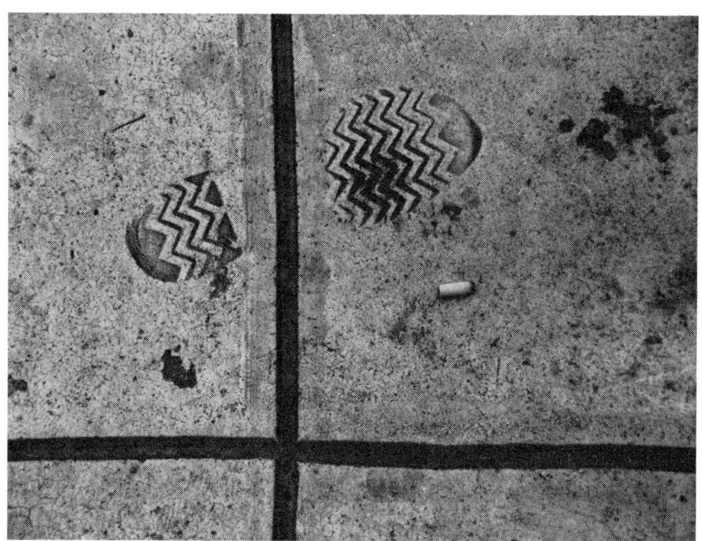

Tracks – taken with a colour print film Konica Color SR-G 100, printed on black-and-white paper.

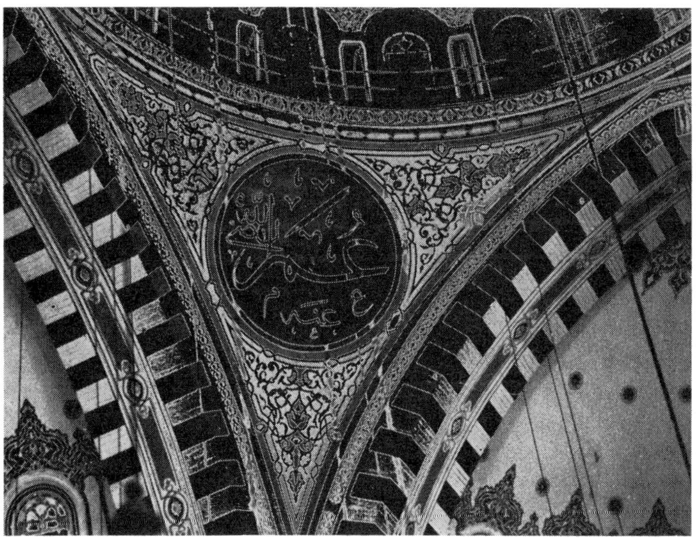

Cupola of a Moshee in Istanbul: pseudo-solarization-graphic– experiment on document film.

slightly, 1600/33° should produce good results. There are also some colour films available with a speed of ISO 1600 which can be used in very poor lighting conditions, such as Fujichrome P1600 Professional slide film. Then there is Scotch Chrome 800/30°-3200/36° slide film which can be pushed to ISO 3200. The same can be done with a colour print film – Konica SR-G 3200.

Compared with the slowest film rating of ISO 25, the ISO 1600 film is 64-times faster! Naturally, the resolution of such a fast film will suffer. On the other hand, you can take snapshots in situations where otherwise you would have to keep your camera stowed away in your bag.

The Kodak Ektapress Gold 1600 is worth mentioning here; this film can be exposed as ISO 6400/39° and push-processed. This must be the extreme limit in pushing film speed at this time. Even if these limits are exceeded, and this must be anticipated in the future, your EOS-1 will be able to cope. In this case you will have to "underexpose" by up to three stops, which is equivalent to a further increase in film speed by a factor of 8.

DX-coding is provided as a matter of course for most standard film types. This is the chessboard pattern on the film cassette, which carries the film speed information that is automatically read-in to the exposure control.

Programming of film speed

If you can see a bar code behind the slit where the film leader protrudes, and behind that the above-mentioned chessboard pattern, then the film is DX-coded and the speed will be programmed automatically.

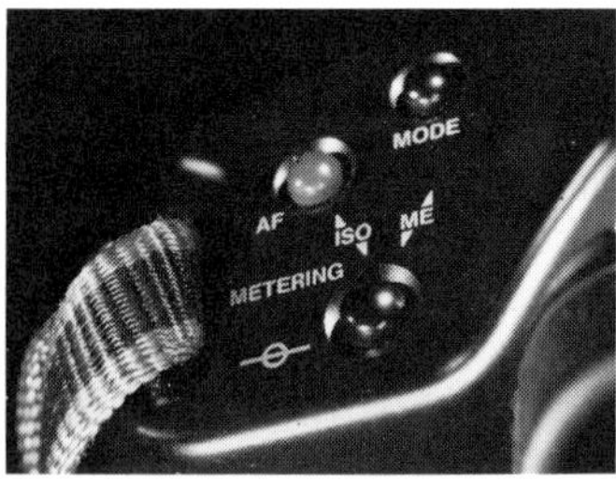

Press the AF and the METERING buttons simultaneously and keep them pressed. The ISO value appears in the LCD panel, which can now be changed by turning the input dial.

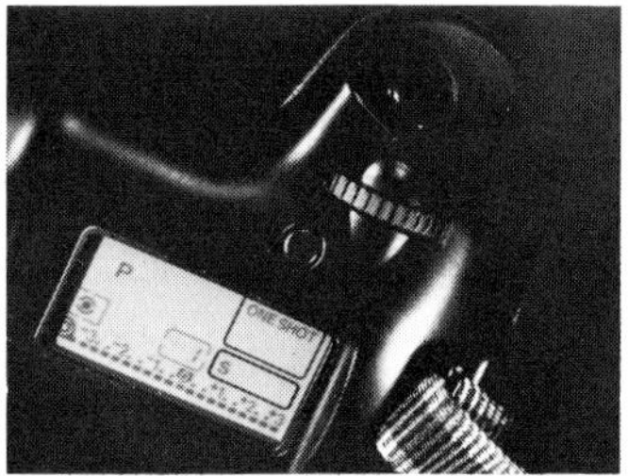

The input dial located between the release and the LCD panel.

If, on the other hand, the film speed cannot be read into the exposure system, perhaps because there is no DX-code, then the legend ISO, together with a previously-set film speed, will blink in the panel to remind you to enter the correct value manually. Manual film speed setting will be necessary whenever a film is supposed to be exposed at a rating different from the nominal one, or when a film is used that can be exposed at different ratings, such as the black-and-white T-Max 3200 or Scotch Chrome 800/30°-3200/36° slide film. In this case the camera cannot automatically know at which rating you wish to expose the film.

Film speed check – film speed correction

To set the film speed the EOS-1 has to be switched on and the AF and METERING buttons have to be pressed simultaneously. Now the currently programmed ISO value is displayed in the panel. You can change this number by turning the main dial behind the release.

- Turning the dial to the left reduces the film speed setting.
- Turning the dial to the right increases it. The selected film speed remains programmed until the film is changed.

IMPORTANT: the film speed setting is the only special function, apart from the reprogramming functions described in the last chapter of this part, that is not cancelled when the white CLEAR button (lowest button behind the palm door on the right side of the camera) is pressed. All other entries are returned to their basic settings.

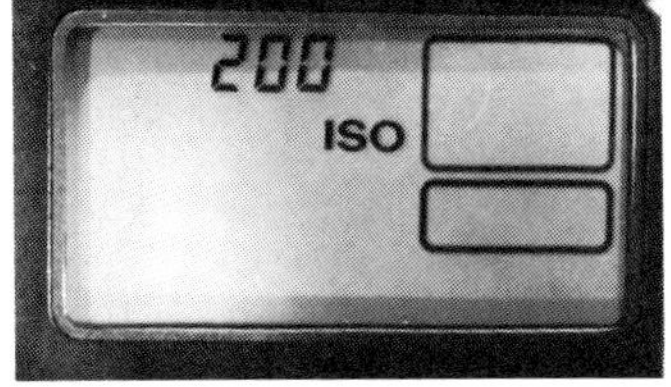

Pressing the A and the METERING buttons simultaneously will display the currently programmed ISO-value in the LCD panel – in this case this is ISO 200/24°. For space reasons only the first part of the speed number, i.e. 200, is shown.

When is it necessary to use the manual override for film speed – i.e., when do we use film speed correction?

- If the film is not DX-coded or if it is designed to be processed at different film speeds.
- If the film is to be processed differently from that required for the nominal film speed (pushed processing of colour slides or black-and-white film)

- If the whole film is supposed to be over- or underexposed by a certain amount.

The last-mentioned case is the most important one. However, I would recommend that you make an exposure test with the film you are going to use before effecting any general exposure compensation.

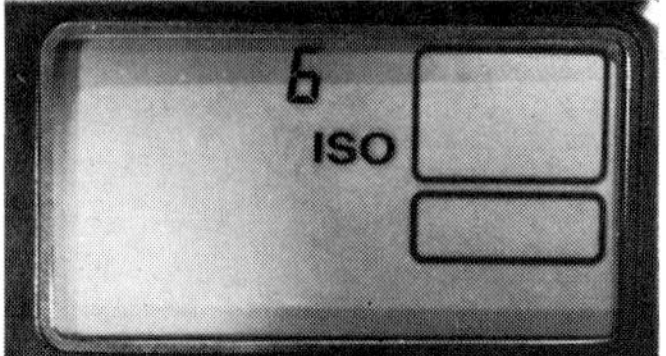

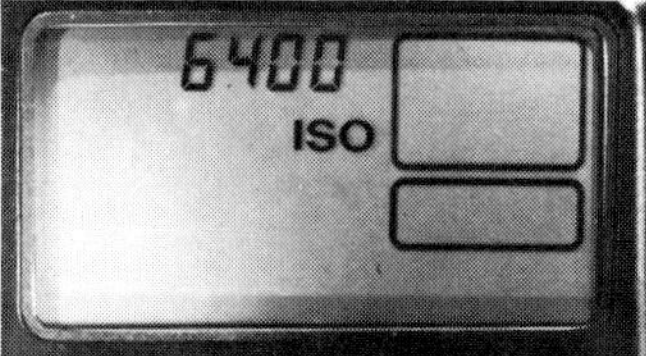

ISO 6/9° is the slowest, ISO 6400/39° is the fastest film speed that can be entered in the EOS-1. They have to be entered manually.

If you intend to expose several films in a row with a different speed setting from the one that is encoded on the film cassette, and if you do not want to change the film speed every time you load the film, you can switch off the automatic programming of the speed. In this case press the CF button behind the palm door and select Custom Function Control 3. This is described in more detail in the last chapter of this section.

The Green Sea of Taiwan. The dark, slightly blurred foliage in the foreground creates a framing for the contrasting subject in the background. It almost seems as if two entirely different pictures have been superimposed.
Suggestion for a suitable exposure for pictures of this type:
1. Meter one of the brighter subject areas in the background by spot-metering method.
2. Press AE lock button and hold.
3. Swing camera round for the desired framing and release.
AF mode: Deactivate! The lens should be focused on infinity, which is easier to do in manual mode.

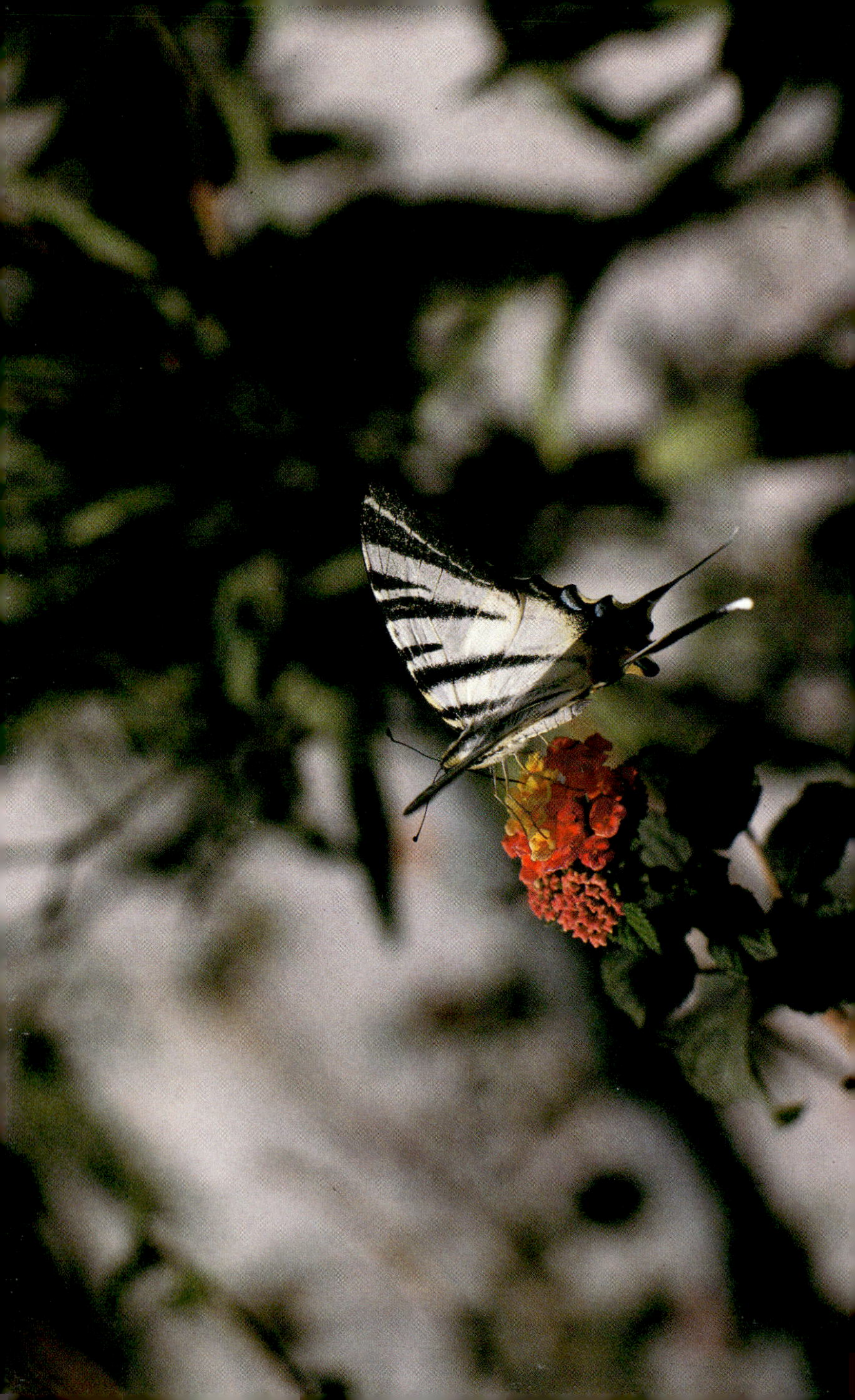

Rewinding partiallyexposed film/reloading partially exposed film

Occasionally it is necessary or desirable to remove a partially-exposed film from the camera and to change it for another, perhaps also partially exposed film. It may be necessary to change the film for a faster one or a colour film for a black-and-white.

First it is necessary to make an adjustment to the basic programming of the EOS-1 which, once done, will remain effective. This is Custom Function Control 2. In its normal programming the film is completely rewound into the cassette. To insert a partially used film, the film leader needs to protrude from the cassette. To reprogram the camera you have to:

- switch the camera on
- press the countersunk black button marked CF behind the palm door. The display F - 1 (or another number), with the number 0 beneath, appears in the LCD panel. This display remains until the release is pressed halfway
- turn the input dial to select the required number. The display changes to F - 2, also with a 0 underneath
- press the CF button again and the 0 changes to a 1 – the function is activated.

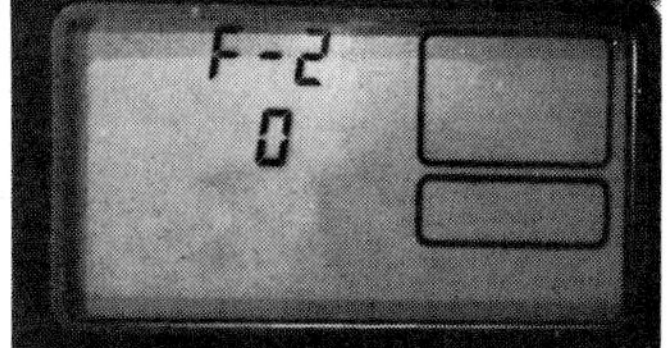

Display for Custom Function Control F - 2 in the LCD panel. If the CF button is now pressed the 0 changes to a 1 and the motorized film rewinding stops short before the film leader is completely retracted into the cassette.

A butterfly on a mulberry blossom. This kind of subject is best captured in servo mode. One word of caution – make sure the butterfly is indeed at the centre of the frame when the release is pressed.

Removing Partially-Exposed Film from a reprogrammed EOS-1
• *Read frame number off LCD panel* • *Note frame number on film cassette or box* • *Press film rewind button at the rear bottom of the camera. The film will be automatically rewound.* • *Put film into box making sure that the leader is not kinked.*
Loading Partially Used Film
• *Read frame number off film cassette or box* • *Load film as usual, allowing automatic film transport to advance film to frame No. 1.* • *Set EOS-1 to manual operation.* • *Attach lens cap to keep light from entering the camera and release shutter repeatedly until the required frame number is displayed in the LCD panel.*

Further information regarding other special functions are contained in the last chapter of this section.

Towards a Clear and Sharp Viewfinder Image...

Dioptre adjustment

It is possible to see the viewfinder image even when wearing glasses – it's not exactly ideal but one can get used to it. The viewfinder of the EOS-1 can be adjusted continuously from +3 to –1 dioptres. The adjustment dial is underneath the rubber frame of the viewfinder eyepiece.

Adjusting the viewfinder eyepiece for your eyesight
• *Carefully remove the eyepiece frame. To do this press down the centre of the top of the frame and push up from the bottom.* • *Using a well-structured, reasonably flat subject, turn the adjustment dial to the left of the eyepiece until the subject appears completely sharp in the viewfinder.*

For photographers with eyesight errors outside this range Canon offer an accessory frame with different eyepiece lenses. Another alternative is to attach a special lens to the viewfinder – this is of particular interest even to normally-sighted people for macro shots. There are also two types of angle finders which magnify the viewfinder image.

The eyepiece cover that has to be attached when taking shots from a tripod is accommodated in the carrying strap of the EOS-1. This can be attached only if the eyepiece frame is removed.

Lens Change – Choice of Focusing Method

The lens release button is situated on the left next to the lens bayonet. This is a large, easily-accessible button which has to be pressed so that the lens can be turned counter-clockwise and removed.
Note: never stand the lens bayonet-side down, this could damage the electrical contacts. Always attach both the rear and the front lens caps when the lens is not in use.

Attaching the lens

Align the red dot on the camera with the red dot on the lens. Then gently push the lens in and turn it clockwise until it clicks into place.

Before starting to take any pictures check that the focus mode switch on the lens is set to the AF position.

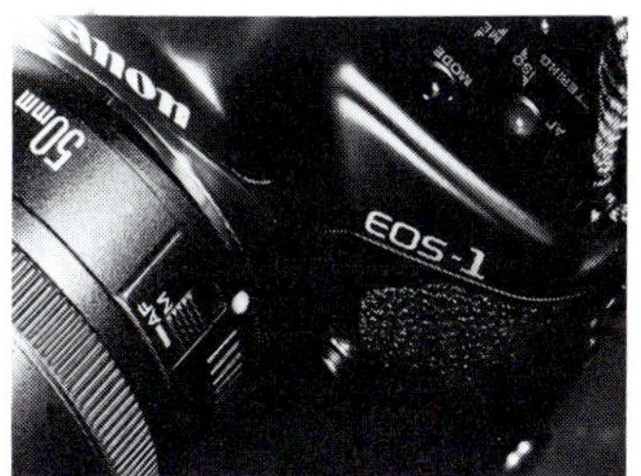

Focus mode switch – set here to manual

Changing the focus mode on the lens: Autofocus (AF) – Manual Focusing (M-FOCUS)

The autofocus function of EOS cameras, and in particular the improved system of the EOS-1, functions quickly and precisely because each lens is equipped with its own AF motor. The focus mode switch on the lens allows you to select either auto or manual focus.

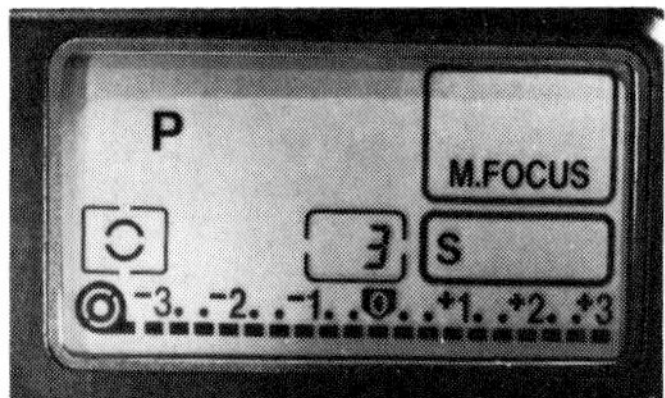

LCD panel showing M-FOCUS mode activated.

Zoom lenses with long focal lengths and macro facility have a range limiter which divides the focusing range between AF macro to infinity and AF 2m to infinity.

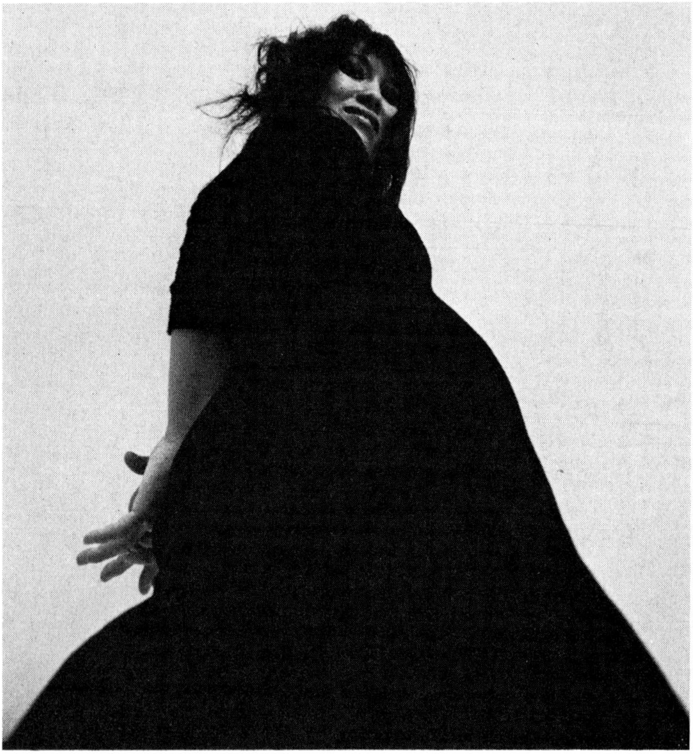

A glare from above. The unstructured black area formed by the clothing is not suitable for AF focusing. Two solutions to this problem; either set lens to M-FOCUS and focus manually or in AF mode focus on the face, lock the setting by keeping the release pressed half-way, and realign for correct framing.

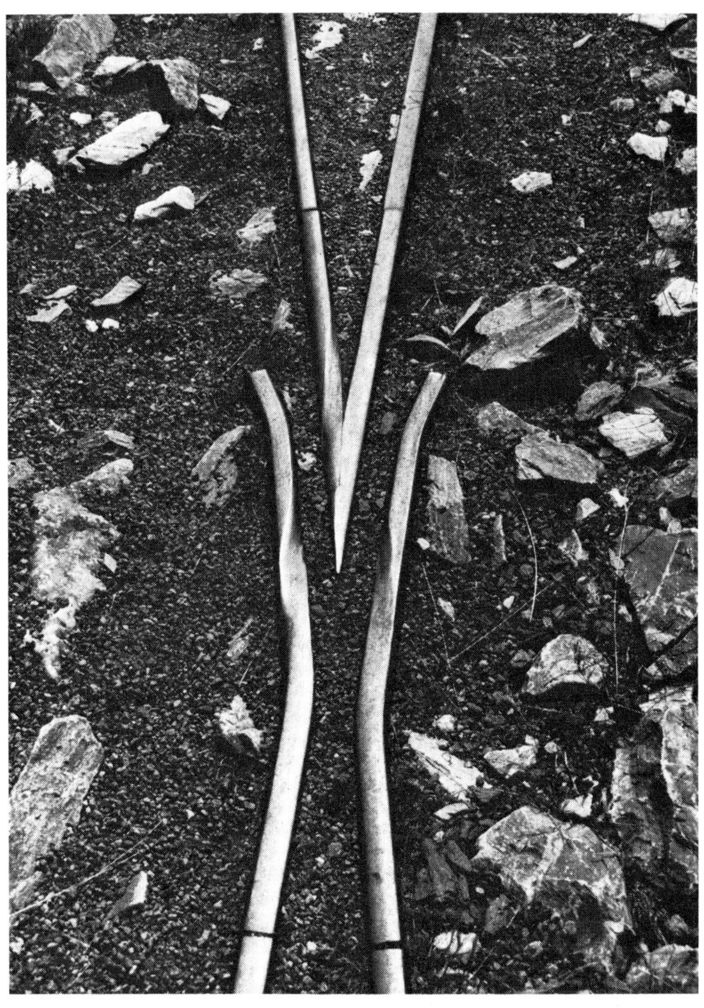

Disused track of a narrow-gauge railway – an ideal subject for a shot in AF mode.

When shooting subjects with a focusing distance of 2m or more it prevents the focusing mechanism having to traverse the entire focusing range, from close-up to infinity, which is time and energy consuming.

Manual focusing is advisable if:

- the lens is supposed to be focused on infinity.
- a large focusing range between macro and infinity has to be bridged (manual focusing can be quicker)
- if a very fast moving subject is to be tracked.
- if subject contrast and structure make it difficult for the AF mechanism to find the correct focus.

Sharp Pictures: Fast Shutter Speed or Supported Camera

Hand-held shots: never slower than 1/250th second

No one is capable of holding a camera totally rigid, while making an exposure of 1/30th sec., without introducing some unsharpness into the picture – even though some people seem to think that they have a particularly steady hand and would be able to do this. Blurred pictures used to be the norm rather than the exception. In recent years the proportion of sharp pictures has increased. This may be due mainly to the introduction of program mode in many cameras, which ensures that relatively fast shutter speeds are favoured. Many amateur photographers snap away in full program mode without ever being aware of what shutter speeds the camera is selecting for them.

If the lighting conditions are good, the EOS program mode will generally select shutter speeds of between 1/500th and 1/250th second. In this case pictures will definitely be sharp.

General Rules for Shutter Speeds with Hand-held Shots:

- *Use 1/250th sec. or faster.*
- *Use 1/200th, 1/160th or 1/125th sec. only if this is absolutely necessary.*
- *Never use shutter speeds slower than 1/500th sec. when using a lens with a focal length longer than 135mm.*
- *1/60th sec is just about possible with wide-angle lenses – lenses with a focal length of 40mm or less.*
- *For flash exposures outdoors – provided the main subject is illuminated mainly by the flash it is possible to use shutter speeds as slow as 1/20th sec but better still use 1/60th sec.*
- *For slower shutter speeds it is essential that the camera is supported either by a tripod or by some other means.*

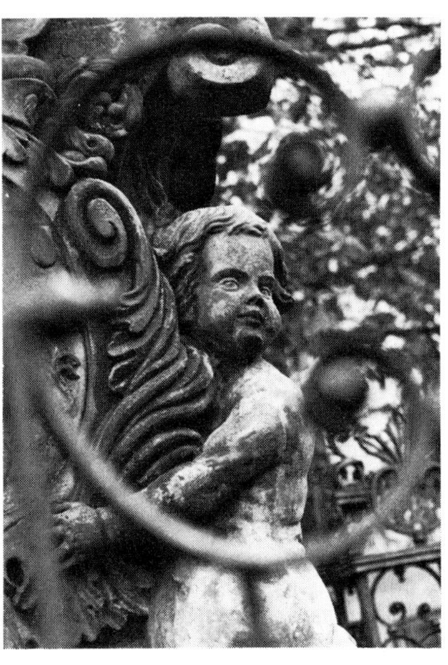

The statue of Putto seen through the blurred outlines of the ironwork in the foreground. Exceptionally, I took this picture at 1/20th sec. This turned out sharp only because I used a 24mm lens and supported my arms against the ironwork.

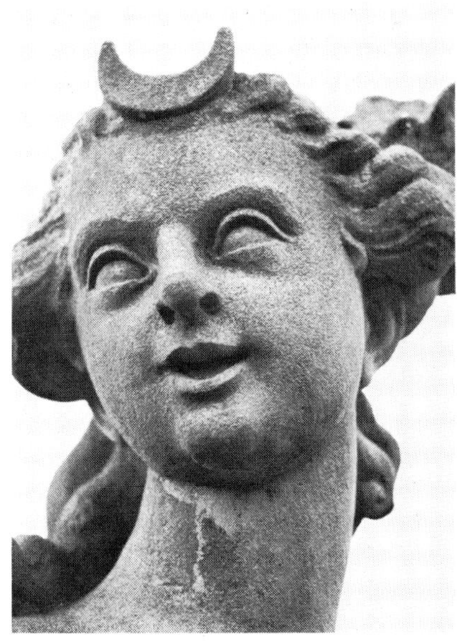

The face of the Rococo Artemis in the rose garden in Bamberg, taken with a 210mm lens. In this case the shutter speed was 1/500th sec, the slowest safe speed for this focal length.

Use of a tripod

Generally speaking you should always use a tripod for shutter speeds of 1/90th second and slower. Journalists are often forced to work without tripods and they resort to methods of supporting themselves and the camera in some way – but for shutter speeds of 1/15th and 1/8th sec., the use of a tripod is essential.

If you support your camera on a sturdy tripod, you can risk releasing with the shutter release button, even if you select a long exposure. If you are worried that the pressure on the release button – either on the camera itself or on a mechanical cable release – could upset both the camera and the tripod then it is better to release by self-timer. Better still, use an electronic remote release 60T3 – the "60" indicates that the cable is 60cm long. Canon offer extension cables up to 10m. The release on the hand unit is a 2-stage switch similar to the one on the camera itself; first pressure point for metering/focusing and limit stop for shutter release. You can lock the shutter in the open position by sliding the release sideways in the pressed-in position. The shutter can be closed only if the release is moved back.

Do not forget the eyepiece cover when you use the remote release. Normally your eye would cover the eyepiece thus preventing any light to enter the viewfinder (see also page 93 on long exposures).

Shutter speeds between 1/90th and 1/8th sec: methods of support

If the light is poor and even a fast film is insufficient to produce fast enough shutter speeds, and a flash is either unsuitable or not powerful enough, then you may be forced to use s hutter speeds between 1/90th and 1/8th sec. without supporting the camera on a tripod. In this case you will have to look for some other form of support – the back of a chair, a balustrade, a wall, a fence, etc. If no rigid surface can be found it helps to lean, legs firmly planted on the ground, against a wall, a tree, or a lamp post. What is important is to support your arms and hands because they hold the camera. Sometimes I crouch down and support my arms on my knees or I kneel down on one leg, with the other bent, as this presents a very steady support for both arm and camera.

The safest method is to support the camera directly on a level surface. This works very well if the camera is used with a remote release, at least for pictures taken in horizontal-format. I have managed to give exposures of several seconds and produce sharp pictures.

For upright format shots, support the base of the camera against a column, a door-frame or a tree. For shots indoors of frescos, ceiling paintings or interesting structures, in a castle or a church, for example, simply put the camera with its back on the floor and release by self-timer or remote release.

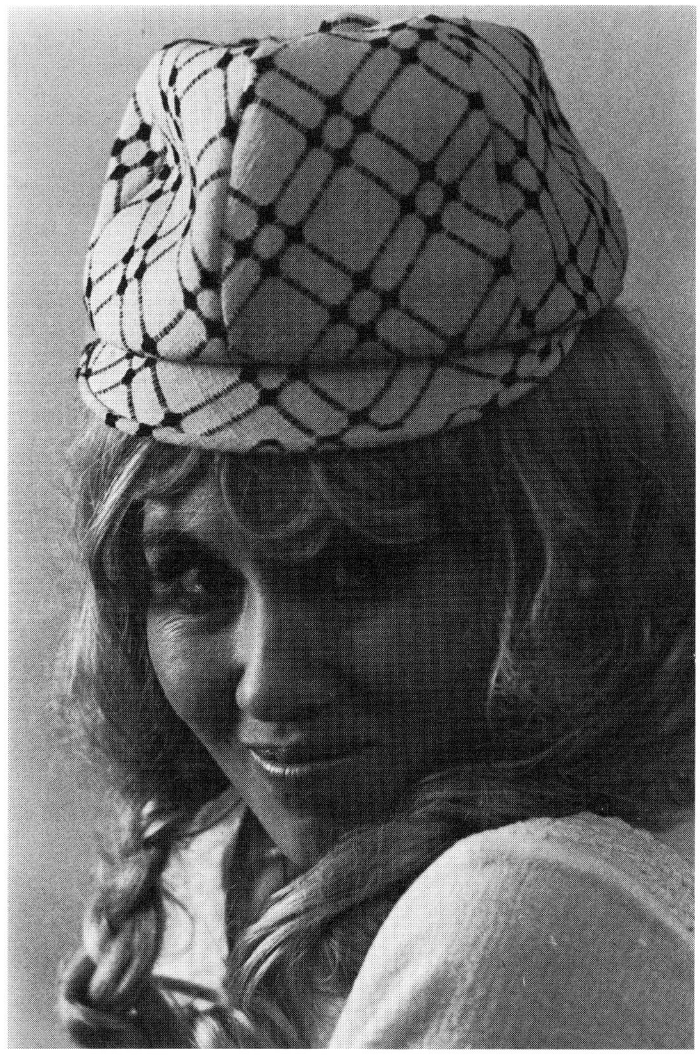

The tripod can be useful even when using fast shutter speeds – perhaps for posed snapshots and portraits. Support the camera on the tripod and release by remote release. In this way the photographer is free to move around, close to the sitter, influencing his or her behaviour and observing the facial expression or pose, choosing exactly the right moment to release.

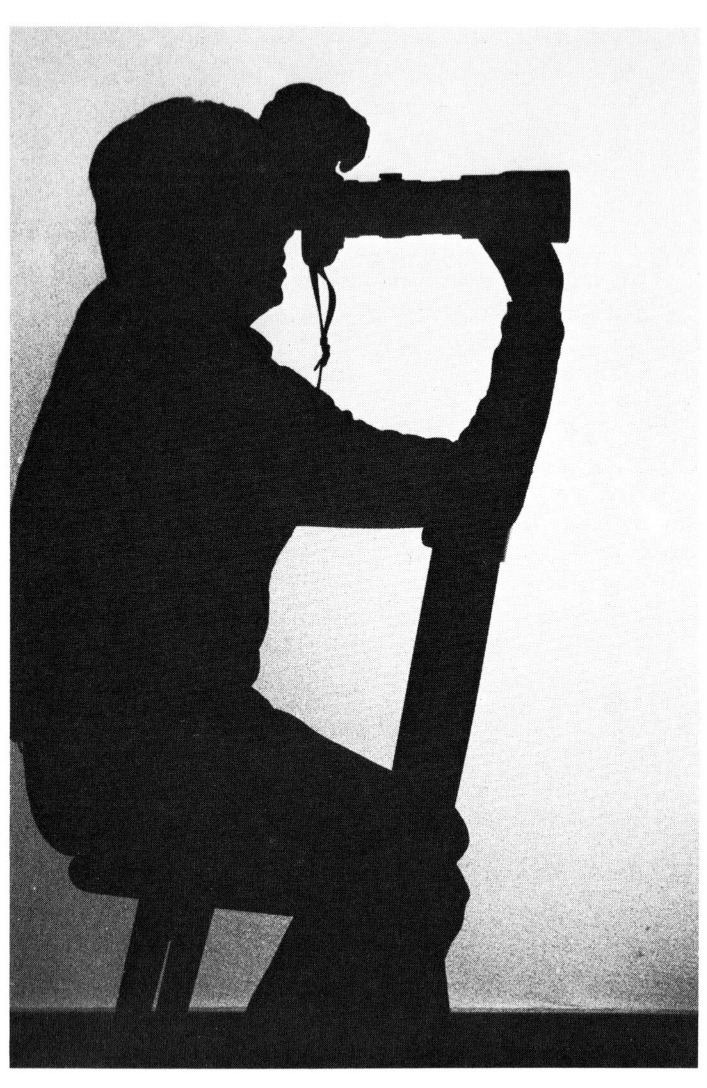

The EOS-1 with a 400mm lens. The left arm is braced firmly on the back of the chair so camera and lens are properly supported.

8 Basic Functions to be Programmed by the Photographer

Programming the EOS-1

Before you use your EOS-1 it may be advisable to consider which of the 8 basic functions are of interest to you and what programming decisions to make.

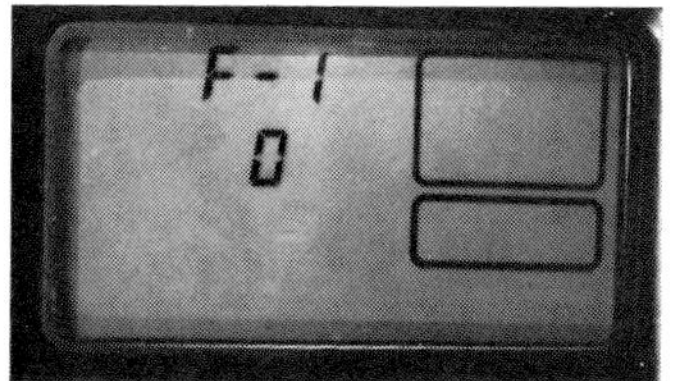

LCD panel when the black CF button under the palm door is pressed. Turning the input dial to the right will display the other Custom Function Controls from 2 to 8. The 0 underneath means that the function is in its basic setting – it has not been activated.

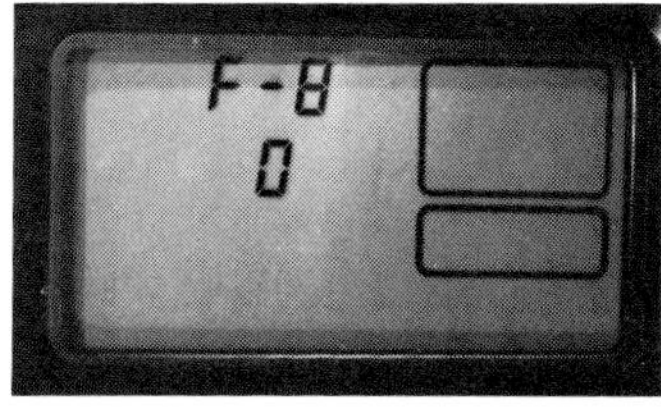

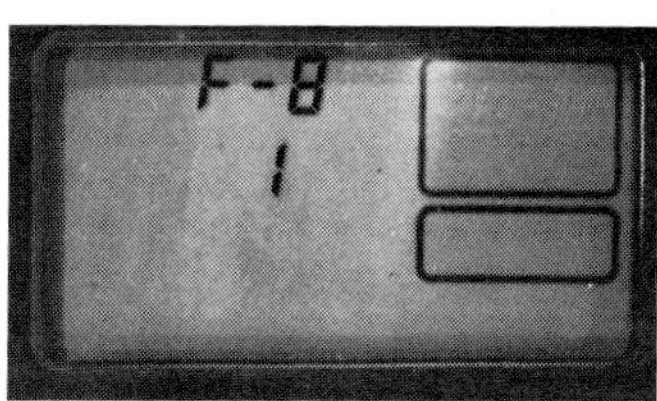

The 1 indicates that the Custom Function Control has been activated. It remains so until the CF button is pressed again.

Control No.	**Normal Setting – Input 0**	**Reprogrammed Function – Input 1**
1	*Film is rewound automatically after the last exposure.*	*Automatic film rewinding de-activated. To activate motorised rewinding, press the rewind button at the rear of the camera.*
2	*Film leader is fully wound into cassette*	*Film is not fully wound into the cassette.*
3	*Automatic reading of film speed (DX-CODE)*	*Automatic reading of film speed cancelled. Film speed has to be entered manually.*
4	*Autofocus mechanism is started when release is pressed half-way.*	*Autofocus mechanism is started only if AE lock button is pressed (either on the EOS-1 or on the Booster).*
5	*Manual shutter speed set by input dial and aperture set by quick control dial.*	*Aperture set by input dial and shutter speed set by quick control dial*
6	*Setting shutter speed and aperture in 1/3rd-step increments*	*Setting shutter speed and aperture in 1-step increments*
7	*Additional manual adjustment to AF setting for USM lenses*	*Function de-activated*
8	*Evaluative metering over the whole frame*	*Centre-weighted metering across the whole frame.*

These functions are described in more detail in the following sections.

Activating the Custom Functions

- Switch EOS-1 on
- Open the palm door on the right side of the camera and press the top button marked CF. This button is countersunk to prevent inadvertent use. The LCD panel will change to F – 1 (or another function number) and beneath that an 0.
- Turn the main dial until the desired function number is displayed.
- Activate the required function by pressing the CF button again. Instead of an 0 in the second line, the number 1 will be displayed. This confirms that this custom function is now selected.
- If the CF button is pressed again, the special function is cancelled, and the 0 will be displayed again to confirm resetting of the normal function.

Note: press the MODE button to revert LCD panel to normal display.

Custom Function 1 – de-activating automatic film rewinding

After the last frame the film transport stops. With this function activated the film is not automatically rewound after the last frame.

Custom Function 2 – film leader is left outside the cassette

This is a very useful function. I keep it permanently activated. The film leader left outside helps to prevent stray light entering the cassette. Moreover, it allows a partially exposed film to be re-wound and re-loaded. Naturally, you will have to identify a partially exposed film by noting down the frame number. A completely exposed film should also be identified.

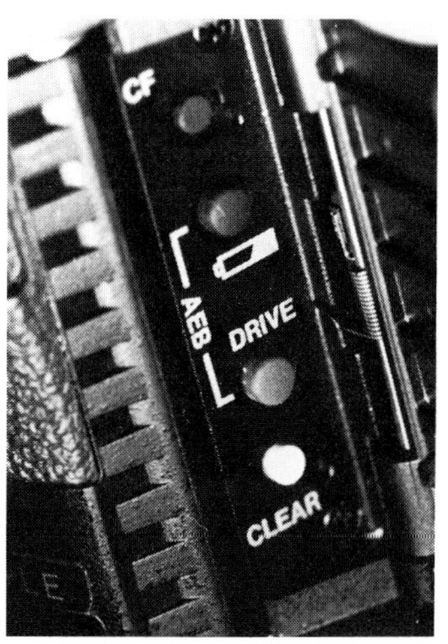

A look behind the palm door of the EOS-1:

1 Topmost button (CF) + main dial: selection of custom functions

2 Battery check button

3 DRIVE button + main dial: selection of film winding mode

4 CLEAR button: reset to basic functions. All special functions are cancelled.

Custom Function 3 – automatic film speed programming de-activated
The use of this function makes sense only if several films of the same speed are to be processed at ratings other than their nominal film speed. For example, I prefer to expose slide film rated at ISO 400/27° as 800/30°. If I intend to expose several films at this rating then I activate this function and enter the appropriate speed. All the films loaded subsequently are then exposed, one after the other, at the same setting, without having to re-enter the film speed every time I load a new film.

Custom Function 4 – AE lock button activates AF mode
Activating this function de-activates the automatic focusing mechanism when the shutter release button is pressed halfway, but instead allows the AF mechanism to work when the AE lock button is pressed. This is useful when working with partial metering as it prevents inadvertent triggering of the release, either on the camera or on the booster. In fully automatic mode this function cannot be activated. I like to use this function in situations when I work with spot-metering or if I want to store the focus setting before re-aligning the camera to place the main subject detail off-centre.

Custom Function 5 – reversal of shutter speed/aperture setting
This function comes in useful for exposure control with:
Tv mode:
The shutter speed is normally preselected by turning the main dial, the camera's exposure control then follows automatically by adjusting the aperture for the metered brightness.
Activating this function changes the preselection of the shutter speed to the quick control dial.
Av Mode:
The aperture value is normally preselected by turning the main dial, the shutter speed for the preselected aperture is adjusted automatically by the camera's exposure control.
Activating this function 5 changes the preselection of the shutter speed to the quick control dial.

Custom Function 6 – shutter speed and aperture displayed in whole stops
The EOS-1 displays almost all the exposure values in 1/3rd-stop intervals. Even the aperture values and shutter speeds entered by the photographer are displayed in the same way. When turning the main dial the appropriate preselected and automatically calculated values are displayed in 1/3rd-step increments. If this appears too confusing you can change the display to the more familiar full-stop aperture and shutter speed sequences. Now the display will jump from one full stop to the next, both

for aperture value and shutter speed. The actual exposure, which changes automatically and continuously along the scale, is not affected and will still be adjusted continuously – the camera will still select intermediate values.

Custom Function 7 – manual AF correction (USM)

This function can be used only with lenses with an ultrasonic motor (USM). In the Canon range these are particularly fast lenses. If a subject is to be shown in sharp focus by reducing the depth of field to a very narrow region within the subject space, it can be useful to make minor corrections to the focus setting obtained by the AF mode. Generally one can override the autofocus setting manually with these special lenses without having to use this function. However, in certain situations it may be advisable or more convenient to focus either only in AF mode or only manually. This would be a situation when this custom function comes in useful. In this case you slide the focus mode switch on the USM lens to AF or to manual, just as with the simpler lenses.

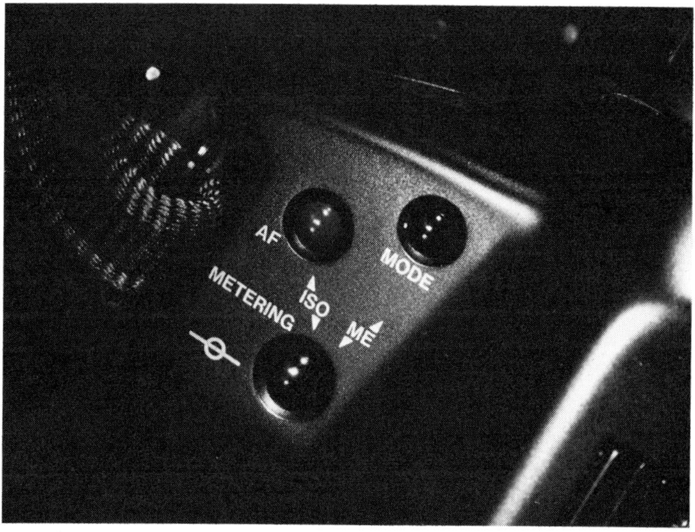

Three buttons with 5 functions on the left shoulder of the EOS 1. The metering method is changed by pressing the metering button and at the same time turning the main dial. The evaluative metering method can be changed to centre-weighted integral by custom function 8.

Custom Function 8

Changing to centre-weighted integral metering

The EOS-1 offers four metering systems. The so-called evaluative multi-field metering is the basic setting of the EOS-1. This metering mode measures light from six different areas within the picture frame and analyses the pattern. In this way all subject parts are equally considered in the metering result. To change over to selective or spot-metering, the metering button on the left camera shoulder is pressed. To reprogram from evaluative to integral metering use custom function 8. In centre-weighted integral metering the whole subject field is measured but the centre of the frame, where the most important subject detail is usually situated, is considered more strongly in the metering result.

PART III

Basic Operation of the EOS-1

Activating Metering Functions and Releasing in Mode P

Releasing – exposure and AF mechanism

Switching the EOS-1 on and off
The small switch at the bottom of the camera back is the main switch. It has three positions: ***L = Lock*** *The camera is switched off. Any special functions selected before the camera was switched off are stored and reactivated when the camera is switched on again* ***A = Activate*** *The camera is switched on with acoustic signal de-activated.* *•))) =* ***acoustic signal*** *activated, all functions can be used. In ONE SHOT mode an audible signal confirms correct focus.*
All programmed functions are retained when the batteries are changed. The same applies when the film is changed, with the exception of the film speed, which is either read-in automatically or set manually.

Turn the EOS-1 on after checking that the focus mode switch on the lens is set to AF. Now you can point the camera at some subject detail that needs to be in sharp focus.

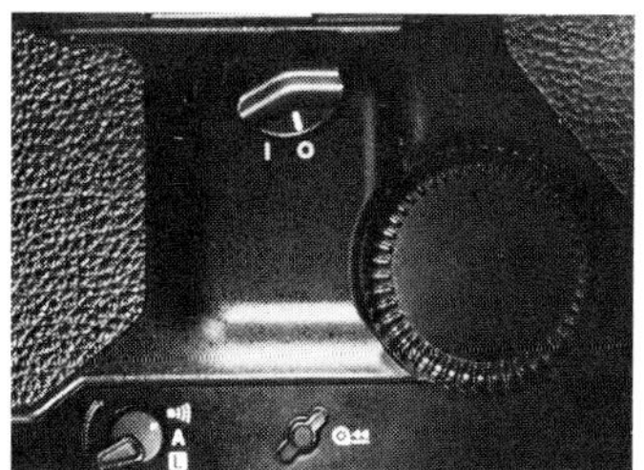

The main switch with its three positions – L, A and •))). Above are the Quick Control Dial and its own ON/OFF switch.

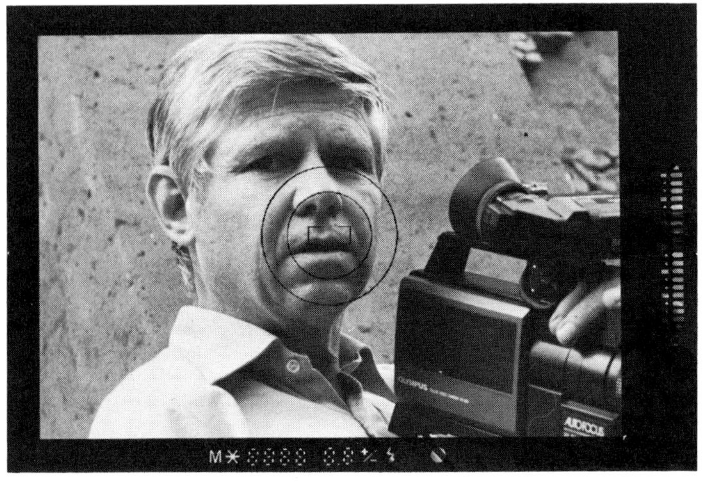

This is how we see the subject through the viewfinder. The small rectangle in the centre of the focusing screen is the AF target field. The small inner circle describes the spot metering field and the larger circle describes the selective metering field.

The small rectangular AF target field is outlined by the two brackets at the centre of the focusing screen. You now have two options:

- you press the release fully home and the following will happen; the camera will automatically read-in the correct exposure and the values will be displayed in the viewfinder, the lens will focus on the subject detail outlined with the AF target field. The green in-focus symbol in the viewfinder will illuminate to confirm that focus has been set as well as the audible signal, if activated. Usually this takes no more than a fraction of a second before the shutter is released. However, the shutter will be released only if the AF mechanism has set the correct focus on the lens. This quick "point and release" method will only work if the important subject detail is placed at the centre of the frame. This will be the case for the majority of pictures but if the main subject is to be placed off-centre the following method has to be adopted.
- you press the release half-way – and the same things happen as mentioned above – but the shutter will not be released until you press the release fully home. The exposure value and focus setting are stored as long as you keep the release pressed half-way. Now you can realign the camera for a more suitable framing. With this method we can place the focusing plane exactly where we want it; it is even possible to produce a totally unsharp picture.

It is also possible to check the exposure data before releasing the shutter in case the shutter speed is too slow – if it is, use the shift facility to open up the aperture for a faster shutter speed.

> ***NOTE:*** *in case of doubt the camera will try to focus on a detail or an outline of the subject that occupies the largest proportion of the target field.*

To adjust the AF focusing and exposure for a new situation take your finger off the release and the settings are cancelled. As soon as the release is pressed half-way down again the AF mechanism will restart the focusing sequence.

> ***"Meter and Check" Method***
> *Press release half-way, then lift your finger off the button:*
> *focus is set. Exposure metering is activated and continually adjusted for changing conditions. Activation and display remains for 8 sec.*
> *Press release half-way and hold:*
> *focus is set. Exposure metering is activated and set.*

If the AF mechanism is too slow or does not function

The AF mechanism of EOS cameras is extremely efficient and quick. It has been further improved in the EOS-1 and is even faster. It can cope with almost every subject and most structures whether vertical, horizontal or oblique. There are only very few subjects or situations when the AF mechanism is at a loss.

- Subjects lacking any structure and uniformly plain surfaces like a completely blue sky, a snow-covered field or heavy fog.

Remedy: set the focus manually.

- Views through fine structures like tree branches. In this case the AF mechanism won't know which is the important subject detail and the lens will traverse the entire range without being able to determine the correct setting.

Remedy: set the focus manually.

- It is too dark. The AF mechanism will work even in twilight. However, there comes a point when even the EOS-1 can't cope.

Remedy: set the focus manually or attach a flashgun and use the infrared metering flash for subjects up to 6m distance. The flashgun can be switched off once the focus has been set.

Releasing with manual focusing

This is not as easy as you might think. When you change the focus mode on the lens, by sliding the focus mode switch from AF to M, not only that mode is changed but also some other operating sequences on the camera.

The freezing of the exposure values with release pressed half-way is cancelled. Now the exposure setting is changed every time the camera is moved or the situation changes. If you want to freeze the exposure value press the AE lock button, situated on the top right of the camera back, and hold in.

Although the AF mechanism is de-activated the camera will still inform you visually and audibly (if set) when you have selected correct focus. Switching the AF mechanism quickly off and on has the same effect as releasing the release button and pressing it again – exposure and focus settings are newly taken and stored.

Program shift: adjusting aperture and shutter speed

If the light is reasonably good and the subject not too unusual we can rely on program mode to select suitable values.

This is fortunate as rapid action makes it impossible to spend too much time on the controls. Moreover, the fast shutter speed of 1/8000th sec. provides an extra safety margin against overexposure, even on the brightest days.

On days or in situations where the lighting conditions are marginal we have to check in the viewfinder to ensure that the hand-held limits are not exceeded. If the depth of field is an important creative element in the composition then we have to keep an eye on the aperture value.

The sharply-outlined fancy red wrought iron handrail with the unsharp outlines of the yellow roofs of a pagoda in the background.

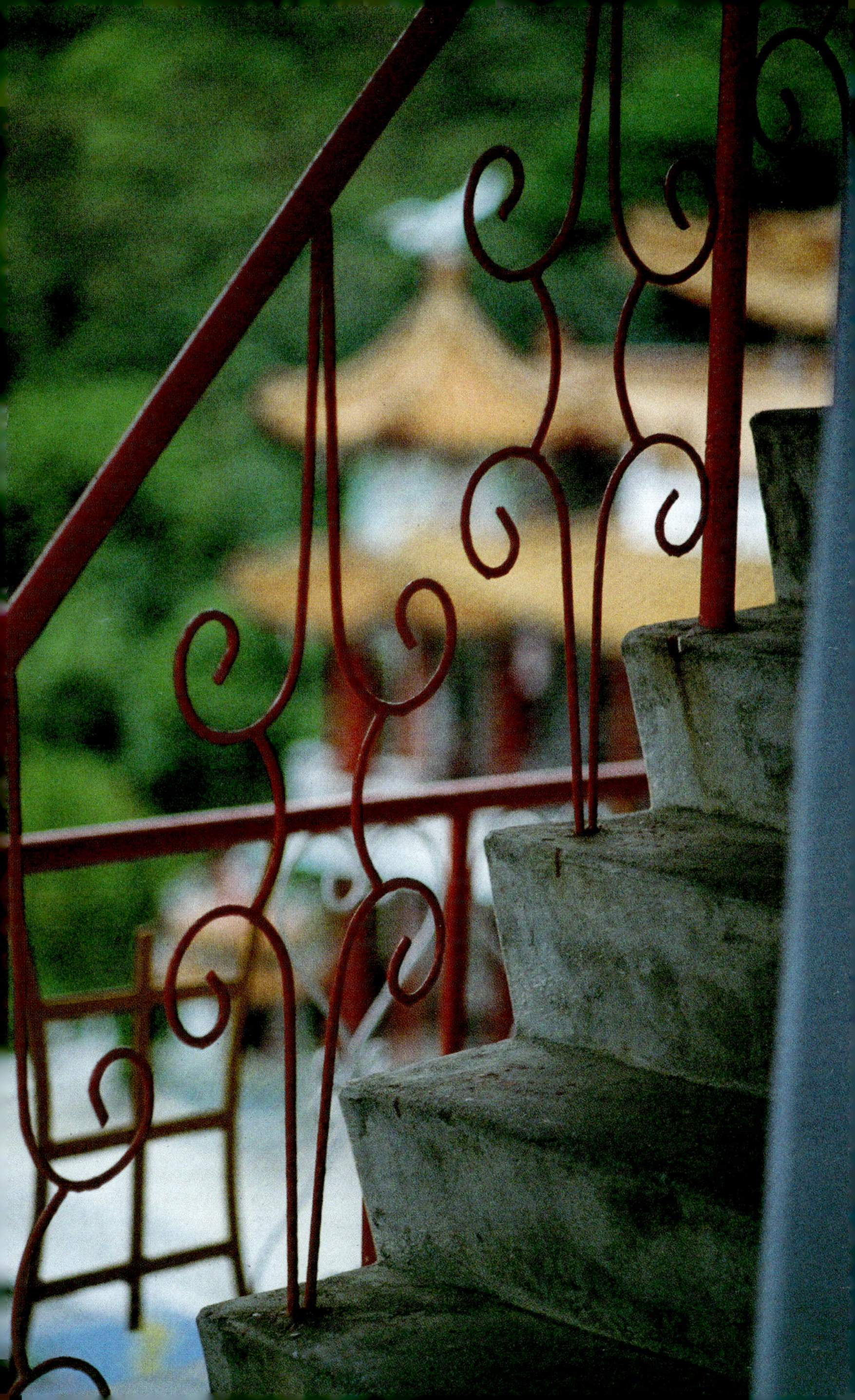

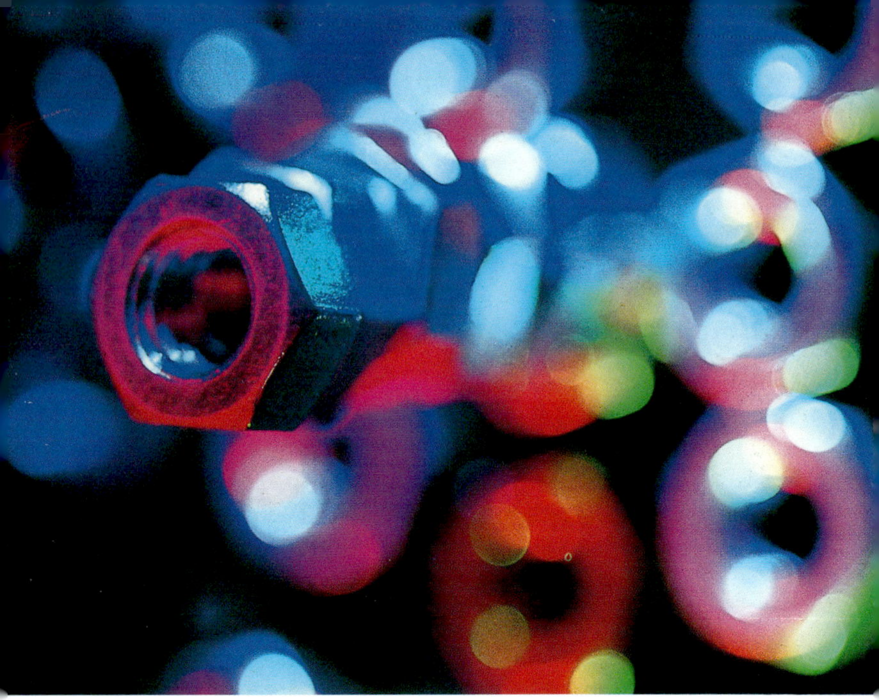

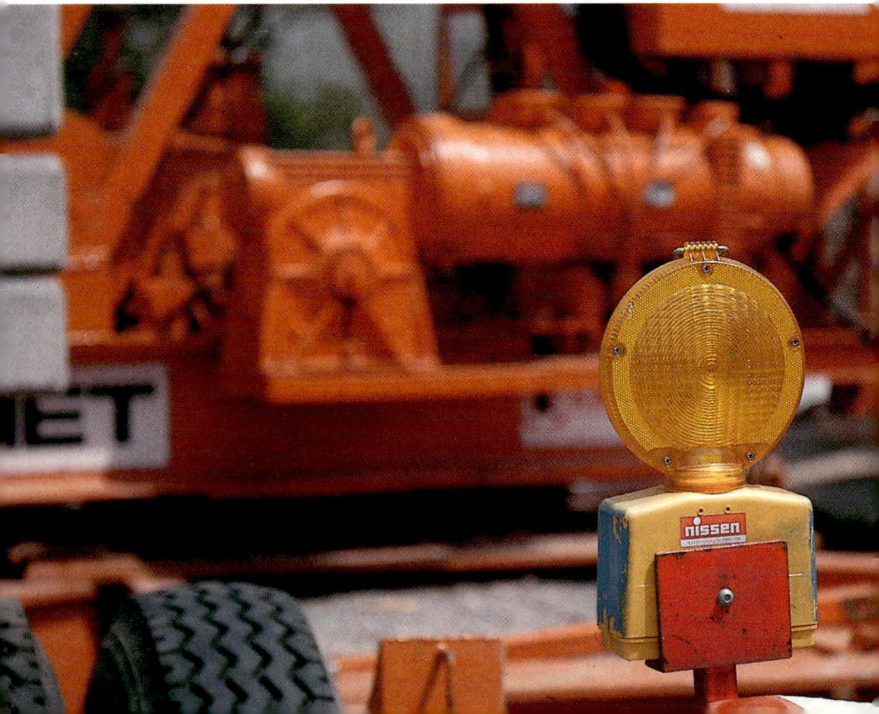

If we are shooting in program mode and the exposure control selects either too large an aperture or too slow a shutter speed, we can shift this towards our desired combination. This is done by turning the main dial while the release is kept pressed half-way.

- main dial to the right – the shutter speed is reduced and the aperture is opened up.
- main dial to the left – the shutter speed is increased and the aperture is reduced.

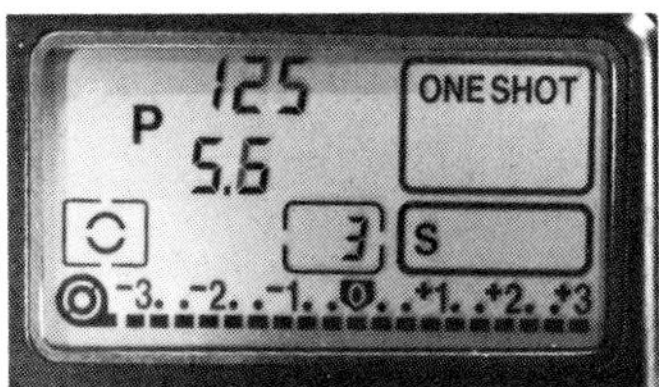

Program mode selected *f*5.6 and 1/25th sec.

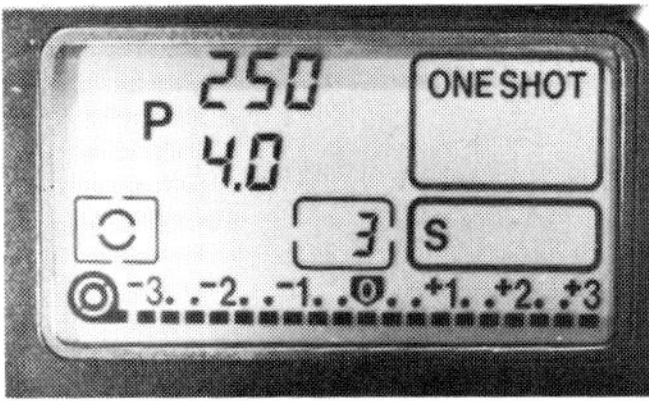

By turning the main dial to the right the shutter speed was reduced and the aperture consequently opened up.
The exposure value remained the same.

When using this function hold down the release with the middle finger so the index finger is free to operate the main dial. Or store the exposure value by pressing the AE lock button.

Top
A pyramid of nuts was illuminated by coloured spotlights.
Bottom
A hazard light sharply outlined and set against the rich ochre shade of the machinery in the background.
To obtain correct focus for these types of subjects it is essential to use focus lock (P mode + release pressed halfway + re-aligning camera or another shooting mode + pressing the AE lock button).

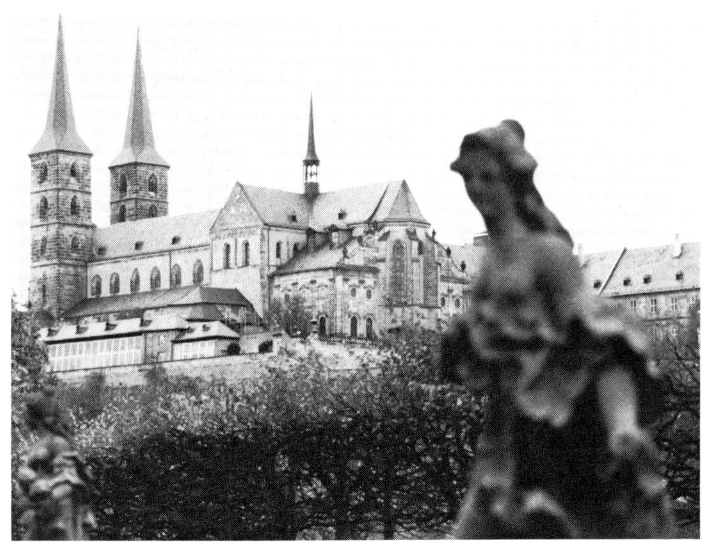

Michaelis Church from the rose garden in Bamberg. Four views for comparison. In this picture I pressed the release fully and the AF mechanism focused automatically on the subject detail at the centre of the frame – the church in the background. The statue in the foreground is outside the depth of field and therefore is unsharp.

To show the statue in the foreground in sharp focus I had to point the AF target field at the statue, press the release half-way and hold down to set the focus and then realign the camera for the desired framing before pressing the release fully to make the exposure. Both these pictures have been taken with a long focal length (250mm) therefore the church is relatively large compared with the figure in the foreground.

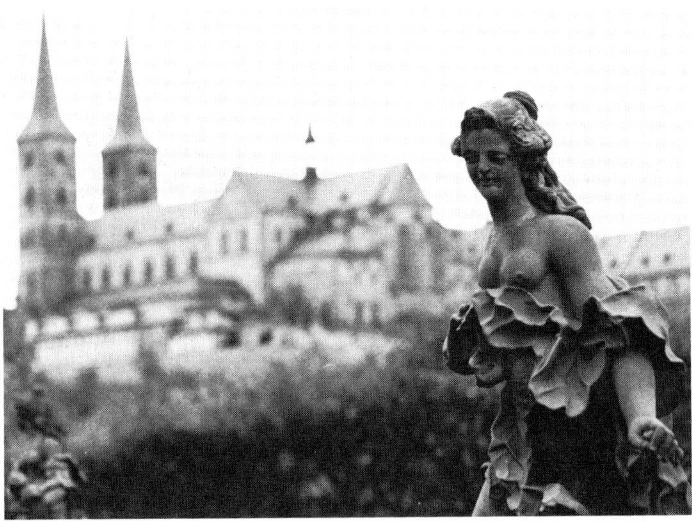

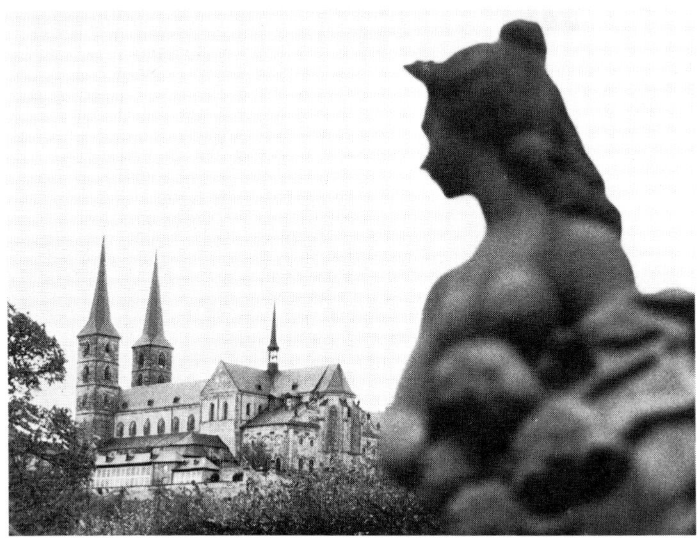

The same subject at a focal length setting of 80mm. The church is much smaller and I am closer to the statue, which now dominates the foreground. As the AF target field is aimed at the featureless sky, one-step release would not have worked. First focus on the church to bring the background into sharp focus, reframe and release.

Autofocus is quite easy even with pictures like this. All you have to do is take care that you focus on the important subject detail first, in this case the statue, and then re-align the camera before releasing the shutter. With a zoom, I focus on the important subject detail with the longest focal length setting, for exact focusing, before bringing the focal length back to the desired setting and adjusting the framing prior to release.

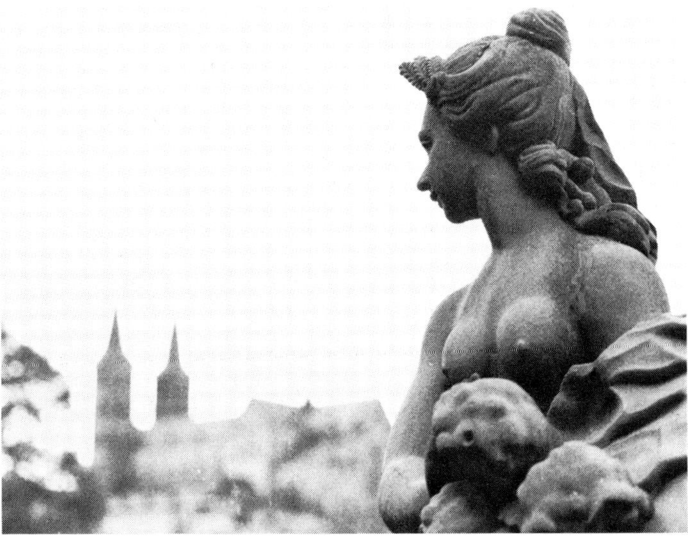

Most important: exposure lock independent of AF

This operating element allows exposure and autofocus to be stored separately and independently from each other. The AE lock button will freeze the metered values even if the release button is not held down.

> *A • is displayed in the viewfinder to the left of the shutter speed to indicate activated exposure lock. The locked value is displayed in the viewfinder and LCD panel. Both the current and the locked exposure values appear in the exposure scale on the right side of the viewfinder.*

The release need not be touched – one touch of the AE lock button activates exposure metering and locks it for 8 seconds. The metering can also be locked for the length of time the button is kept pressed. The AF mechanism can then be reactivated by pressing the release.

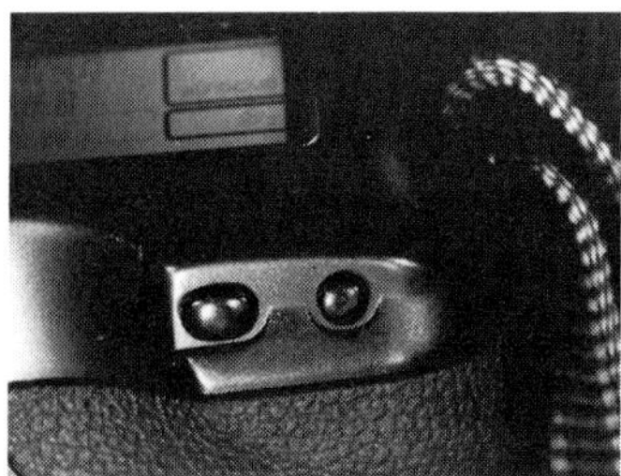

These two buttons are situated on the top right of the camera back. The left one is the AE lock button and the right one is the exposure compensation button.

Example: the exposure is supposed to be metered for an area on the right side of the subject space, the focus set for a subject detail on the left side of the frame.

This is how you proceed:

1. Point the camera to the right and press the AE lock button.
2. Move the camera to the left, bring the important subject detail within the AF target field and press the release lightly to focus the lens.
3. Move the camera around to obtain a suitable framing for the subject, (perhaps adjust the focal length setting at the same time) and then press the release fully home.

The most important operating elements are:

- the release button
- the main input dial
- the AE lock button (operated by the thumb)

65% of all shooting situations can be successfully dealt with by the use of these buttons.

General rule: use of flash by day or night
The use of flash is described in detail in Part VI "Use of Flash and Halogen Lighting". You may note the following: An exposure correction of –1 should be applied with 90% of all flash photographs with SLIDE FILM – and this applies really only to slide film!

Exposure Correction: Under- and Overexposure

Subjects and situations that require compensation

One of the special characteristics of the professional EOS camera is that override facilities are easily accessible to the photographer. Exposure compensations are applied quite frequently by experienced photographers. Particularly to slide film which requires more precise exposure than print film. Colour print film requires compensation only if presented with a rather contrasty subject or if a special effect is to be achieved. With critical subjects most photographers take exposure sequences provided the subject keeps still long enough. In this case the EOS-1 will accept settings different from the measured ones quickly and easily.

Subjects where underexposure is recommended – especially if slide film is used – are the following: bright details in front of an extensive and very dark background (a situation which arises frequently when flash is used (see Part VI). These subjects should be underexposed by about one stop (the exposure is halved). Then there are bright highlights in front of a dark background – sunsets and sunrises belong to this group – usually require a compensation of up to –1 to –2 *f*-stops.

Subjects where Exposure Compensation is Advisable
The following subjects should be underexposed by 1 or 2 stops, particularly if slide film is used:

- *Against the light landscapes*
- *Sunsets*
- *Stained glass windows*
- *Silhouettes*
- *Shots from an aircraft*
- *Bright details against a dark background*

The following should be overexposed by up to 1 stop:

- *Hazy views of distant subjects*
- *Snowscapes (white on white)*
- *Lit streets at night*
- *Dark details in front of white background*
- *People dressed all in black, animals with dark fur*

Subjects where overexposure is recommended are: dark details in front of a bright background or large, white areas such as clouds or snow. When using slide film you should expose for the brightest subject detail, when using colour print film expose for the darkest subject detail. In this sense colour slide film has to be slightly underexposed when taking against-the-light landscapes, and colour print film should be slightly overexposed.

Compensation by the button!

Exposure is activated by pressing this button but compensation is not stored. If the button is held down and the main dial turned at the same time then the amount of correction is determined.

Turning the main dial to the left: the exposure is reduced in 1/3rd step increments. In the LCD panel the amount of compensation is indicated by the marker moving towards the left along the dotted line. In the viewfinder the marker moves downwards on the scale at the right of the focusing screen. Turning the main dial to the right: the exposure is increased in 1/3rd step increments. In the LCD panel the amount of compensation is indicated by the marker moving towards the right along the dotted line. In the viewfinder the marker moves upwards on the scale at the right of the focusing screen.

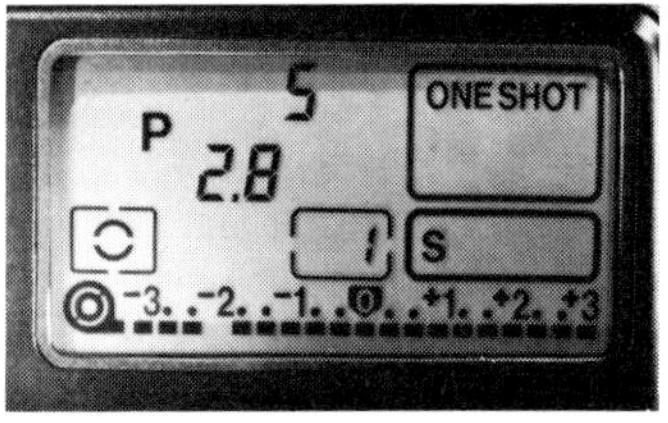

Display of underexposure compensation by –2 *f*-stops on the scale at the bottom edge of the LCD panel. Exposure compensation is also indicated in the viewfinder.

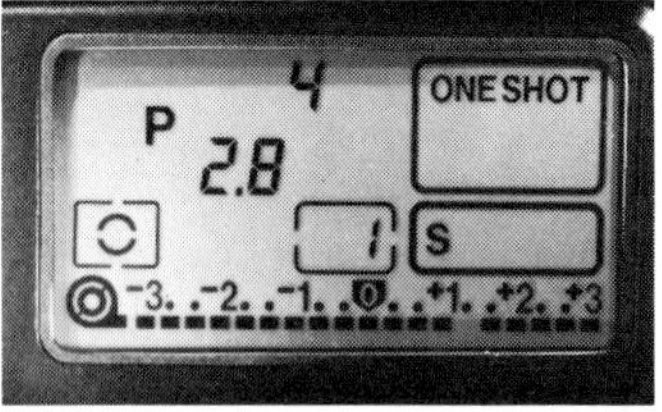

Display of overexposure compensation by +1 1/3rd *f*-stops on the scale at the bottom edge of the LCD panel. Exposure compensation is also indicated in the viewfinder.

Keep the exposure compensation button pressed and simultaneously turn the main dial to enter and store the required compensation. This can be done also by pressing the release half-way and turning the quick control dial. The amount of over- or underexposure will remain set, regardless of changing lighting conditions, until it is cancelled.

> ***+/– Display in the Viewfinder***
> *The +/– symbol in the viewfinder next to the exposure values indicates that a compensation has been entered. The amount of compensation is indicated on the scale at the right of the focusing screen. Underexposure: arrow moving downwards from the midpoint marker Overexposure: arrow moving upwards from midpoint marker*

Compensation by quick control dial

This dial is at the rear of the camera and is used as follows:

1. Set the quick control dial switch to "I".
2. Activate exposure metering by pressing the release halfway

- when pressing the release or the exposure compensation button, continuous exposure metering (adjusting continuously with changing lighting conditions) is activated.
- any metered and stored exposure value is activated when the AE lock button is pressed.

3. Turn quick control dial – to the left for underexposure and to the right for overexposure.

Exposure compensation is again in 1/3 step intervals up to +/–3 stops. The display is the same as described above, both in the LCD panel and in the viewfinder.

When setting an exposure compensation by using the quick control dial, it is activated by a short pressure on the release or the exposure compensation button. They need not be kept pressed in.

> ***Cancelling the Exposure Compensation:***
> - *Press release half-way and return exposure compensation to zero by turning quick control dial.*
> - *Press and keep pressed the exposure compensation button and return exposure compensation to zero by turning main dial.*
> - *Press white CLEAR button under the palm door on the right side of the camera. In this case the entered exposure value need not be activated. Any other stored functions, such as spot metering, multiple exposures, servo mode, etc., will be cancelled at the same time.*

Exposure compensation by changing film speed setting

The third method of changing the metered exposure is by manually overriding the film speed setting. This special function is not cancelled by pressing the CLEAR button. I would recommend this method whenever a whole film is to be over- or underexposed.

The Different Metering Methods and How To Use Them

Evaluative multi-field metering – when and how?

This is the standard metering method for your EOS-1. It is the preferred method whenever you have to react quickly with a fast moving subject, or for taking snapshots, animals in the wild, etc. For pictures of subjects with high contrast this method is generally not the best. If it is used then one has often to apply some exposure compensation. If you are used to this metering method and have plenty of experience with exposure compensation then you will be able to use this method successfully for almost every subject. The evaluative multi-field metering method is the standard metering method of the EOS-1. The entire frame is considered almost equally in the metering result. The camera evaluates six different subject areas and calculates an average. The metering method can be changed by Custom Function 8 to centre-weighted integral metering. In centre-weighted integral metering the subject part at the centre of the frame is considered more strongly in the metering result than the areas around the sides. The latter metering method is the most common metering method used in modern SLR cameras. The reason for weighting the metering result in this way lies in the fact that the subject area at the centre of the frame is usually the most important part of the composition. However, this is not always true and a lot of compositions are particularly impressive or charming just because they do not follow this rule. Personally I use the following rule with the EOS-1: for slide film I use the centre-weighted metering method, for print film the evaluative method. For copying I definitely use the evaluative metering method.

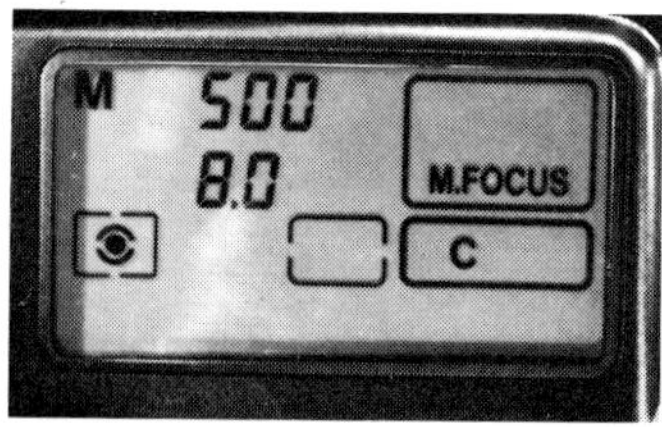

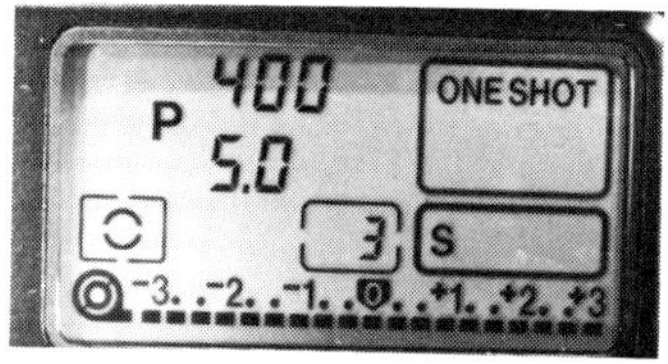

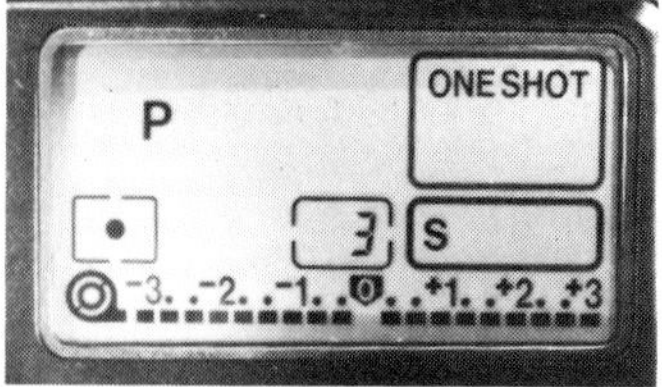

Top left: panel display for whole field metering – multi-field or centre-weighted.
Top right: selective metering.
Left: spot metering.

Selective metering – when and how?

In the selective metering method only 5.8% of the frame is considered – covered by the larger of the two circles at the centre of the focusing screen. It is useful for pictures, particularly when using slide film, such as landscapes with high contrast, stage scenes, a circus, illuminated street scenes and buildings at night or in the dusk – in short, for all situations when it is important to meter small, bright highlights in a generally dark subject space. Backlit scenes, for example, when a face in the shade against a bright background is supposed to show sufficient detail, are another important group of subjects that benefit from selective metering. If you want to produce a true silhouette, then you can meter the background against which the main subject will be outlined with this method.

Selective and spot metering render exposure compensations unnecessary – at least this is the rule but rules do have exceptions! If we meter the setting sun in selective or spot metering mode then we should not apply the previously recommended exposure compensation of between –1 to –2 stops, which applied only to evaluative and integral metering, otherwise the whole background will be very underexposed.

- To change over from the basic evaluative metering to selective or to spot metering, press the METERING button on the top left shoulder of the camera and turn the main dial until the required symbol appears in the LCD panel.
- To return to the basic setting, repeat this process or press the CLEAR button (the white button under the palm door).

Genuine spot metering – when and how?

Spot metering means that only 2.3% of the frame, namely the smaller of the two concentric circles at the centre of the focusing screen, is metered. This allows very precise metering of even tiny subject areas; perhaps the tip of a cliff illuminated by the last rays of the sun, the face of the singer on stage lit by a single spotlight, or the luminous detail of an interesting stone in a dark recess.

If you are using a zoom lens, then the metering result may be even further improved by using a long focal length setting for the metering process (don't forget to bring the setting back to the desired framing). You may think that this metering method is rather unusual and you may never use it. Let me assure you it is very useful and I tend to use it quite often.

Part IV

The Programs of the EOS-1

P: Program Automatic

Exposure by program mode

Overexposure is a thing of the past with the EOS-1. If the light is very bright, the exposure program simply stops down the aperture and increases the shutter speed, if necessary down to 1/8000th sec. It will therefore hardly ever be necessary to use a neutral density or polarising filter to prevent overexposure.

How, in fact, does the EOS-1 program mode work?

I suggest that you attach a zoom lens to the camera and point it at a reasonably well-lit subject. You will notice that as you change the focal length setting on the lens, the shutter speed and aperture value also change. This is as it should be, as the program mode works in conjunction with the focal length setting of the lens.

Let's assume the subject is only dimly-lit and becomes gradually brighter. To start with, program mode will ensure that the aperture is fully open when the exposure is set. With increasing brightness the aperture stays wide open and the shutter speed is constantly decreased until the reciprocal value of the focal length setting in mm on the lens is reached:

for focal length 30mm, 1/30th sec
for focal length 50mm, 1/50th sec
for focal length 100mm, 1/100th sec, etc

As the brightness increases further, program mode will alternately increase the shutter speed and stop down the aperture, in 1/3rd stop intervals.

For lenses with longer focal lengths, program mode chooses faster times and wider apertures. For shorter focal lengths preference is given to slower shutter speeds combined with smaller apertures.

This means:

- when using longer focal length lenses, when the limit of safe hand-held shooting is reached, program mode will endeavour to set fast enough times provided the subject brightness is sufficient.
- when using shorter focal length lenses, where shutter speeds are less critical, program mode can stop down for greater depth of field.

Program mode aperture/shutter speed combinations with increasing subject brightness

Focal length 30mm, maximum aperture ƒ4

aperture	4	4	4	4	4	4	4.5	4.5
speed	1/10	1/13	1/15	1/20	1/25	1/30	1/30	1/40
aperture	5	5	5.6	5.6	6.3	6.3	7.1	7.1
speed	1/40	1/50	1/50	1/60	1/60	1/80	1/80	1/100
aperture	8	8	9	9	10	10	11	11
speed	1/100	1/125	1/125	1/160	1/160	1/200	1/200	1/250
aperture	13	13	14	14	16	16	18	18
speed	1/250	1/320	1/320	1/400	1/400	1/500	1/500	1/640
aperture	20	20	22	22	25	25	29	29
speed	1/640	1/800	1/800	1/1000	1/1000	1/1250	1/1250	1/1600
aperture	32	32	32	32	32	32	32	32
speed	1/1600	1/2000	1/2500	1/3200	1/4000	1/5000	1/6400	1/8000

Focal length 100mm, maximum aperture ƒ5.6

aperture	5.6	5.6	5.6	5.6	5.6	6.3	6.3	7.1
speed	1/50	1/60	1/80	1/100	1/125	1/125	1/160	1/160
aperture	7.1	8	8	9	9	10	10	11
speed	1/200	1/200	1/250	1/250	1/320	1/320	1/400	1/400
aperture	11	13	13	14	14	16	16	18
speed	1/500	1/500	1/640	1/640	1/800	1/800	1/1000	1/1000
aperture	18	20	20	22	22	25	25	29
speed	1/1250	1/1250	1/1600	1/1600	1/2000	1/2000	1/2500	1/2500
aperture	29	32	32	32	32	32		
speed	1/3200	1/3200	1/4000	1/5000	1/6400	1/8000		

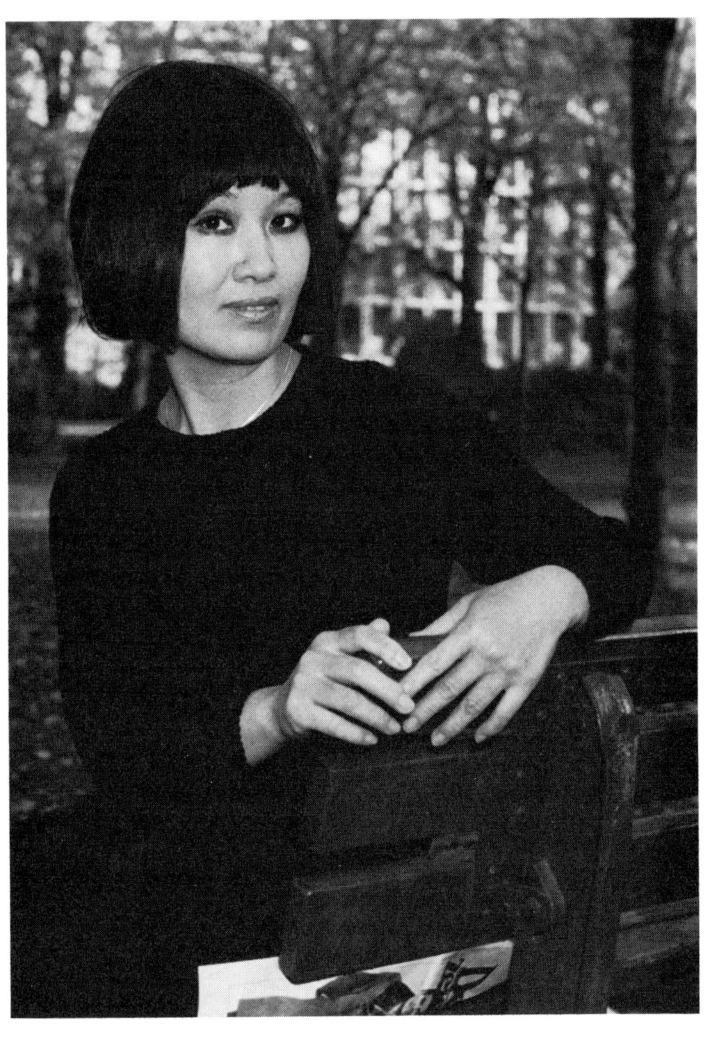

Flash in daylight. The flash output was kept low to fill in the foreground.

Flash in program mode

Flash photography could not be easier if you are using a system flash with the EOS-1 (see also Part VI):

- *for uniform illumination of the subject use flash in daylight or in a bright room.*
  As soon as the flashgun is switched on, the shutter speed is set to a suitable time for flash photography – between 1/250th and 1/60th sec – but the camera will still adjust the settings to take account of the available light. The flash is used only to fill-in the foreground otherwise the picture will look the same as if no flash has been used.
- *the general lighting level is relatively low and the camera selects a shutter speed slower than 1/60th sec – at least as long as the flash is not switched on.*
  As soon as the flashgun is switched on, the camera will automatically increase the shutter speed to 1/60th sec. The flashgun emits an infrared metering flash, effective for a subject at between 8m and 11m from the camera. This flash provides the data for both the automatic focusing of the lens and the exposure control. The size of the aperture will be chosen in relation to the distance of the subject at the centre of the frame. The closer the subject, the smaller the aperture. This means that a close-up subject will be shown brightly against a dark background – the closer the subject, the darker the background.
- *for dimly-lit backgrounds at long distances. This includes shots at night outdoors or in large, dark halls:*
  The same applies as above. A brightly-lit main subject is set against a dark background - the greater the proportion of dark subject details, the more overexposure. When using slide film in this type of situation, you should apply an exposure compensation between –2/3rd and –1 2/3rd then the background will be darker, with a brightly-illuminated foreground. It is also possible to modify the flash output directly on the flashgun, which allows the foreground illumination to be reduced while keeping the rendering of the background unaffected.

Experience shows that the majority of flash photographs on slide film, taken in P mode, require a compensation of –1. This does not apply to copying. However, if the original contains a large proportion of dark areas then it may instead require an exposure increase of 1/2 a stop.

Av: Aperture Priority

You select the aperture – the shutter speed is calculated automatically

I use the aperture priority mode particularly in the following two – entirely different – situations:

1. Whenever I need to shoot with a predetermined, wide-open aperture. This situation occurs, for example, when working indoors, or in the dusk, with fast films and without a flash. Particularly if I wish to obtain pin-sharp images within a narrow depth of field, to emphasise the sharp main subject against an out of focus foreground and background.
2. Whenever I need to stop down the aperture to obtain sufficient depth of field.

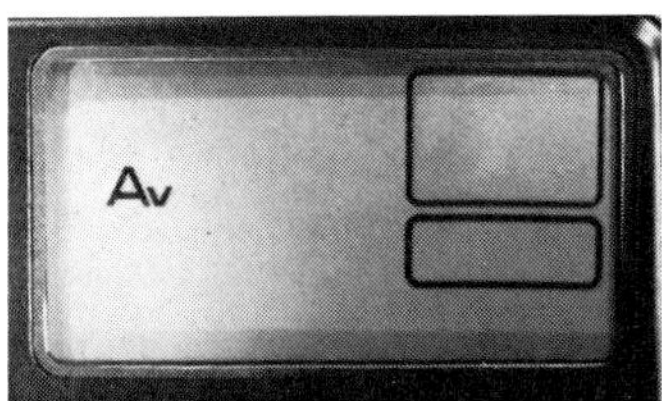

Holding down the MODE button while turning the main dial will select aperture priority mode, and Av will be displayed in the LCD panel.

Changing from P to Av:

Press the MODE button, situated on the left shoulder of the camera, and simultaneously turn the main dial until Av is displayed in the LCD panel. The aperture displayed at this time will be the value set when the camera was last in either Av, M or bulb mode. This value stays in memory even if the CLEAR button is pressed, the camera is switched off (L = lock) or the batteries are changed.

Returning to P:

Press the CLEAR button under the palm door, or press the MODE button and simultaneously turn the main dial until P is displayed. (Note: pressing CLEAR will cancel all other special settings at the same time, such as compensation, etc.)

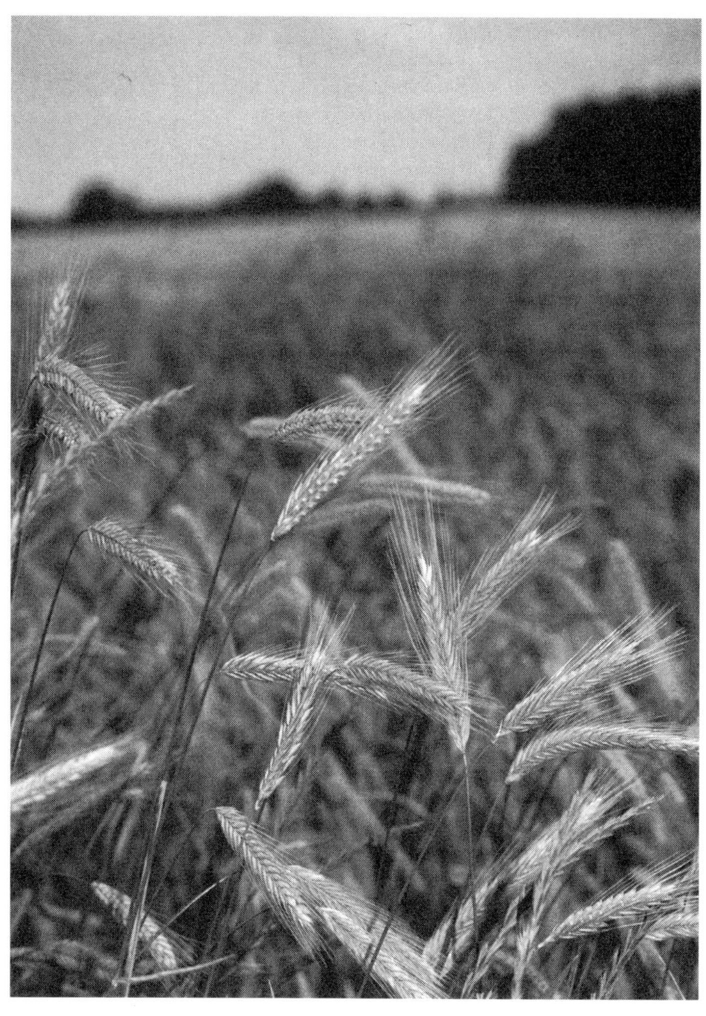

Ears of Corn – taken in aperture priority mode, with wide-open aperture. I intended to obtain a clear contrast between the sharply depicted ears of corn and the unsharp background.

Free choice of aperture values

The aperture can be changed in third-stop intervals by turning the main dial. Turning to the left (counter-clockwise) closes the aperture, to the right (clockwise) opens the aperture. Only aperture values available on the lens that is attached can be selected. To conclude; the aperture value is adjusted manually; it is not influenced by the exposure metering.

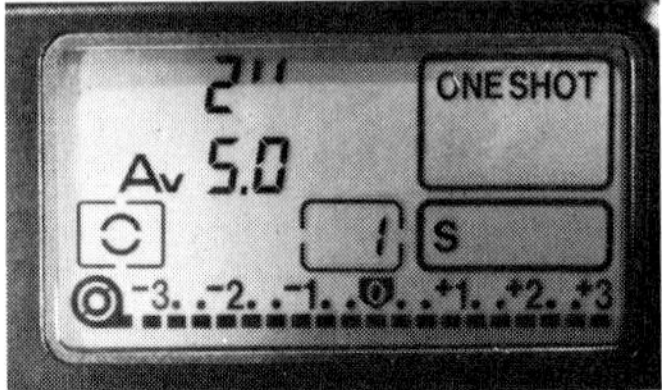

The LCD panel with EOS-1 set to Av mode and exposure metering activated. The aperture setting may be changed by turning the main dial.

The exposure times follow automatically for the given lighting conditions and the reading of the chosen metering system (evaluative, integral, selective or spot-metering). The metered exposure value can be stored by pressing the AE lock button (the button on the left behind the LCD panel).

Exposure compensation for intentional over- or underexposure:

- reducing the exposure level means in this case that only the shutter speed is increased, the aperture remains at the preset value.

To affect exposure compensation:

- press the exposure compensation button and turn the main dial to set the required level.
- press release half-way and turn the quick control dial to the left (underexposure) or the right (overexposure).

Display for Danger of Underexposure:

- shutter speeds as slow as 1/2 minute are automatically set, if this is still insufficient, then 30" (30 sec) will blink in the LCD panel.

Remedy: open up aperture, change to long exposure (bulb) or use flash.

Display for Danger of Overexposure:

- most unlikely – the 8000 (1/8000th sec.) blinks in the LCD panel.

Remedy: stop down aperture.

Flash in Av mode

Using flash in Av mode means basically that the metered exposure is left as it is but subject detail in the foreground is additionally illuminated:

- it has to be remembered that switching on the flash can alter the shutter speed setting, but in lighting conditions where a shutter speed of 1/250th sec. or slower has been determined, this speed will not change when the flash is switched on and the aperture cannot be changed by the exposure mechanism as it is manually preset. I always consider the available light, even if it is quite low and requires exposure times of 20 or 30 seconds. The resulting picture will be a composition of available light and flash light. If the shutter speed is slower than 1/20th, down to 1/8th sec., the sharply-depicted flashed outlines may be superimposed by blurred outlines due to camera shake. This may be exactly the effect you wanted to achieve, or not, as the case may be. If not, you will have to support the camera on a tripod.
- if the exposure mechanism calculates a shutter speed between 1/320th and 1/8000th sec., then this speed will be automatically changed to 1/250th sec. if a flash is attached and switched on (naturally, this has to be an EOS system flash unit). In this case the 250 (1/250th sec.) will blink in the LCD panel to remind you to stop down, otherwise the picture will be overexposed.

Experience has shown that for the majority of pictures taken in Av mode using slide film, an exposure compensation of –1 has to be entered.

Tv: Shutter Speed Priority

You choose the shutter speed – the camera determines the aperture

Shutter speed priority mode is useful whenever a fast speed needs to be set to freeze movement, or if a slow speed is required to lend impact to movement by showing it as more or less blurred. Tv mode is also well suited for flash photography.

Changing from P to Tv:

Press the MODE button and simultaneously turn the main dial until Tv is displayed in the LCD panel. The shutter speed displayed at this time will be the value set when the camera was last in either Tv or M mode. The shutter speed can be changed manually by turning the main dial only when either one of these shooting modes are selected. This value stays in memory even if the CLEAR button is pressed, the camera is switched off (L = lock) or the batteries are changed.

Returning to P:

Press the CLEAR button under the palm door, or press the MODE button and simultaneously turn the main dial until P is displayed. (NOTE: pressing CLEAR will cancel all other special settings, such as compensation, etc.)

Free choice of shutter speeds

The shutter speed may be changed in third-stop intervals by turning the main dial. To the left (counter-clockwise) increases the speed, to the right (clockwise) decreases the speed. To conclude: the shutter speed is adjusted manually, it is not influenced by the exposure metering.

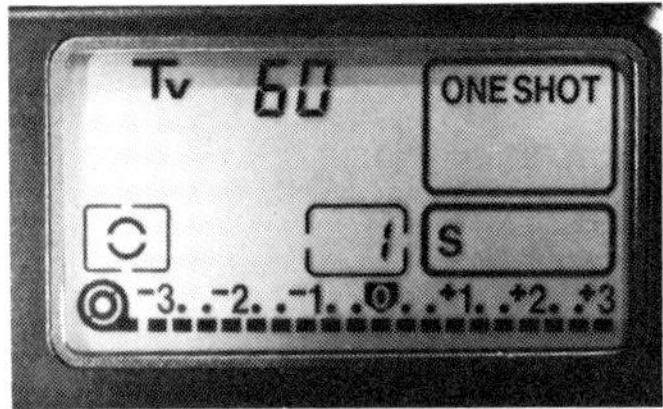

The LCD panel with EOS-1 set to Tv mode and exposure metering activated. The shutter speed setting may be changed by turning the main dial, the aperture is calculated automatically.

The aperture value follows automatically for the given lighting conditions, always in accordance with the chosen metering system (evaluative, integral, selective or spot metering). The metered exposure value can be stored by pressing the AE lock button (the button on the left behind the LCD panel).

Exposure compensation towards intentional over- or underexposure:

- reducing the exposure level means that only the aperture is reduced, the shutter speed remains at the preset value.

To affect exposure compensation:

- press the compensation button behind the LCD panel and turn the main dial to set the required level.
- press release half-way and turn the quick control dial to the left (underexposure) or the right (overexposure).

Display for Danger of Underexposure:

- the maximum aperture of the attached lens, for example 1.8, blinks in the LCD panel.

Remedy: use slower shutter speed or flash.

Display for Danger of Overexposure:

- the minimum aperture of the attached lens, for example 22 or 32, blinks in the LCD panel.

Remedy : faster shutter speed.

Flash in Tv mode

When using flash in Tv mode you can ensure that the shutter speed is fast enough to avoid blurring due to camera shake:

- if you entered a shutter speed between 1/250th and 1/60th sec. for sufficiently bright subjects and the camera calculated a suitable aperture, these settings will not change if a flash is attached. Only the main subject in the foreground will be filled-in by the flash. The aperture can be changed (shifted) within the limits of correct exposure. For example, if the original combination was 1/250th sec. and *f*5.6, I could change the shutter speed to 1/60th sec, and the aperture would be automatically stopped down to *f*11.
- if I preselect a shutter speed between 1/250th and 1/60th sec. in poor lighting or in complete darkness, and the camera sets the largest available aperture value (value blinks), then the flash will illuminate the foreground quite sufficiently but the background will be lost in a greater or lesser degree of darkness. The faster the preselected shutter speed, the darker the background.
- if I preselect a shutter speed between 1/8000th and 1/400th sec for a reasonably bright subject, and the camera calculates an average or even maximum aperture, then the shutter speed will be slowed down to the fastest flash synchronization time of 1/250th sec.; the aperture will be stopped down at the same time to compensate. If it is still too bright, the smallest aperture value blinks in the LCD panel. In this case too the background behind the brightly-lit main subject in the foreground will be rather dark.

Depth of Field Control and the dEP Mode

Checking the depth of field in the viewfinder

The depth of field preview button is situated on the lower left of the lens mount. If you place your index finger in the usual way on the release button, you can reach the depth of field preview button quite easily with your little finger. Pressing this button stops down the aperture to the selected value. Although the image in the viewfinder gets darker, usually you can still see how much of the subject depth is shown in acceptablc focus.

Automatic depth of field Selection – depth mode

The depth mode is also selected by pressing the MODE Button and turning the main dial to display dEP in the LCD panel.

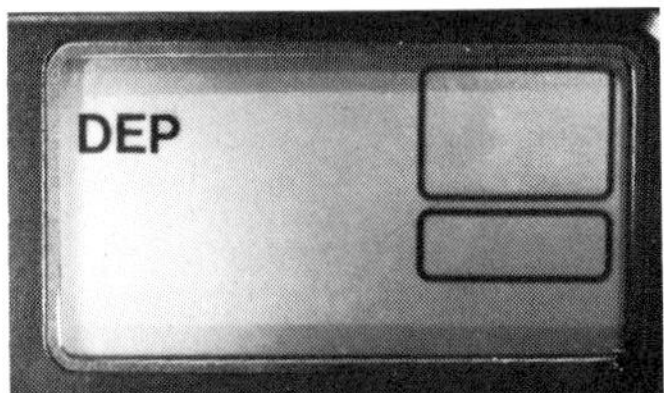

Press the MODE button and simultaneously turn the main dial until dEP is displayed to confirm selection of depth mode.

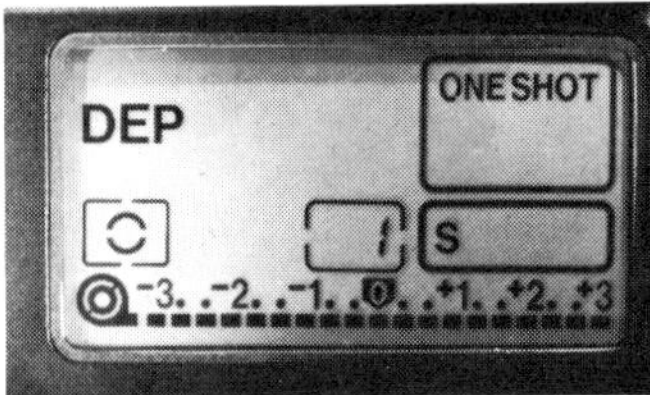

Continuous display for depth mode whenever the EOS-1 is switched on and a film is loaded.

Dancing figures:
Clad in luminous strips and illuminated with two 125W UV beams. Taken at 4 sec which produced this luminograph (tracing of movements of light). The strong blue hue could have been reduced by using a UV filter.

Overleaf:
This apple demonstrates how fill-in flash outdoors can be used to good effect. Top left: without a flash. Top right: flash exposure without any compensation. Bottom right: flash exposure with –1 exposure compensation. Bottom left: flash exposure with –2 exposure compensation. The exposure compensations were set on the camera, not on the flash unit.

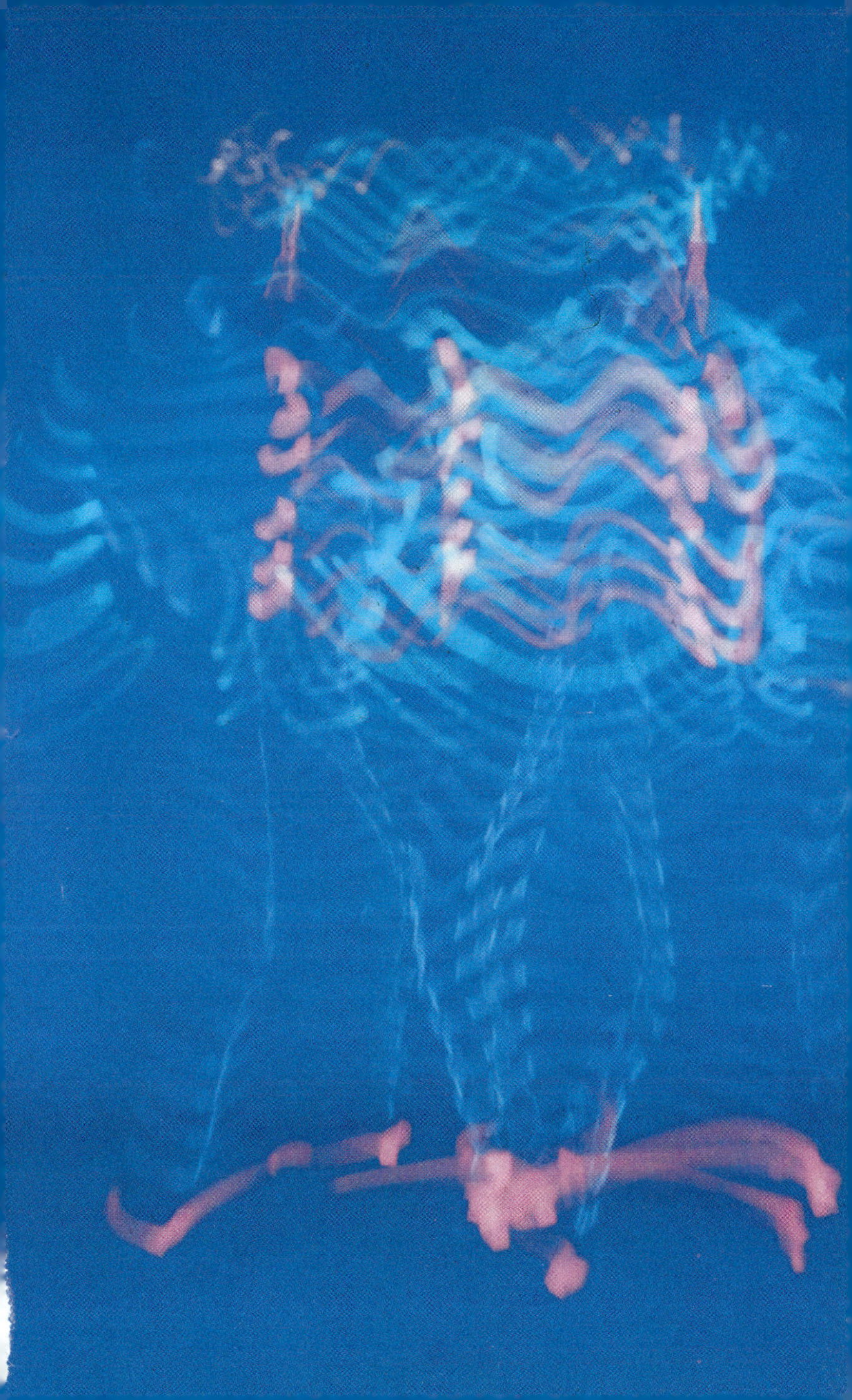

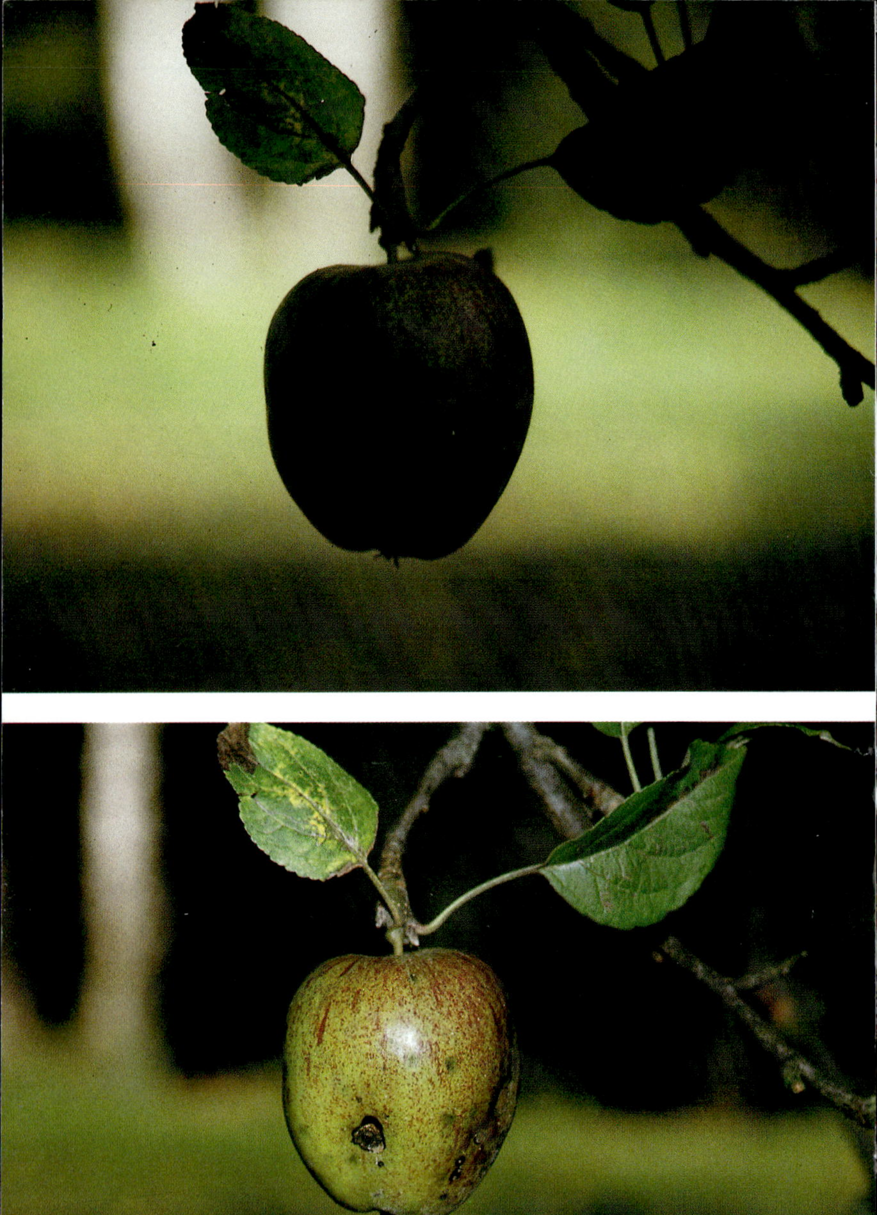

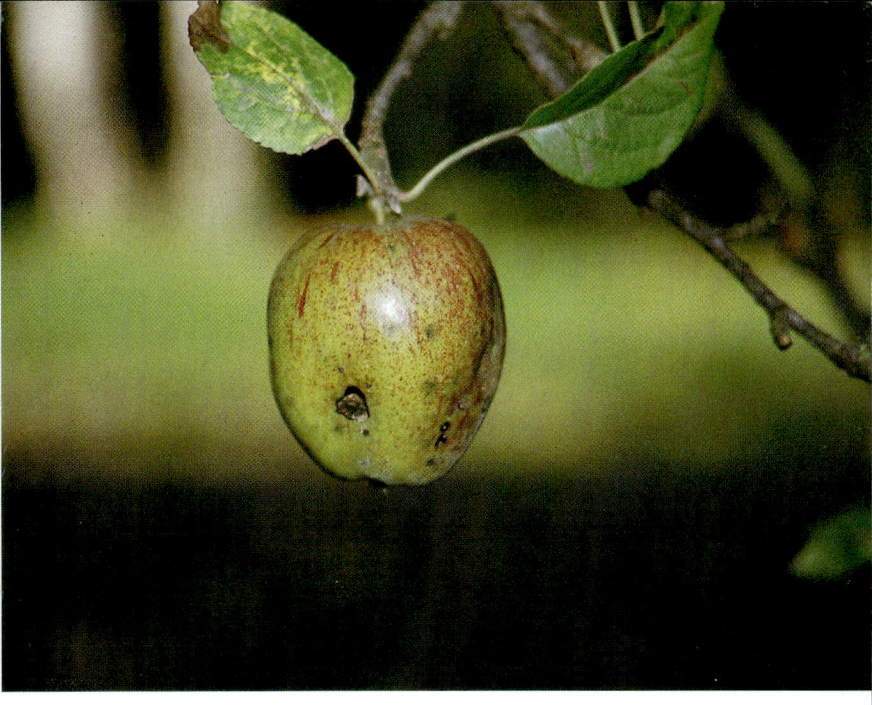

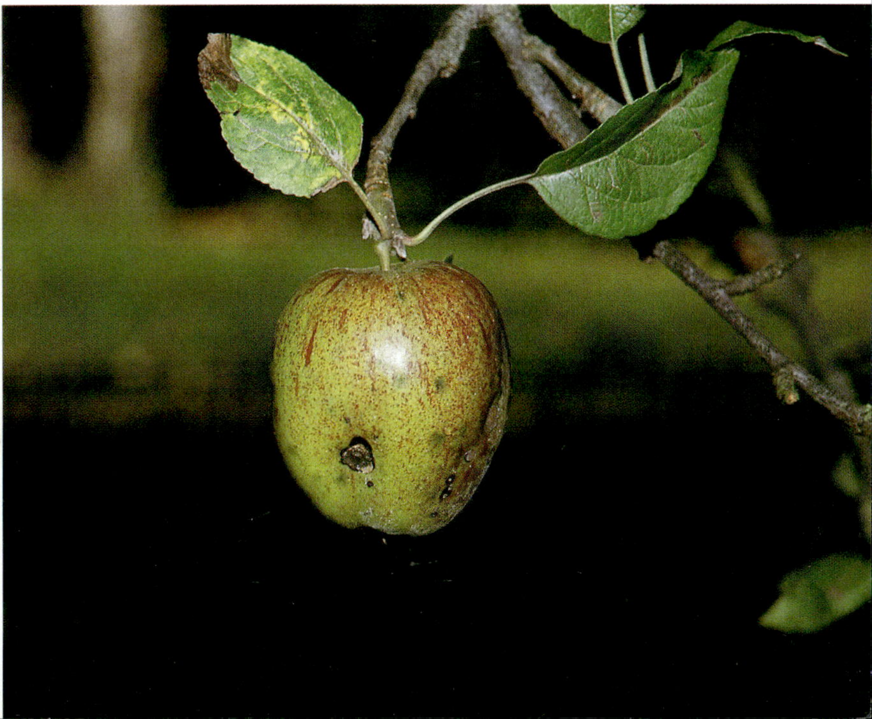

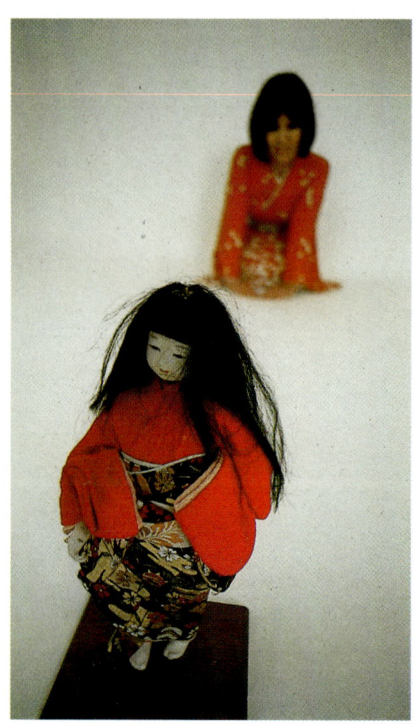

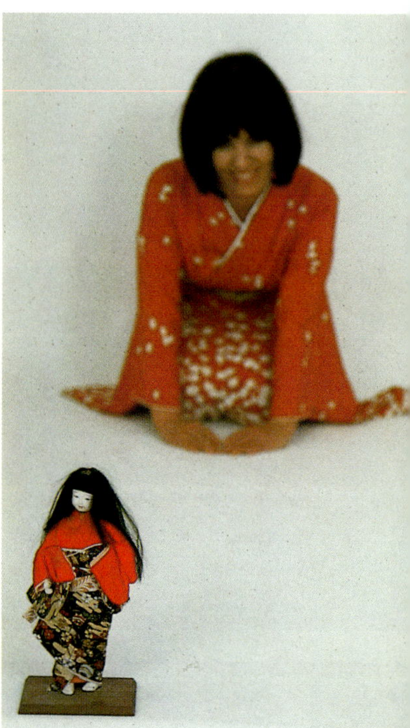

The Japanese doll and model demonstrate most impressively the effect of different focal lengths. Picture on the left: wide-angle shot at close range (to the doll) which makes it seem disproportionally large and the woman in the background very small in comparison. Picture on the right: at long range (from the doll) with a long lens. Now it is overshadowed by the larger woman in the background. And what is the actual size of the doll? 20cm! A good example of the "objectivity" of photography.

1. Point camera at the closest limit of the subject depth that needs to be shown in sharp focus and press the release halfway to activate AF mechanism. dEP1 will be displayed both in the viewfinder and in the LCD panel.
2. Point camera at the farthest limit of the subject depth that needs to be shown in sharp focus, and press release half-way again. dEP2 will be displayed both in the viewfinder and the LCD panel.
3. Align camera for correct framing. It is even possible to adjust the focal length setting, the dEPth mode will allow for this.
4. Press release fully. The camera will calculate and set the appropriate average values and display both aperture and shutter speed. In many cases the resulting shutter speed may be too slow for hand-held shots and you will either have to select a shorter focal length on the zoom lens or put the camera on a tripod and start again.

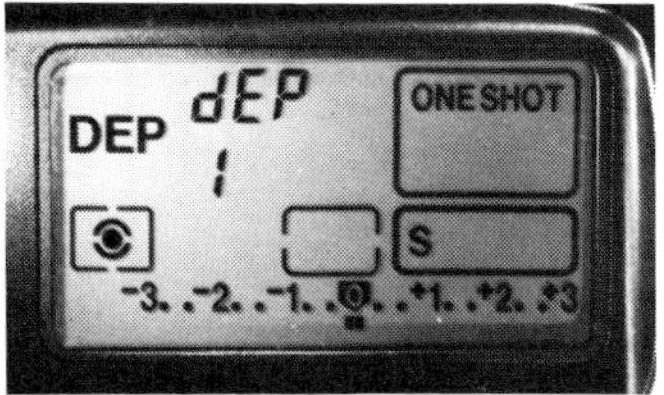

Depth mode display after taking the first reading. An appropriate display will also appear in the viewfinder.

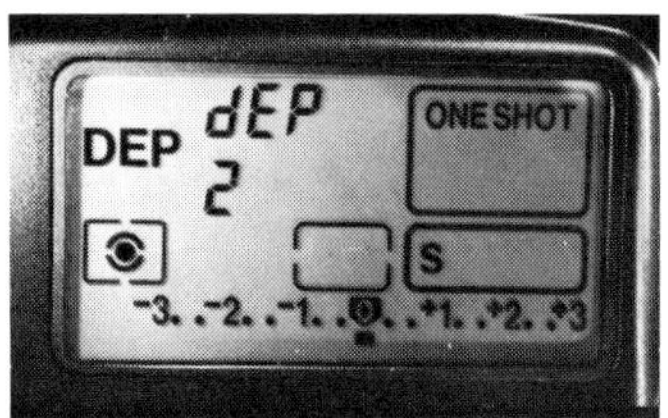

Depth mode display after the second reading. An appropriate display will also appear in the viewfinder.

M: Manual Mode – with Exposure Metering

Often used – the manual mode

Procedure: press MODE button and turn the main dial until M is displayed in the LCD panel. A clearly visible, green M will appear in the viewfinder. Now you can turn the main dial to adjust the shutter speed – to the left for slower speeds, to the right for faster speeds.
The aperture is adjusted either by:

- turning the main dial and simultaneously pressing the exposure compensation button (the button on the right behind the LCD panel), or
- pressing the release half-way and turning the quick control dial. Turning the dial to the left opens up the aperture, turning it to the right stops it down.

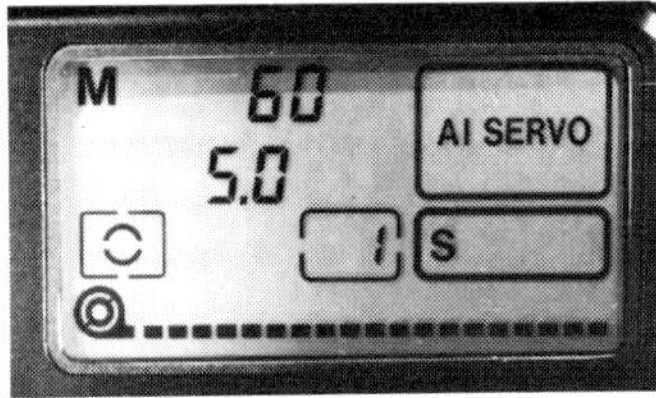

LCD panel with manual setting of aperture and shutter speed.

Manual mode with exposure level display

Even though the aperture and shutter speed have to be set manually the EOS-1 will still keep you informed as to whether the chosen settings correspond to the correct exposure level. Check the scale on the right of the focusing screen; if the arrow is at the centre of the scale on the green triangle the exposure level is correct. Overexposure of up to three stops is indicated by the arrow pointing to the top half the scale, underexposure by the lower half of the scale.

Flash in M-mode

Even in M-mode the flash – provided it is an EOS system flash – will work fully automatically.

To use a flash changes nothing as far as the aperture setting is concerned. Neither will there be any changes to the shutter speed for values between 1/250th and 1/30th sec. Shutter speeds faster than 1/250th sec, will be slowed to 1/250th sec. For the given aperture value the flash will automatically calculate the appropriate flash output for the subject in the foreground.

Sources of Error:

- underexposures due to too great a distance: if, for example, you use a slow film (ISO 50), select *f*32 for a subject at 30m distance, then you will not record anything on the film. The flash is not powerful enough to illuminate a subject at this great distance. I should think 10m at aperture *f*4 with an ISO 100 film is the limit for successful flash illumination.
- too slow a shutter speed together with a large aperture for subjects illuminated by available light, the result – overexposure. Always when the arrow in the viewfinder climbs up the scale, you should watch out for overexposure. In this case, increase the shutter speed to 1/250th sec. and if this is still insufficient, stop down the aperture.

Please note:

- if the arrow points at the central green triangle on the exposure scale, then the general lighting determines the exposure level. The flash is used only to fill-in the foreground.
- as the arrow moves down the exposure scale, the general lighting contributes less and less and the flash illumination dominates the exposure. From an underexposure indication of 3 stops, the available light contributes practical nothing to the exposure.

Long Exposures with or without Bulb

Automatic exposure up to 30 seconds

In P, Av and dEP mode, the EOS-1 will automatically calculate and set shutter speeds up to 30 sec. (30"). In Tv and M mode the shutter speeds can be entered manually in 1/3rd step increments, again up to 30 sec.

Long exposures of any duration

Press the MODE button and turn the main dial until bulb is displayed in the LCD panel. For long exposures you will definitely need to use a tripod and perhaps also remote release 60T3. This remote release is 60cm long and it can be extended by a 10m cable. The remote release has a slide switch on the handgrip which is used to lock the shutter in the open position.

The elapsed time appears in the LCD panel in a sequence of numbers (1-30) and bars, which represent each half minute, up to 120 seconds. After which the display is cancelled and, if necessary, the sequence starts again.

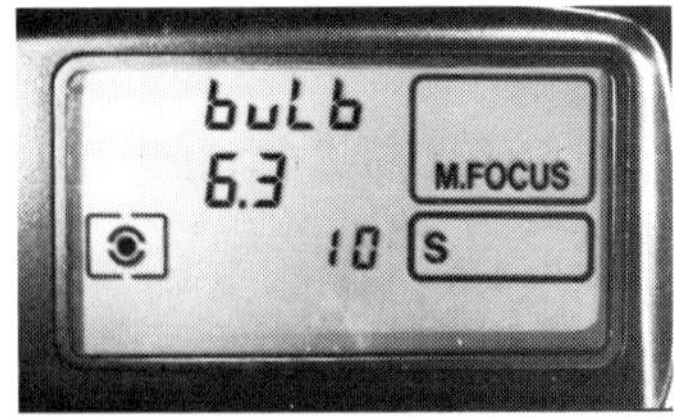

Long exposure at "bulb" setting. The shutter is open, 10 seconds have elapsed.

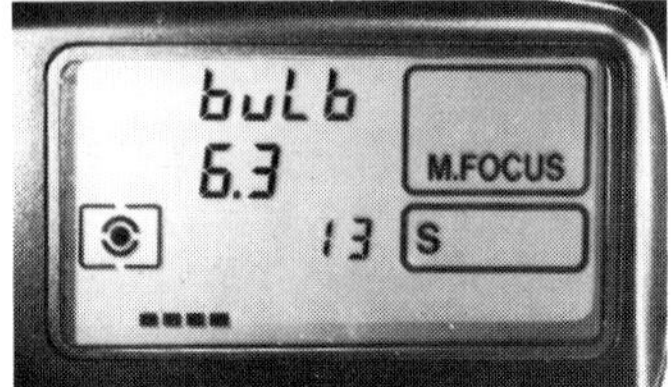

Long exposure at "bulb" setting. The shutter is open, 30 seconds plus 13 seconds have elapsed.

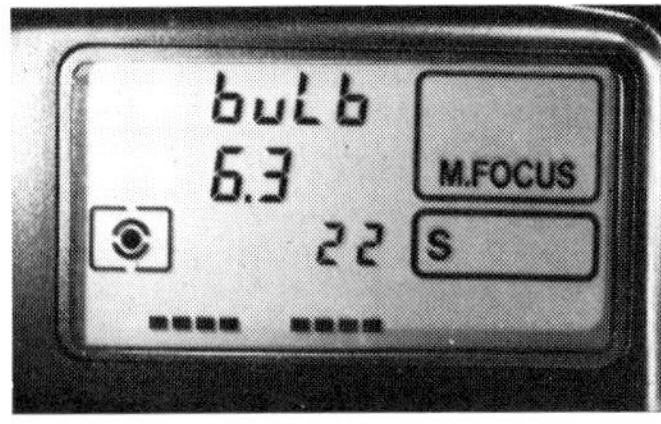

Long exposure at "bulb" setting. The shutter is open, 2 x 30 seconds plus 22 seconds have elapsed.

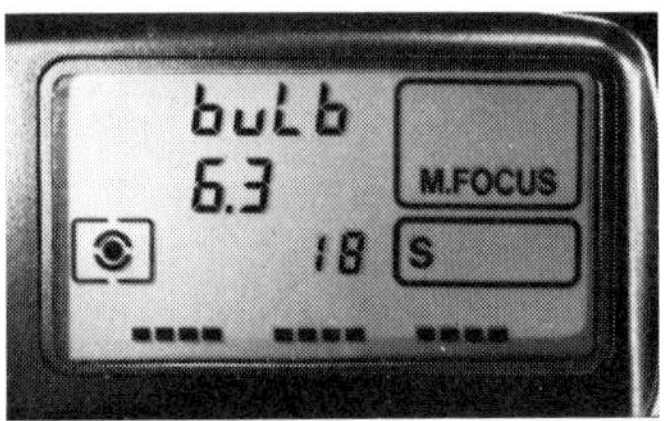

Long exposure. The three bars and the number indicate that 3 x 30 plus 18 seconds have elapsed. After a total of 120 seconds the count-down sequence is started again.

The LCD panel illumination does not work in long exposure mode. This with good reason, as the power drain would be too great during a long exposure sequence.

> *Please note: when giving long exposures from a tripod the eyepiece has to be covered to prevent stray light entering the viewfinder and confusing the metering, particularly if a strong light source is behind the camera. In the shoulder pad of the carry strap you will find a small rubber pad which fits over the eyepiece.*

Flash can be used with long exposures of any duration.

Part V

Special Features and Refinements of the EOS-1

Snappy Picture Sequences

AF SERVO mode for moving subjects

The most vociferous objections to autofocus cameras came from snapshot and sports photographers.

It used to be the case that an AF mechanism allowed the shutter to be released only after the lens was successfully focused. In snapshot and sports photography one often has to act almost instantly to get a good shot, to capture a movement or a fleeting expression. In situations like these it is often better to take the shot even if the subject is not perfectly focused, it may still be within the depth of field, particularly if a small enough aperture was preselected.

The objection against the AF mechanism holds true – but only for cameras which use the ONE SHOT mode in combination with the S (single frame) mode. As far as the EOS-1 is concerned, the shutter release block is automatically cancelled in continuous shooting mode C, and in single frame shooting it can be cancelled by changing over to SERVO.

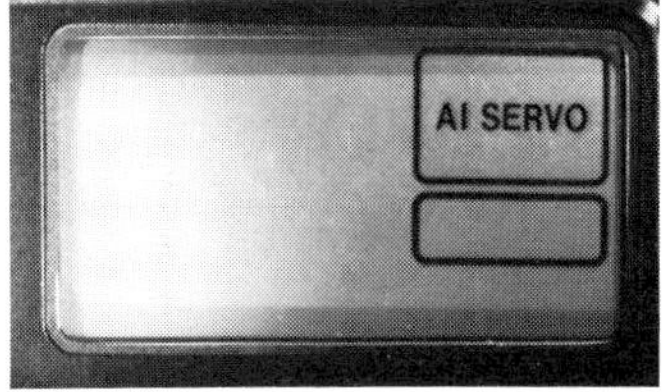

Press the AF button on the left shoulder of the camera and turn the main dial at the same time to select either ONE SHOT or SERVO.

To set SERVO:
- press AF button.
- rotate the main dial in either direction to replace ONE SHOT with SERVO in the LCD panel.

To reset ONE SHOT:
- press the AF button and turn main dial until ONE SHOT is displayed.
- press white CLEAR button behind the palm door. All special functions will be cancelled.

The autofocus setting cannot be stored in SERVO mode. When the release is pressed half-way the AF mechanism will focus always on the subject detail within the AF target field and it will continuously re-adjust to even the smallest changes. The shutter can be released at any time, even if the focusing procedure has not been completed. Automatic exposure lock is also de-activated. However, the exposure can be stored for a particular framing by pressing the AE lock button.

SERVO mode is useful for fast-moving subjects or for portrait studies to capture fleeting expressions. As the focus is set for the centre of the frame, it is vital that the important subject detail is in the AF target field.

Whenever it is more important to arrange the subjects details carefully within the subject space and to find the correct framing, then ONE SHOT mode is better.

C-mode – the continuous snapshot mode

It is possible in single shooting mode to achieve quite a rapid shooting sequence. Press the release fully and release the button – the camera will make all the settings and release the shutter – the process can then be repeated. In favourable conditions when the subject can be easily focused and there is sufficient light, you can achieve 3 frames per second.

If we change over from S (single shot) to C (continuous) then we only need to press and hold the release – one shot after another will run through the camera. The EOS-1 will take up to 2.5 frames per second in C-mode; 36 pictures in 14 - 15 seconds.

To select C:

- press and hold the blue DRIVE button under the palm door.
- turn the main dial until C is displayed in the rectangle in the LCD panel.

Cancellation of C:

- press DRIVE button again and turn main dial until S is again displayed.
- or press CLEAR – this will cancel all special functions.

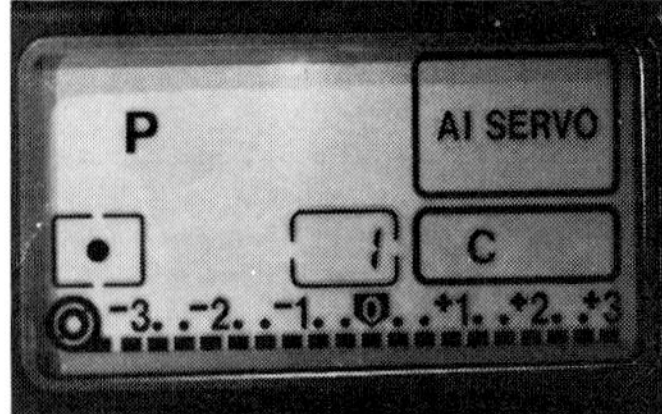

LCD panel for continuous shooting C + SERVO (autofocus continuously tracking subject).

C + ONE SHOT (normal AF mode):

if you wish to take a sequence of shots, up to ten, then the release is initially blocked until the focus is set for the first picture of the sequence. Thereafter one shot after the other is taken without any readjustment of focus setting. This combination ensures the fastest shooting sequence.

C + SERVO:

holding the release down when the EOS-1 is programmed with this combination of functions, a series of pictures will be taken but the focus setting is continuously adjusted for the detail within the AF target field. However, even if the focus could not be set within a reasonably time, the shutter will still be released. If you are tracking a moving subject with this setting, then the shooting frequency will be uneven, perhaps in short bursts. The shooting frequency is not so fast, perhaps 1 or 2 frames per second. It may take about half a minute to use up a 36-exposure film.

Conclusion:

- in single frame mode S + ONE SHOT the shutter release is delayed until the AF mechanism has focused the lens.
- in C + ONE SHOT mode the shutter release block is cancelled after the first shot of the sequence.
- in C + SERVO the shooting frequency is reduced because the AF mechanism tracks the subject and adjusts the focus between each frame.

Fast shooting frequencies with flash are possible under the following circumstances:

- the system flashgun has to be loaded with fresh batteries.
- the flashgun has to be set to reduced output, i.e. 1/8, 1/16 or 1/32 of its total output
- the subject distance must not be too great.

It is better to use fast films as this increases the effective range of the flash.

Four times the film speed means twice the flash range.

The sequence of movements is relatively slow, the main subject does not move from the centre of the frame, it is therefore quite easy to keep it in the centre of the frame. This is the ideal situation for S + SERVO. For faster movements C + SERVO is better.

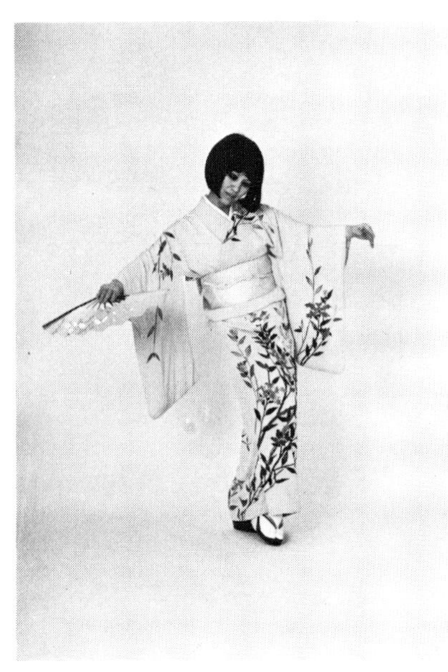

The high and the low C with booster operation

If you are using the booster then the frame frequency is greatly increased. If you are selecting C mode by pressing the DRIVE button and turning the main dial not just a C, but CH or CL is displayed. CH (continuous high) means fast shooting sequence up to 5.5 frames per second. If you press the release fully with this setting it is almost impossible to take only one frame. Before you can take your finger off the button, 2 or 3 frames will have been exposed. CL (continuous low) means continuous slow shooting of 2.5 frames per second. Naturally it is possible to take single pictures in C mode with a remote release; the release is pressed and quickly released. Fast shooting sequences with flash are possible.

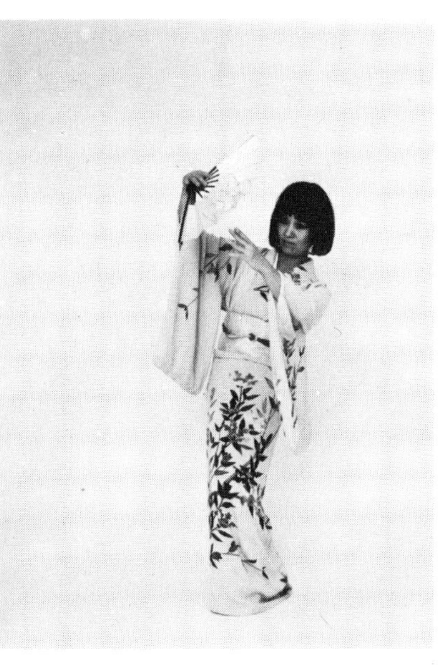

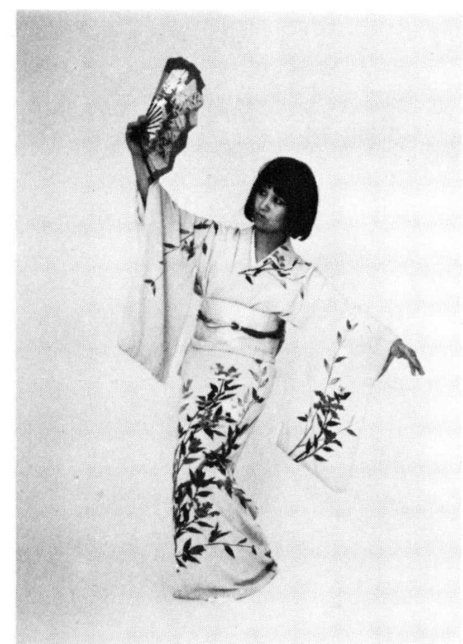

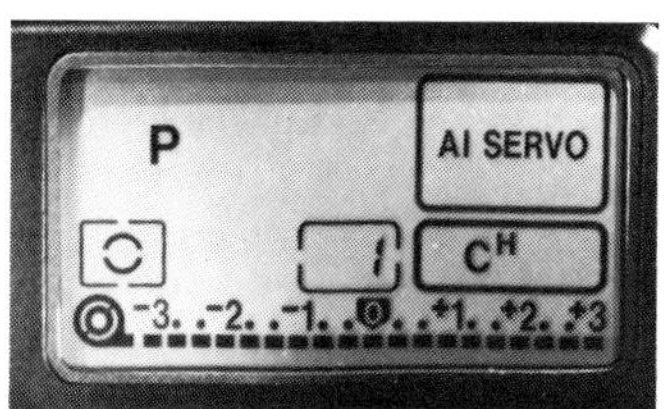

Display for booster CH shooting sequence of 5.5 frames per sec.

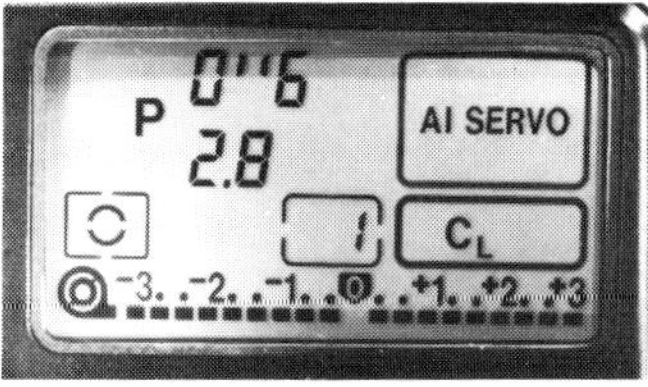

Display for booster CL shooting sequence of 2.5 frames per sec. Exposure metering is activated.

Release Specialities

Self-timer – with 2 or 10 seconds count down

Two further functions can be selected with the DRIVE button and main dial; these are the two different count-down times for self-timer operation:

- clock Symbol 10: self-timer with 10 seconds count-down
- clock symbol 2: self-timer with 2 seconds count-down

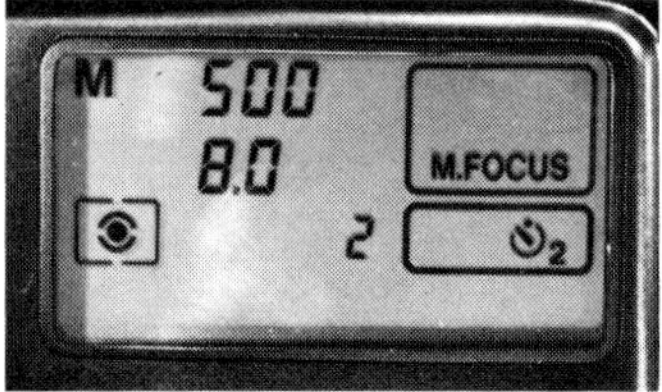

Self-timer with 2 seconds count-down. The number 2, without frame, means that the count-down has just started, time remaining is 2 seconds.

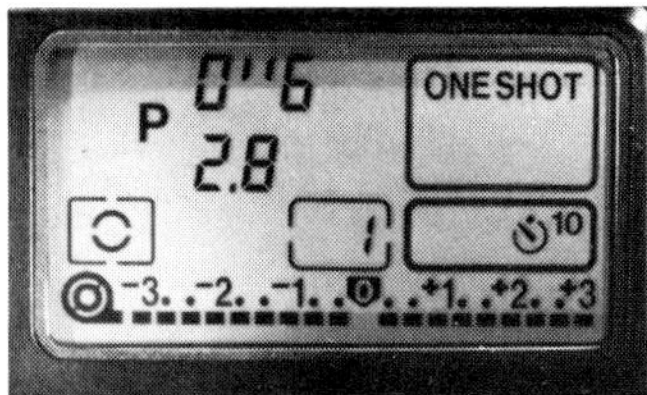

Self-timer sequence with 10 seconds count-down. The number 1 in the box indicates that the first frame can be exposed. The count-down has not yet started. The numbers of the count-down run down without a box.

The sequence is started by pressing the release. The seconds are then counted down in the LCD panel. A red light next to the lens blinks at the same time, first slowly, and shortly before the shutter is released, more rapidly.

Please note when using the self-timer:
the AF mechanism sets the focus after the first pressure on the release. The focus is now set and can no longer be changed until the shutter is released (even SERVO mode cannot change anything in this situation). If you wish to include yourself in the picture, it is best to arrange a substitute in exactly the place where you will be, set the focus for this distance, and then move into position.

To cancel the self-timer function:

- press DRIVE button and turn main dial until S or C is displayed;
- alternatively; press the CLEAR button to cancel all special functions.

To interrupt the self-timer sequence:

- simply switch the EOS-1 off (L). This cancels the count-down. You can then switch on again and start a new sequence or cancel the self-timer function altogether.

The self-timer function is not only suitable for self portraits. I use it frequently to release the shutter when the camera is supported on a tripod; this ensures a shake-free release with long exposures.

ME – double and multiple exposures

The multiple exposure function ME allows between two and nine exposures on one frame.

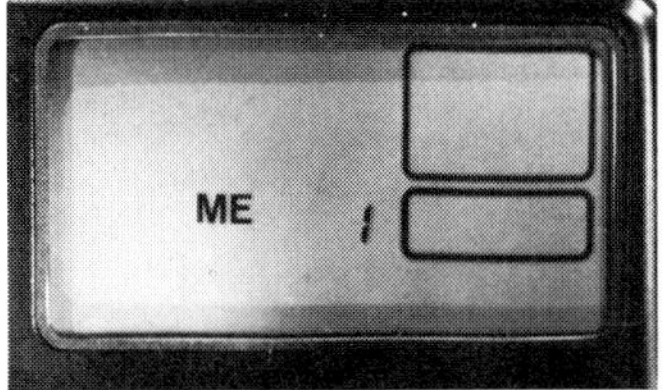

Simultaneously pressing the MODE and the METERING buttons displays ME and 1, without box, in the LCD panel.

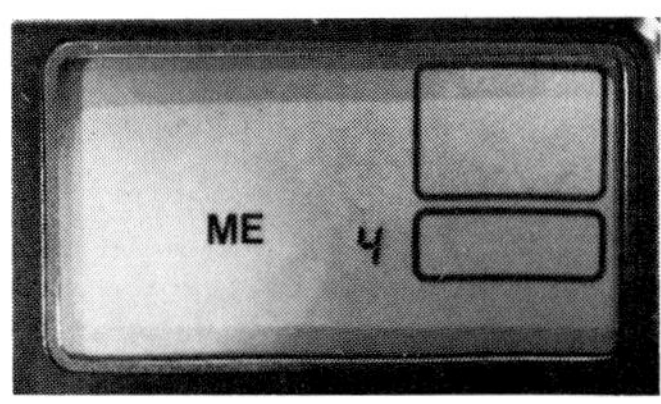

The number of exposures on one frame – between 2 and 9 – can be selected by turning the main dial. In this case 4 exposures has been selected.

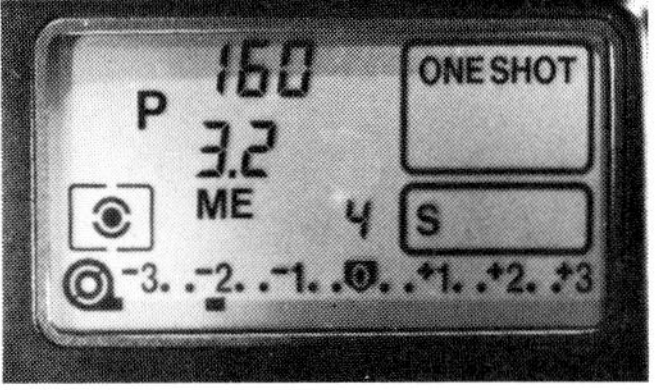

An exposure compensation of –2 has been programmed for this 4x multiple exposure.

Setting ME:

- simultaneously press the MODE and the METERING buttons on the left shoulder of the camera. ME appears in the LCD panel and in the viewfinder when the release is pressed half-way. The number 1 beside it can now be changed to a number between 2 and 9 by turning the main dial.

After each individual shot the exposures are counted down in the LCD panel so you always know how many shots you can expose on this particular frame. This is important because the individual partial exposures may be made at quite long intervals.

To cancel the ME setting:

- once a multiple exposure has been completed, the ME function is automatically cancelled.

To cancel or even interrupt the sequence:

- press the MODE + METERING buttons again and turn the main dial until 1 (or another, more suitable value) is displayed in the LCD panel. For total deletion together with all other special functions, press the white CLEAR button under the palm door.

Correct exposures for double and multiple exposure pictures

Whether or not one superimposes the individual subjects in such a way that the finished picture looks interesting is not only a matter of creative skill but also of luck.

We have to distinguish between two quite different situations with regard to exposure:

- multiple exposures without overlapping.
  We wish to show four flowers delicately arranged against a black background, each of the blooms to be placed in a different corner of the frame. In this case the images do not overlap, they are arranged next to each other. Each individual subject requires its own full lighting. That means exposure compensations are not required.
- multiple exposures with overlapping.
  We are photographing four landscape subjects, each of which fill the whole frame, in this case each subject must receive somewhat less exposure. In our particular case only 1/4 of the light that the subject would normally receive if taken on its own. If, however, we are piling up a larger number of exposures, then it is better to allow each a little more than just the proportional amount. The following table offers a rough guide; you will have to perform your own experiments to achieve good results.

Compensations for Multiple Exposures		
No. of Exposures	*theoretical compensation*	*practical compensation*
2	*–1*	*–1*
3	*–1.5*	*–1*
4	*–2*	*–1.5*
5	*–2.5*	*–2*
6	*–2.5*	*–2*
7	*–3*	*–2.5*
8	*–3*	*–2.5*
9	*–3*	*–2.5*

The above values should serve as a rough guide and must be adjusted according to the particular situation

The first time you experiment with multiple exposures I would recommend that you use brightly-lit subjects against a dark background. An interesting variation; use a different colour for each exposure. Perhaps use a different filter, either in front of the lens or in front of the light, to produce a colour palette. It is also possible to use flash.

AEB – 3 frame auto exposure bracketing

With this function you are taking three pictures with exposure variations by pressing the release once. In particular, one picture is exposed exactly according to the metered value, one will be overexposed and one underexposed, always by a pre-determined amount in 1/3rd steps up to 3 stops.

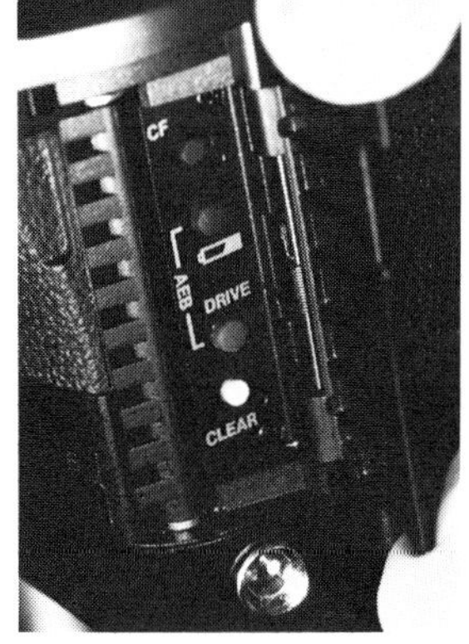

Press the 2nd button (battery check button) and the 3rd button (DRIVE) under the palm door to display AEB in LCD panel for six seconds to enable you to remove your fingers and turn the main dial to select exposure increments between +/– 0.3 and 3 stops.

Setting AEB:

- simultaneously press the black battery check button and the blue DRIVE button under the palm door. In the LCD panel AEB and 0.0 will be displayed.
- turn the main dial to the right and select a value between 0.3 and 3.

If you select 3.0, then one of the pictures will be overexposed by 3 stops and one underexposed by the same amount. If you select 0.3 the pictures will show little difference as the difference in exposure level is small.

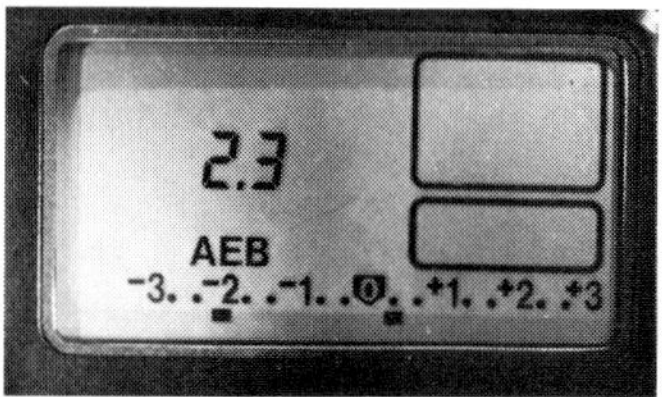

Automatic exposure bracketing by a factor of 2.3 with an exposure compensation of + 0.3. The actual exposure values are –2, +0.3 and +2.7.

Normal AEB operation – AEB + S (SINGLE SHOT):

Each of the pictures is individually exposed. The release button has to be pressed between each exposure. The legend AEB blinks as long as the AEB sequence has not been completed. After the three pictures are taken AEB stops blinking.

Continuous AEB operation – AEB + C:

In this setting it is also possible to determine the point of release for each frame, simply press the release down and quickly let go. In this case check whether AEB blinks (sequence not yet finished) or if it has stopped blinking.

Holding the release button down will make all three exposures in quick succession -

- for C (with normal handgrip) at 3 frames/second
- for CL at 2.5 frames/second
- for CH at 5.5 frames/second.

AEB with Self-timer:

If the auto exposure bracketing sequence is initiated by self-timer, regardless of whether 2 seconds or 10 seconds count-down is chosen, then it suffices to press the release only once. The three exposures will be made in quick succession, without booster at a rate of 3 frames/second, with booster at 5.5 frame/seconds.

Quick AEB sequence:
AEB + ONE SHOT: no focus adjustment between individual shots.
AEB + SERVO: focus adjustment between individual shots (not with self-timer function). However, this reduces the shooting rate.

An exposure bracketing sequence with a factor of 2. One picture is correctly exposed, one is underexposed by a factor of 4, the bottom one overexposed by the same amount.

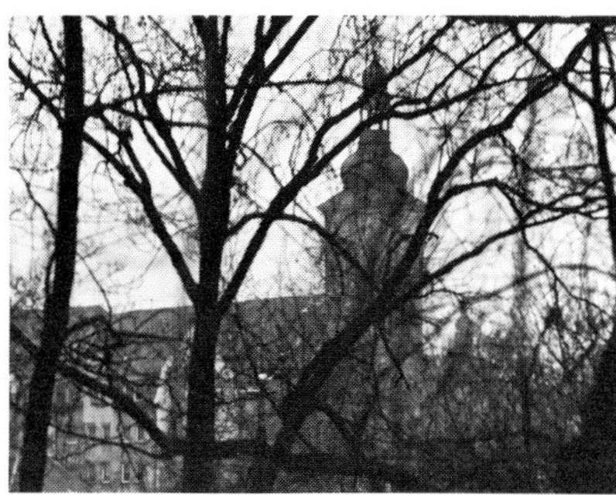

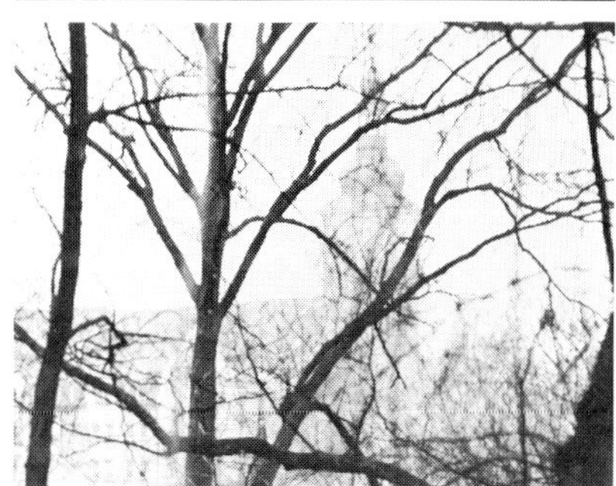

The AEB Exposure Variations in Combination with the Different Exposure Modes
P Program: shutter speed and aperture are changed between the individual shots. *Tv mode: only the aperture setting is changed.* *Av mode: only the shutter speed is changed.* *M program: only the shutter speed is changed. The initial exposure can be set independently of the metered value.*

To cancel AEB:

- either press the black battery check button and the blue DRIVE button and turn the main dial to the left until 0.0 is displayed.
- or, more simply, switch the EOS-1 off (L) and, if required, back on again. If the film is changed, this will also cancel the AEB function. However, in both cases the set exposure variation remains. A short pressure on both of the above mentioned buttons will re-activate the AEB function. The AEB function is retained if the battery is changed.
- another easy way: switch to “bulb”.
- another possibility: attach a Canon EOS system flashgun and switch it on. As soon as the flash is charged, and the release pressed half-way (or the exposure compensation button or the AEB lock button) the AEB function is cancelled. Flash can be switched off again. In this case too, the exposure variation is retained, and AEB can be re-activated.
- or, as previously, press the CLEAR button to cancel all special functions.

AEB sequence with exposure compensation

As already indicated, the exposure bracketing can also be shifted towards under- or overexposure by the additional setting of exposure compensation. If an exposure compensation is set with the same factor as the AEB variation, but with a minus sign, then I get two pictures which are underexposed to different degrees, in addition to my correctly-exposed shot. If I choose the plus factor, I shift everything towards overexposure. The combination of AEB and multiple exposure is particularly interesting.

The Special Box of Tricks

Self-timer with AEB

As mentioned earlier, the AEB function is particularly well suited for use in combination with the self-timer. Should you wish to take a self-portrait choose the 10 seconds count-down and AEB 0.3, to get three pictures with similar exposures.

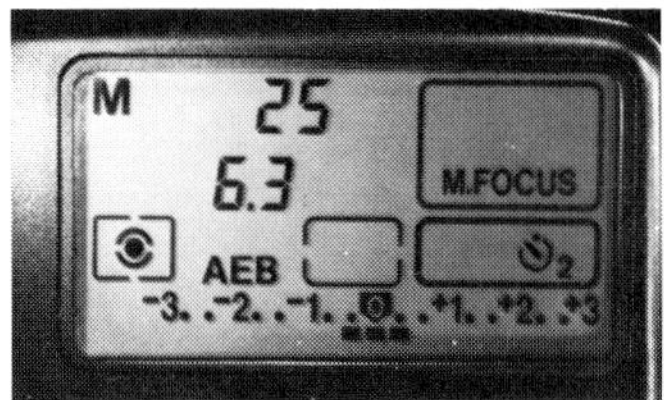

AEB with a factor of +/– 0.3 and self-timer. After 2 seconds three pictures are automatically exposed.

Three movement phases in one picture

Three individual shots on one frame can be taken as follows:

- AEB 0.3 + ME + self-timer with 2 seconds count-down (or C or CH)

Triple exposures of fast-moving subjects taken in this way produce a stroboscopic effect – three phases of a movement are captured on one frame of film.

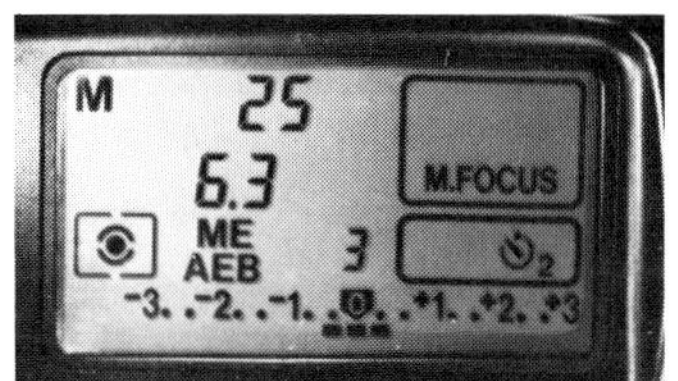

Entry for 3-picture stroboscopic effect: AEB 0.3, ME 3, self-timer with 2 seconds count-down and manual focus.

With flash

Flash is possible with AEB/self-timer and AEB/ME – provided no EOS system connector is used. It is possible to use Canon system flashguns and to set them to produce three flashes, but only if the Canon flashgun is connected by a normal two-core centre contact adapter to the PC terminal on the front, left side of the camera.

Part VI
Artificial Light and Flash Photography

EOS System Flash Photography

The use of EOS flashguns and/or other flash units

In this section on EOS flash photography, the most important flashguns are discussed and, in addition, all the other hints on flash photography, which are scattered throughout the book, are once more systematically summarized.

The EOS-1 has two flash adapters:

1. The accessory shoe accommodates a variety of flashguns with centre-contact adapter. All special functions of EOS flash mode can be utilized whenever an EOS system flashgun or another flash-unit with EOS system contact is connected. As soon as the attached flashgun is ready and the release has been pressed half-way, the following happens:

- the correct flash exposure is automatically calculated and set;
- a suitable shutter speed is set automatically;
- the flash symbol is displayed in the viewfinder;
- in poor lighting the infra-red metering flash is fired to assist the AF mechanism.

The entire flash sequence is fully automatic.

If, on the other hand, a flashgun is connected by a simple two-core cable, or a non-compatible flashgun is attached, then the camera has to be set manually.

2. A normal, two-core cable can be attached to the PC terminal at the left side of the camera. Again, flashguns attached in this way will de-activate the special functions, flash synchronization time and aperture have to be entered manually. EOS system flashguns can be attached to the PC terminal by shoe adapter to the end of the two-core cable but they will function as ordinary, non-automatic flash units.

In principle it is possible to use two flashguns with the EOS-1; a combination of a system flash in the hotshoe plus a second or third flashgun triggered by photocells.

Dedicated flashguns make flash photography really foolproof. If the flash does not work the reason could be that the flashgun is not properly mounted in the camera's accessory shoe. Check this by turning the mounting wheel on the foot of the flashgun counter-clockwise. Push the flashgun firmly into the shoe, as far as it will go, and screw the wheel down tightly.

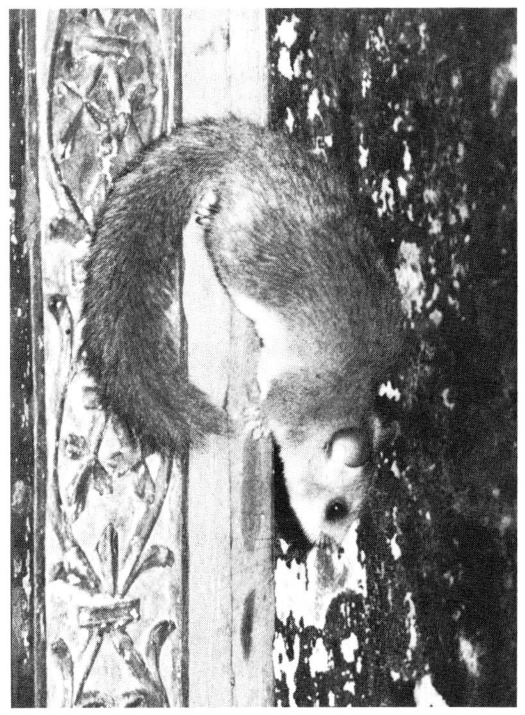

I was just photographing post-byzantine frescos in a dark, Greek church. Suddenly I heard a noise behind me. I turned and spied this fat dormouse. I raised the EOS to my eye and pressed the release. Without the AF mechanism I would never have been fast enough to capture this picture.

Flash synchronization: from long exposure to 1/320th seconds

I consider it very important that a fast shutter speed can be set in flash mode. Only if the flash synchronization time is fast enough is it possible to use flash for fill-in purposes in bright sunshine. The fastest possible shutter speed for flash is when both shutter blinds are completely open. For the EOS-1 this is 1/250th sec. At faster speeds such as 1/1000th sec. the second blind starts to cover the film before the first one has reached the other side. If the flash is triggered at 1/1000th sec., then the picture will not be completely exposed, only a narrow band will capture the flash illumination. Under very bright conditions the EOS-1 is capable of using even faster shutter speeds than 1/250th sec., even if the time indicated in the LCD panel and viewfinder is still 1/250th sec.

Should I have set a faster shutter speed than the shortest flash synchronization time then the EOS-1 will automatically override this time. In P mode the shutter speed will be set to a time between 1/250th and 1/60th sec.

Shift Function with Flash:
Shifting the aperture/shutter speed combination by turning the main dial works perfectly with the camera set to Av or Tv.

However, if the camera is set to P mode the shift function is inoperative whenever the flashgun is attached.

Autumn leaves. This is an ideal subject for AF focusing regardless of whether the camera is set to ONE SHOT or SERVO. Manual focusing would also have worked perfectly with this subject, however, AF focusing is faster and very simple. The photographer can concentrate fully on the subject, its composition and framing as the hands are placed steadily around the controls, the camera can be held firmly.

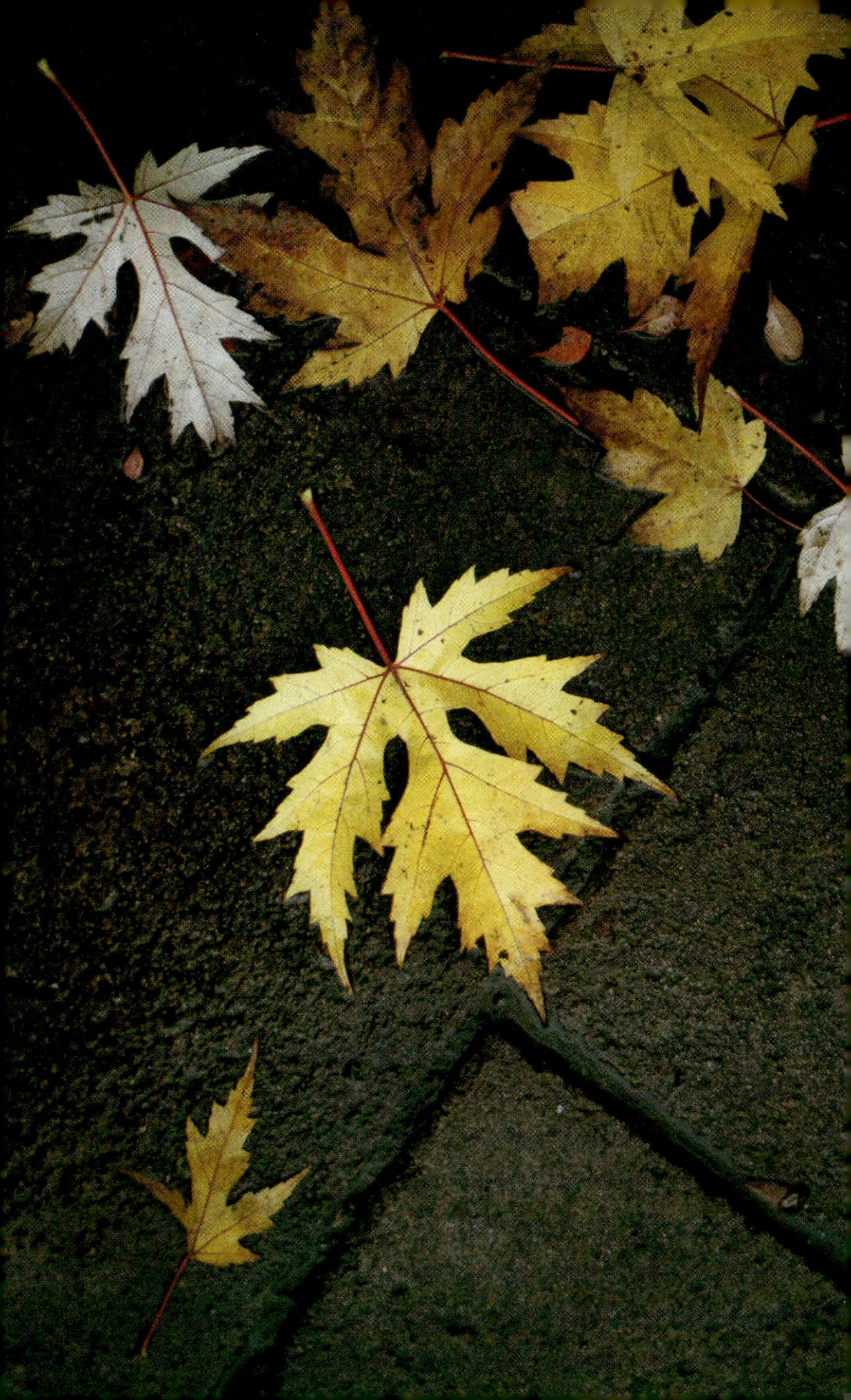

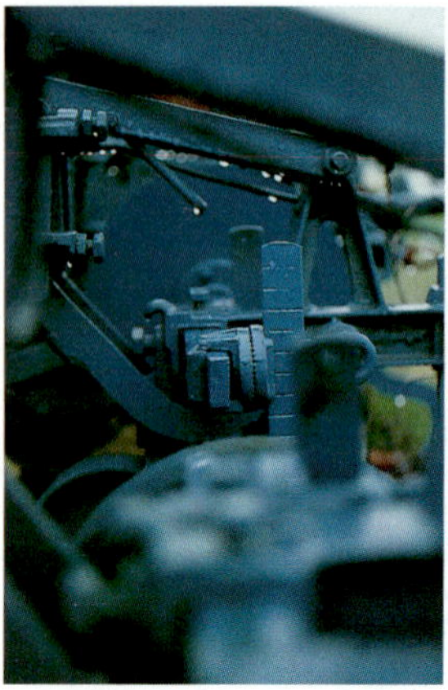

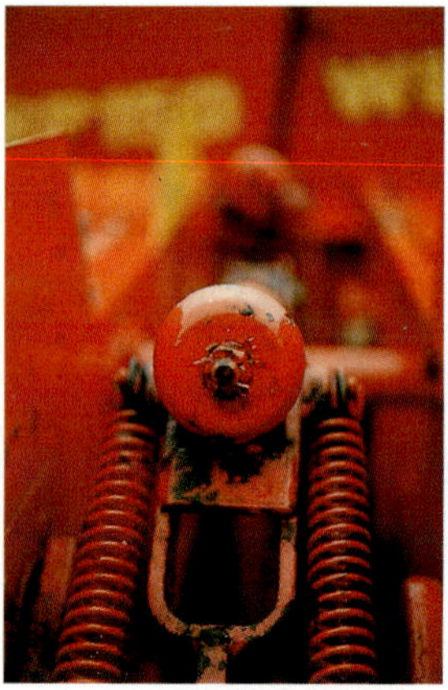

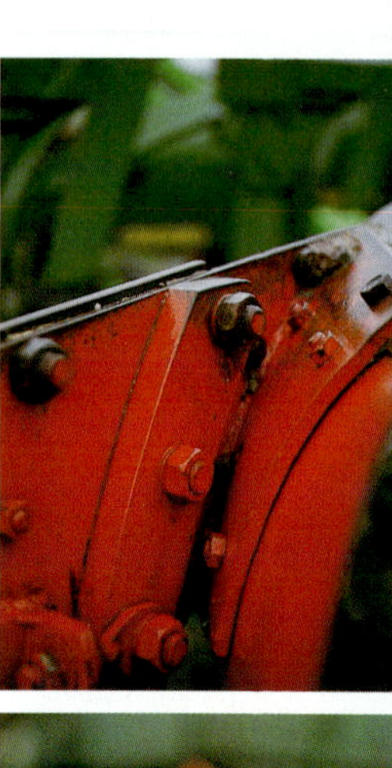

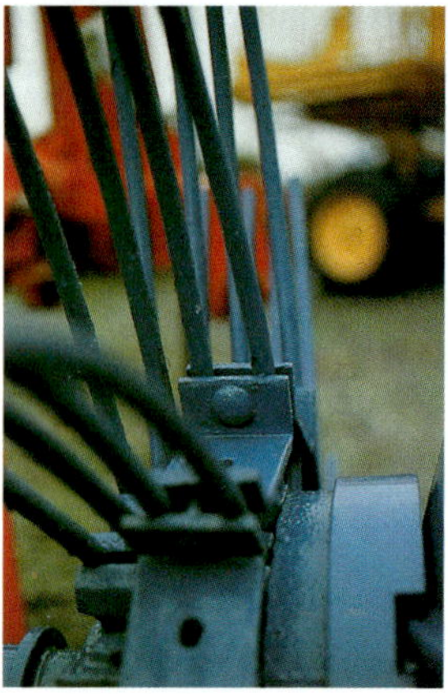

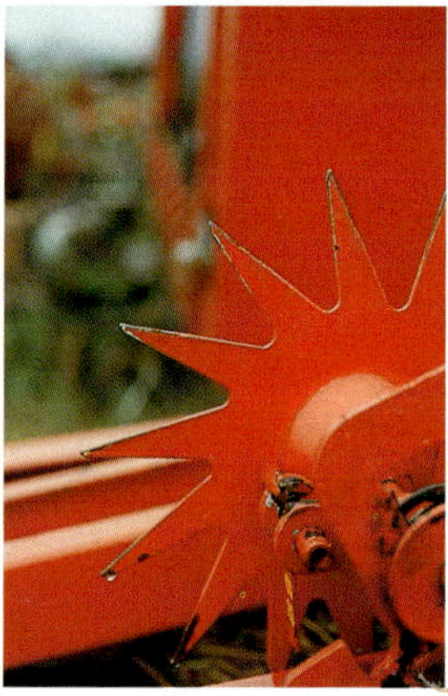

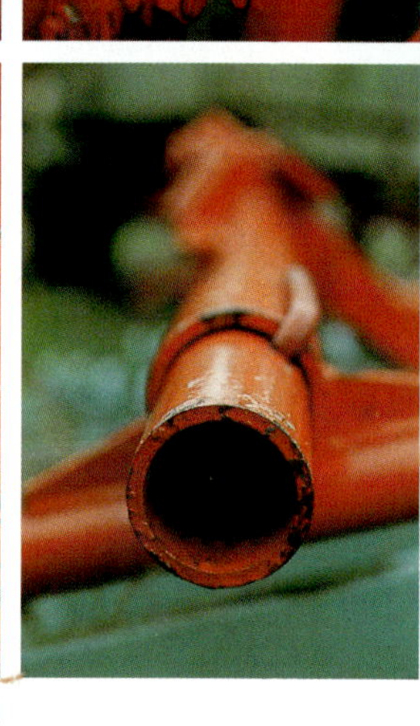

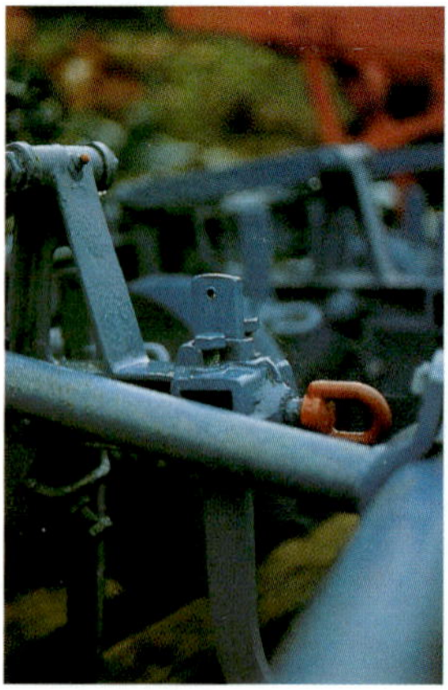

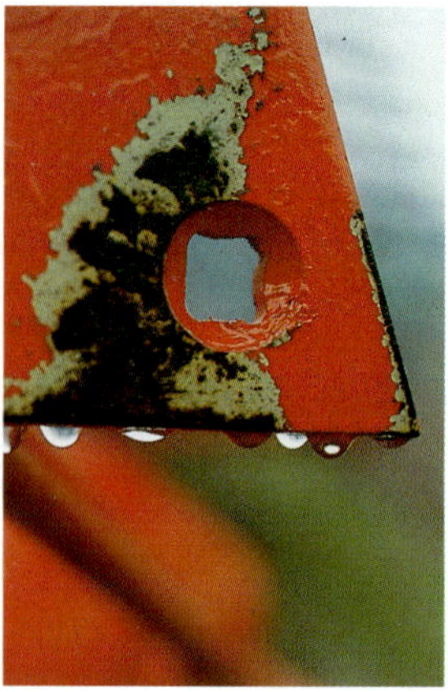

This is how the exposure mechanism works

The automatic exposure mechanism of the EOS-1 works perfectly – even better than that of the previous EOS models.

In daylight the flash output is accurately measured, the foreground subject is adequately filled-in.

- If the frame covers a large proportion of distant background, then the foreground subject will be overexposed. In the majority of cases this situation necessitates an exposure compensation of –1 or perhaps even –2. If this compensation is programmed into the EOS-1 the surroundings will turn out rather dark, the foreground subject brightly outlined against the background. If I enter the compensation in the flash (this is possible with the 430 EZ), then the background remains bright, only the foreground illumination will be stopped down – this is often the desired solution.
- If the foreground subject fills the majority of the frame and I enter an exposure compensation of –1 or –2 in the EOS-1, then the effect of the available light is reduced, the flash output is hardly affected. The flash-illuminated details are highlighted, the rest increasingly darkened.
- If I want to correct the flash output towards underexposure, then I have to enter a faster film speed into the camera, or – as is possible with the Canon Speedlite 430 EZ – I enter the flash compensation directly on the flashgun. Flashguns that have no compensation facility should be changed over to manual and the output level adjusted.
- Subjects closer than 90cm may cause problems. How these may be dealt with is described in the section "Flash for Macro Shots".
- If you are using a Speedlite 420 or 430 EZ a small white metering flash is emitted with indirect flash which is used to calculate the correct exposure (active metering).

A series of pictures taken in an agricultural machinery yard. For all of these shots I used a 70-105mm zoom. The EOS-1 was set to Av mode to be able to select as large an aperture as possible.

AF and exposure metering with infrared metering flash

In poor lighting or total darkness, for subject distances up to between 6 and 11m, depending on flashgun, an automatically emitted infrared flash is used to focus automatically and to set the aperture (active metering). In this situation the setting of the aperture is calculated for the subject distance (short distance – small aperture, long distance - large aperture). A weak level of available light will be ignored in the calculations. The poorly-lit background will be quite dark in the picture.

Distance and exposure metering in darkness function perfectly. I have taken a number of pictures in dark churches and the pictures taken with flash always turned out correctly exposed and perfectly focused. However, I generally have to apply exposure compensations or set a faster film speed, because of the prevalent dark tones of the paintings. If you use a flash in near or total darkness then you might as well enter the compensation straight into the camera; this usually turns out exactly the same as if the flash output had been reduced.

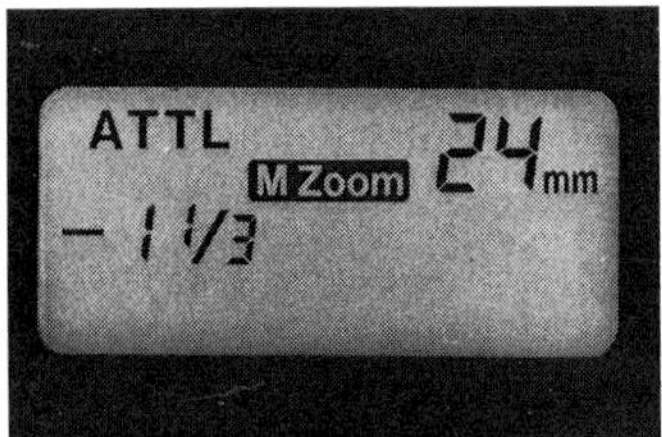

Display on the LCD panel of the Canon Speedlite 430 EZ:
automatic exposure control with exposure compensation –1 1/3rd and manual zoom reflector setting to 24mm focal length.

> ***Bounced Flash***
>
> *The reflectors are adjusted automatically (Canon EOS system flashguns) or manually to the focal length of the lens. This makes it possible, on the one hand, to light the whole subject for wide-angle shots and, on the other hand, to achieve a considerable flash range for shots with longer focal length lenses or longer focal length settings of a zoom lens.*
>
> *The combination of a long focal length lens and a wide-angle reflector setting presents no problems for the lighting quality as long as the resulting limitation on flash range is still acceptable. This actually provides particularly even lighting. I sometimes set the reflector manually to 35mm although I use a 70mm lens for photographing frescos or mosaics; this ensures that the entire subject area is lit right to the edge, and the illumination is even. (This will cost a little extra battery power).*
>
> *The combination of a short focal length lens and the reflector set for lenses with a long focal length must be avoided unless you want a spotlight-type illumination of the centre of the subject field as a special effect.*

Choice of Flashguns

EOS system flashguns by Canon

Canon supply the following EOS system dedicated flashguns:

- Speedlite 300 EZ: GN 25 (guide number for ISO 100/21° film with reflector setting to 35mm). A compact unit, lightweight and very simple to use.

Disadvantage: no adjustable reflector.
Advantage: particularly large number of flashes per set of batteries.

- Speedlite 420 EZ: GN 30 (guide number for ISO 100 film and focal length setting of 35mm) – more powerful but still compact. Reflector angle adjustable through 90° upwards and 180° backwards. Features a stroboscope facility. White light metering flash to meter for indirect flash.
- Speedlite 430 EZ: GN 30 (ISO 100, 35mm). A further development of the 420 EZ. Offers the same excellent facilities as its brother model, such as fully adjustable reflector, and white-light metering flash for indirect flash illumination as well as exposure compensation selectable on the flash-unit within the range +/– 1/3rd to +/– 3; shorter re-charge time; strobe effects selectable between 1 and 10 flashes/second; connection for power pack.
- Macro Ring Lite ML3: special macro ring flashgun for automatic exposure at distances of between 2 and 400cm. Without IR metering flash control but with modelling lights. To be used only in combination with the macro EF 50mm *f*2.5 lens.

The reflector of the three Speedlites adjusts automatically to the focal length of the lens being used – a very useful facility available only with Canon EOS system flashguns. With the 420 EZ and the 430 EZ the reflector can also be adjusted by hand. The Canon flashguns are particularly well designed and easy to use.

It is now possible to get an extension cable system, consisting of a TTL Hotshoe Adapter 2 (with its own battery CR-2025) and a 60cm and a 300cm cable and an OFF-Camera Shoe Adapter, to be attached to the flash unit. This equipment allows a flashgun to be attached to the camera and positioned at any desired angle to the subject, while at the same time retaining full automatic functions. It is possible to mount a second flash unit in Hotshoe Adapter 2, to be used as frontal fill-in flash.

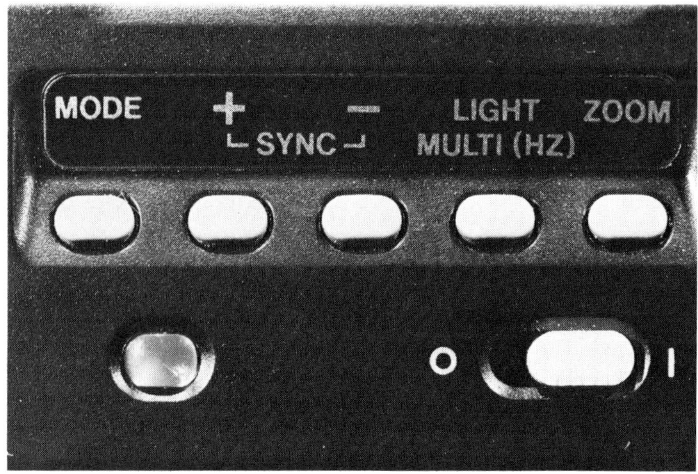

The buttons on the Speedlite 430 EZ, from left to right:

1. auto/manual
2. + exposure compensation
3. – exposure compensation

These buttons are also used to modify manual partial exposures. Simultaneously pressing buttons 2 and 3 will cause the flash synchronization to be transferred from the first shutter blind to the second shutter blind.

4. Switch for flash panel illumination, also for strobe mode and strobe frequency between 1 and 10 flashes/second.
5. Switch to select between manual zoom reflector adjustment for focal lengths between 24 and 80mm and automatic zoom reflector adjustment.

System-compatible flashguns by other manufacturers (SCA)

Flashguns offered by other manufacturers for the EOS system can be used with the EOS-1, as with any other EOS camera. As far as the EOS-1 is concerned, Canon engineers have been particularly generous by providing the two-core connector (PC terminal), which allows the connection of any simple flashgun. This provision invites us to use any flashgun that we might possess. One word of caution though; should the use of a non-Canon flashgun cause any damage or malfunction to the EOS-1 then you would have no claim against the manufacturer. The warranty provided by Canon applies only to Canon equipment and the compatibility of accessories within the system and this is only reasonable. The same applies also to lenses and other accessories.

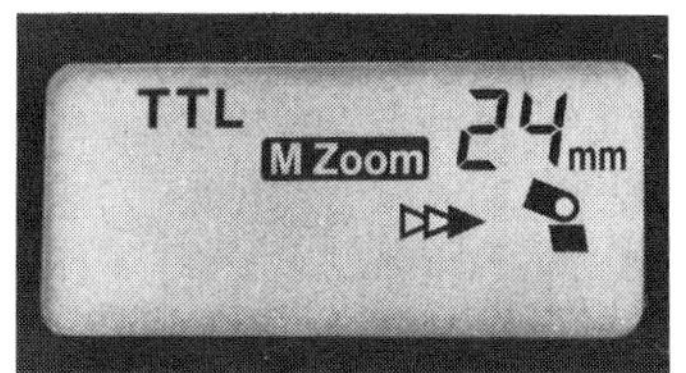

The multiple arrow in the LCD panel of the 430 EZ, and also of the other EOS Speedlite flash units, means that the flash will be triggered just before the second shutter blind is released to cover the film. The flashgun symbol appears whenever the reflector is tilted – and a white metering flash is emitted to meter the indirectly illuminated subject.

Power Pack: *an additional container that can be attached to hold more batteries. To be recommended for long shooting sequences with rapid flash rates (W = winder operation).*
Autofocus IR metering flash: *small adapter with EOS connector (SCA 312) to be plugged into the EOS hotshoe, the flashgun is mounted on top of that (without adapter), or a V-cable (SCA 307 A). This accessory allows automatic focusing even in total darkness. It has its own 1.5 V, AAA battery.*

Simple, non-EOS system compatible (computer) flashguns

Connection strictly forbidden: flashguns from the photographic stone-age must not be connected to the EOS because of their high triggering voltages (acc. to DIN 19014 up to 400 Volt). The use of such flash units could damage the camera.
Connection permissible: any of the more modern flashguns with low trigger voltage and thyristor circuitry.

Second Flash Socket on lower left side of camera (PC terminal):

This connection can be used for:

- *any flashgun with a simple, two-core standard cable (PC).*
- *cable with two-core standard adapter hotshoe which can be connected to any flashgun, regardless of which system.*
- *standard cable connections of the SCA adapter system.*

Any flashgun connected to the second socket, regardless as to whether an automatic or a manual model, will work but without any of the automatic functions.

I have used flashguns with a normal two-pole centre contact, with Leica R5 and Olympus system connections, and noted the following:

- it is possible to use these flashguns with the EOS-1 in manual mode (and also in Tv and Av mode). The aperture should be calculated from the guide number of the flash (see below "M-mode + flash").
- switching over to M, extremely fast shutter speeds can be selected – 1/320th sec. – provided the slight loss in width of the frame (unexposed narrow strip at the bottom) can be tolerated (even shutter speeds of 1/400th and 1/500th sec. are possible)

Flash Photography in the Different Exposure Modes

Flash photography in P mode

Exposure Time:

The connected and charged system flashgun automatically sets a shutter speed of between 1/250th and 1/60th sec. (in very bright conditions the shutter speed set may actually be as fast as 1/320 sec, but this is not indicated in the display as such).

For Shutter speeds set for ambient light:

- ***between 1/60th and 1/250th sec.*** *there is a tendency to decrease the shutter speed if a flash is switched on (down to 1/60th sec.) and to stop down the aperture – so that the exposure level is always maintained.*
- ***between 1/8000th and 1/400th sec.*** *the shutter speed will be decreased to 1/250th sec. when a flash is switched on, consequently the aperture will be stopped down (if it cannot be stopped down sufficiently to avoid overexposure, then the smallest available aperture value (22 or 32) blinks in the LCD panel and viewfinder – provided the flashgun used is a Canon Speedlite.*
- ***+++ from 1/30th and slower****, the shutter speed of EOS-1 will be set to 1/60th sec. The infrared metering flash is automatically triggered. This metering flash is used to set the focus and aperture – the aperture value depends on the subject distance. In this case the background will be rather dark, the darker, the shorter the distance from flash to subject.*

Aperture value and level of exposure:

The aperture setting is adjusted to the amount of ambient light in relation to the shutter speed. The amount of light to be delivered by the flash is based on the foreground subject on which the lens is focused. If there is sufficient light, ambient brightness and flash lighting are combined. A flash used in daylight or a brightly-lit room will deliver only enough light to fill-in the foreground.

Aperture setting and exposure level in poor light and in darkness:

In dark interiors and at night (always when 1/60th sec. is set as flash synchronisation speed due to the level of ambient light) flash lighting takes precedence. The shutter speed is automatically set to 1/60th sec., AF and aperture settings are set by IR metering flash. Distant backgrounds remain dark. The aperture setting then depends on the subject range – the shorter it is the more the aperture is stopped down. The range of the metering flash for the Speedlite 300 EZ is between 90cm and 6/7m, the two other more powerful units reach as far as 10/11m.

Canon EOS-flashguns:

If the subject distance is too great, shutter speed and aperture value blink in the viewfinder and the LCD panel. The difference in ambient light illumination in the direction of over- or underexposure against flash illumination is indicated in the viewfinder by an arrow pointing at the scale on the right of the focusing screen. Better results can usually be expected for deviations by one or even two stops.

The distance-related exposure control also works when the lens is set to manual focus.

Exposure compensation:

To apply an exposure compensation on the EOS-1 has a considerable effect on how the ambient light is reproduced in the picture; it has little effect on the actual flash illumination. (This applies whenever strong ambient lighting plays a rôle but not if the flash is used in near or total darkness!). Applying exposure compensations between –1 and –3, the brightness of the background can be "pushed aside" in bright daylight situations. If, however, the flash is supposed to be reduced, then it is better to set a faster film speed on the EOS-1 in order for the flash to emit a smaller flash. If you are using the Speedlite 430 EZ it is possible to enter these compensation values directly on the unit (in 1/3rd step increments up to 3 stops).

Exposure error warning when the release is pressed halfway (only for EOS Speedlites):

Shutter speed and aperture value blink in the viewfinder – subject is too far away, move closer and try again.

Only the aperture value blinks; ambient light causes overexposure of the background. A shaded subject in the foreground will nevertheless be correctly lit by the flash.

> *The effective range of flashguns is from 70cm up to 12m. For flashguns used with SCA adapters no exposure error warnings are displayed in the viewfinder. In this case fire the test flash. If the green OK signal at the rear of the flash lights up then the illumination level is sufficient.*

When using flash in P mode it is not possible to use the shift function.

Flash photography in Av mode

- Shutter speed: once the aperture value has been preset, the shutter speed is set automatically in the range between 1/250th and 30 sec. In darkness, slower shutter speeds may result. In Av mode the aperture setting is not changed when a flash is switched on, it has to be set manually to a suitable value. The shutter speed, initially calculated, will also not be changed unless it is too fast for flash synchronization, i.e. between 1/8000th and 1/400th sec; in the latter case the speed will be decreased to 1/250th sec.
- Aperture and illumination level: the aperture value is manually preset and the amount of flash required is determined accordingly.
- Incorrect exposure warning when release is pressed halfway (only with Canon flash-units): shutter speed and aperture values blink in the viewfinder: subject distance is too great.
- 250 display (1/250th sec) blinks: subject surroundings will be overexposed, shaded subject in foreground will be correctly illuminated by flash. If appropriate, reduce the aperture.
- 30" display (30 sec) blinks: main subject will be correctly exposed, background will be dark despite the long exposure time.

Please note: when using Av mode with flash illumination check the shutter speed as the camera often calculates rather slow shutter speeds which could cause camera-shake. However, if a subject in the foreground is sharply depicted by the flash, it does not matter if the background details are blurred. In this situation one can generally try hand-held shots with speeds up to 1/8th sec., although theory forbids such slow speeds. Attractive contrasts between sharp- and soft-focus can be achieved by the combination of flash and long exposure times in the range between 1/4 to 1 sec. Av mode will generally be selected if either particularly large or small apertures are desirable.

- Shift: is operative.
- Exposure compensation on the EOS-1: possible in principle. Only the shutter speed will be changed. This means that the background will turn out darker with a minus correction, and lighter with a plus correction.

When using Av flash mode, larger apertures than ƒ4 should be avoided otherwise exposure errors may occur.

In principle it is possible to use non-system flashguns with integrated sensor in Av flash mode. In this case the aperture set on the camera has to be entered into the flashgun. Do not forget to check the shutter speed, as this will not be automatically set to flash synchronization speed on the camera.

Flash photography in Tv mode

- Shutter speed: is set manually between 1/250th and 30 sec.
- Aperture and illumination level: the aperture setting and flash intensity are automatically adjusted to the shutter speed setting. The IR metering flash is used to set a perfect focus for subjects in the close range up to 10 or 11m; the aperture setting is determined by the subject range.
- Incorrect exposure warning with release button halfway (only for Canon flashguns):
- Shutter speed and aperture values blink: subject too far away, move closer!
- The largest available aperture value blinks: the background will be correctly exposed, the main subject itself will be overexposed.
- Shift facility: possible.
- Exposure compensation entered on the camera: possible. In this case only the aperture value is changed. Consequently only the effect of the ambient light is affected.

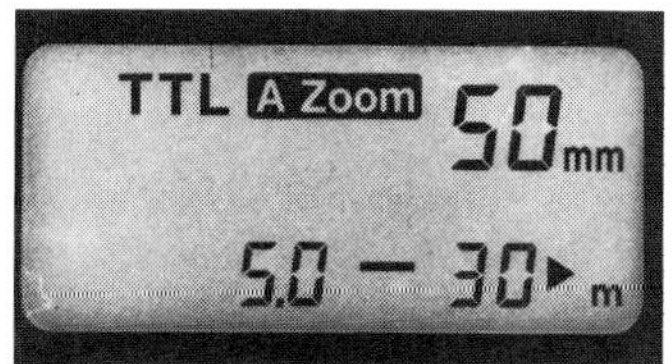

Flashgun LCD panel, with EOS-1 in M mode and aperture set to ƒ22 (film ISO 100), showing flash range.

Flash photography in M mode

- Shutter speed: is set manually by main dial between 1/250th and 30 sec. If an EOS-system flash is attached the selected shutter speed is automatically limited to 1/250th sec. If a non-compatible flashgun or an EOS flashgun is connected via non-system adapter then it is possible to enter faster shutter speeds - intentionally or by mistake.
- Aperture: the aperture is also set by hand by turning the main dial and simultaneously pressing the exposure compensation button, or by turning the quick control dial. The exposure metering needs first to be activated.
- Level of illumination: the flash intensity is automatically controlled for different distances so that the main subject in the foreground is always correctly exposed. In darkness the IR metering flash will be triggered.

The flash exposure is therefore automatically controlled even in manual mode.

- Flash exposures in the macro range: M mode makes correct automatic exposure possible even at close range. With the Canon 420/430 EZ (reflector setting to 24mm), for example, a subject somewhere at a range between 50cm and – depending on film speed (even up to ISO 1000) – 1 to 5m, will be correctly exposed automatically with an aperture of *f*22. The distance range appears on the flashgun's LCD panel when the release is pressed halfway.

Guide numbers for manual flash photography (ISO 100/21 °)

Canon 430 Reflector	*normal*	*1/16th output*	*1/32nd output*
50mm	*35*	*8.8*	*6.2*
80mm	*42*	*10.8*	*7.6*
Canon 420 Reflector	*normal*	*1/16th output*	*1/32nd output*
50mm	*35*	*8.8*	*6.2*
80mm	*42*	*10.5*	*7.4*

In fully automatic operation the flashgun is also switched to M and the aperture must be set by hand. If no display is available use the guide number. This, divided by the distance in metres, gives the aperture to be set; alternately, dividing the guide number by the aperture that has been set gives the distance in metres which must not be exceeded. Guide numbers, unless expressly marked otherwise, refer to ISO 100/21° films. In order to determine the guide numbers for a film of twice the speed, it must be multiplied by 1.4, or by 2, for a film of four-times the speed. (See rapid flash sequences in C-mode, page 126).

> *When using automatic M flash mode you should never use larger apertures than f4 otherwise exposure errors may occur. Any aperture can be used when it is set by hand and if the flashgun is also switched to M.*

Flash photography in DEPTH mode

When flash is used, depth of field mode switches automatically to program mode. It is not possible to use DEPTH and flash at the same time. As soon as the flash is switched off the camera reverts to the DEPTH mode setting.

Flash photography with long exposures (bulb)

At dusk and in darkness the IR metering flash is used to set the focus and exposure level in accordance with the preset aperture. (The effective range of the attached flash 420/430 EZ can be read-off the flashgun's LCD panel). Do not forget to ensure that the long exposure does not cause overexposure.

Special Flash Situations

Flash subjects with dark backgrounds – by night or day

An extensive, dark background misleads the exposure metering to assess the subject as poorly-lit and as a result a small subject in the foreground would be bombarded with a rather powerful flash. The same problem occurs if a small subject is to be shown against a distant background.
Remedy: if you don't want highlights and side-lighting to be drowned in a powerful flash, set the film speed to twice its actual value, or, if you are using the 430 EZ Speedlite, enter a compensation value between –0.3 and –0.6.

Specially for Slide film: Exposure compensation with Flash	
Bright subject, in front of dark background:	*–2/3rd to –1*
At night outdoors:	*–2/3rd to –1*
Inside, the background at some distance:	*–2/3rd to –1*
A predominantly dark subject:	*–1/3rd to –2/3rd*
Close subject in daylight, outdoors:	*–1/3rd to –1*
Very small subject in front of dark/distant background:	*–1 to –2*

Flash subjects with bright backgrounds – by night or day

A very bright, close background filling the whole format may result in a rather dark main subject. Compensation, as above, but in this case from +1/3rd to 2/3rd.

Natural illumination with bounced flash

Indirect lighting is a tried and tested flash method giving good illumination recommended for indoor locations with white walls. Under these circumstances the best shooting modes are P or Tv. The flashgun's reflector is pointed directly at the ceiling if the subject is close, or at an angle if the subject is further away. This results in a diffuse light source which bathes the subject in a soft light without hard shadows. However, this method requires a powerful flash. If you are using a Speedlite 420 EZ or 430 EZ, these flashguns will emit a white metering flash when the release is pressed halfway. As a result, a sufficiently large aperture will be determined by the exposure control. Close-up subjects can be satisfactorily illuminated by indirect flash.

A particularly good way to illuminate a portrait is by indirect front light. This can be done by turning the reflector of the flashgun through 180° towards the back, where a white screen should be placed to bounce the light back towards the subject. The light reflected by the screen (or wall or ceiling) provides the actual illumination for the subject. The larger the lighted area, the more even the resulting illumination. For this purpose you can set the reflector to the widest wide-angle setting on the flash.

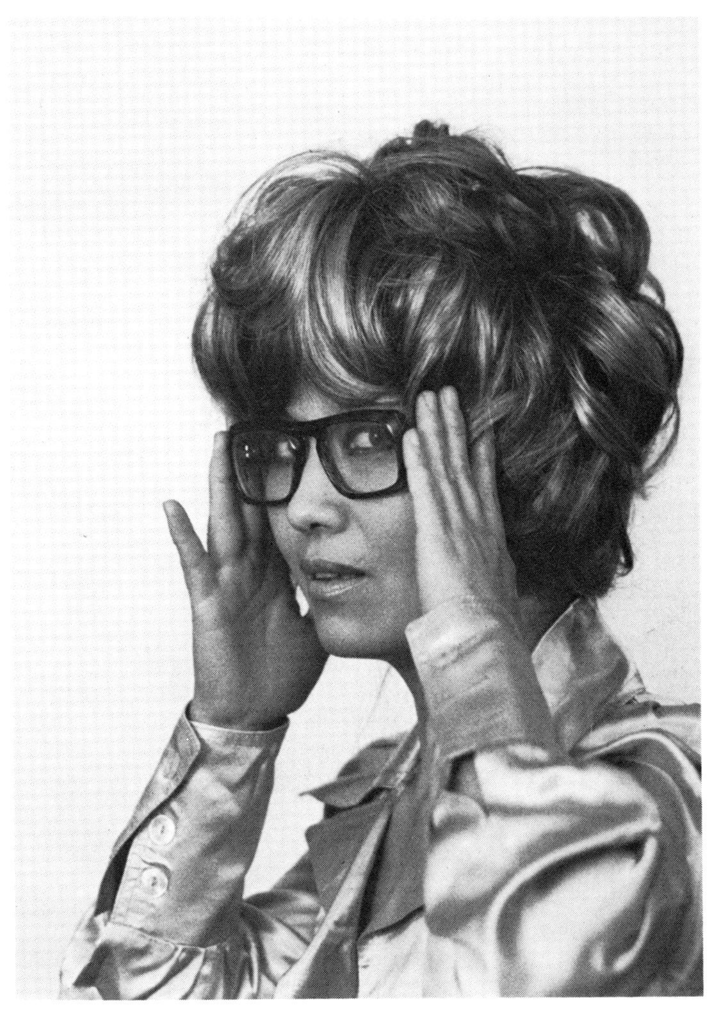

Indirect flash with the reflector pointed at the ceiling ensures uniform, soft illumination of the main subject.

Flash with several flashguns

Flashguns connected by extension cable:

- Two flashgun combination: one flashgun mounted on the camera and one connected by cable: camera Hotshoe Adapter 2 (with battery CR-2025), cable (either 0.6 or 3m) and an Off-Camera Shoe-Adapter.
- For a combination with up to four flashguns – all independent of the camera (connected by cable): Hotshoe Adapter 2, cable and TTL Distributor.

All flashguns connected in this way will be controlled by the metering system, there is no need to interfere with the exposure settings.

- For EOS system flashgun mounted on camera and non-system flashgun connected by cable: an additional flashgun may be connected with a standard adapter to the camera's PC terminal. Under no circumstances attach several flashguns by a generally-available standard distributor, this would definitely damage the camera contacts.
- Cordless triggering of additional flashguns: small slave units (for example Hama, Kaiser, or Metz) can be used to connect up to three flashguns, depending on type and size. The sensor of this tiny gadget is pointed at the main flashgun, attached to the camera. The flash from the main flashgun provides the trigger for the slave units. Before you buy such a unit I would recommend that you try it out to make sure that your flashgun will be triggered.

Rapid flash sequences in C-mode

I have been able to fire off fast flash sequences in continuous mode C, CL (Booster) and CH (Booster). The EOS flashguns manage 2.5 and 3 frames per second quite well. Even the faster booster sequence of 5.5 frames/second was quite successful with the more powerful flashgun although one has to accept that it did not recharge in time for some of the frames in the sequence.

Always set the flashgun to M and reduce the flash output, i.e. flashgun to W (manually reduced output set to M 1/16 or M 1/8), better still M 1/16 or M 1/32. The less light is emitted with each burst, the quicker the recharging and the greater the shooting frequency.

Always wait for the flash to be fully recharged, before releasing (Canon EOS flashguns), i.e. change from green light to red.

If the recharging time is longer than 6 seconds, replace the batteries, or use NC cells.

In principle continuous rapid flash in C-mode is possible also in the P, Av and Tv modes. However, to determine the correct exposure, it is best to set the EOS-1 to M. The aperture has to be calculated for the subject distance and set by hand. The 420 EZ and the 430 EZ show the maximum flash range for the respective aperture settings. With these Canon flashguns the aperture setting on the EOS-1 is even displayed automatically on the flashgun's LCD panel. Do not release if the aperture value in the LCD panel blinks after AF focus has been set, otherwise the picture will be incorrectly exposed. The same applies also if the shooting distance is greater than the displayed range. In these events change the aperture until the value stops blinking or move closer.

Guide numbers (GN) for manual operation of 430 (420) EZ and film speed ISO 100/21°.

		zoom reflector position for focal length (mm)					
		24	**28**	**35**	**50**	**70**	**80**
	1/1	25	27	30	35	40	43 (42)
	1/2	17.7	19.1	21.2	24.7	28.3	30.4 (29.7)
reduced	**1/4**	12.5	13.5	15	17.5	20	21.5 (21)
output	**1/8**	8.8	9.5	10.6	12.4	14.1	15.2 (14.8)
	1/16	6.3	6.8	7.5	8.8	10	10.8 (10.5)
	1/32	4.4	4.8	5.3	6.2	7.1	7.6 (7.4)

For different film speeds multiply the above values by the following values:

ISO 50/18°	x 0.7
ISO 100/21°	x 1
ISO 200/24°	x 1.4
ISO 400/27°	x 2
ISO 800/30°	x 2.8
ISO 1600/33°	x 4
ISO 3200/36°	x 5.6
ISO 6400/39°	x 8

The range of the flash depends on the reflector position, the aperture setting and, most importantly, on the film speed. Using a slow film the close-up range lies between 50cm and 3 to 4m (for the 420/430 EZ Speedlites); if a faster film and wide open apertures are used, distances up to 15 to 20m can be reached.

Flash with macro

The close-up limit for EOS system flash lies somewhere between 75 and 90cm. This is no problem if you are using a longer lens, say the EF 35-70mm, *f*3.5-4.5 or the 35-105mm zooms lens, as these produce a reasonable reproduction scale even at slightly greater subject distances. You may also consider the possibility of using supplementary achromatic lenses which produce reproduction scales of up to 1:2.5 even from considerable subject distances.

Moreover, the shooting distance and the flash distance need not always be the same. Let's assume you move to within 15cm of the subject with the Macro EF 50mm, *f*2.5, then the flashgun connected via a cable could be placed quite easily at a distance of 0.7 to 1m.

To move really close with the EOS-1 and attached system flashgun, to within 50 cm and in the best case even 10 cm, then both the camera and the flashgun have to be set to manual operation.

If you have a Macro Ring Lite, flash photography within a range of 2cm to 4m is particularly simple, even in P mode. This special macro flash unit provides particularly uniform lighting. Disadvantage: this flash has to be used with the Macro EF 50mm, *f*2.5 (reproduction scale without additional accessory 1:2). This ring flash has two extra lights which can be triggered separately, and allows the illumination to be arranged from left and right, or from top and bottom.

Nice blue eyes

The dreaded red eyes that often stare at you from portraits are caused by frontal flash, i.e. the flashgun attached to the hotshoe of the camera pointing directly at the sitter. Whenever the shooting axis coincides with the direction of the incident light then the light will be reflected from the retina through the wide open pupil – a quite common occurrence as the pupils are wide open in the dark and this is often when flash is used.

To avoid this you have to:

- either use a hand-triggered flash, to one side, which you can then point at the person's face.
- illuminate your sitters with a video lamp (e.g. Kaiser 6 V 20W), which will cause the pupils to close before the actual shot is taken and only a small part of the incident light will be reflected.
- or use bounce flash
- or connect the flash via cable and illuminate your sitter from an angle.

Part VII

Image Creation Technique with EOS Lenses

Lenses for the EOS-1

Fixed focal length lenses

Since the introduction of the EOS system, Canon have developed a reasonable range of lenses with fixed focal lengths.

Most of us will favour zoom lenses for their easy handling and convenience. However, a good set of fixed focal length lenses is indispensable to most photographers. The advantages of fixed focal length lenses are:

- they possess better reproduction qualities than zoom lenses. It must be mentioned here, however, that the special, apochromatically corrected zoom lenses are just as good in this respect;
- they are generally much faster, the maximum aperture of fixed focal lengths is *f*1, for zoom lenses the maximum aperture is *f*2.8;

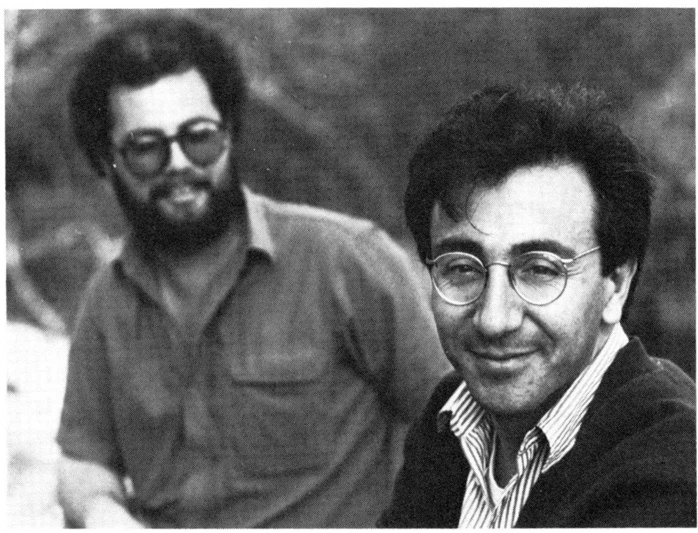

A double portrait, taken with a 135mm lens, from a distance of 2m. The combination of large aperture focusing on the foreground allowed me to depict the head in the foreground as absolutely sharp against the blurred outline of the second head.

Constraints in optical construction mean that zoom lenses have a greater number of elements, therefore the fixed focal lengths allow more light through. The effective amount of light passing through the lens for a given aperture is therefore greater for a fixed focal length than for a zoom;

- the fixed focal length lens is generally more compact and lighter in weight.

The 24mm, *f*2.5 lens presents the border between wide-angle and super wide-angle lenses. For its short focal length it is very fast, particularly compact and light and has a close-up limit of 18cm. It is therefore possible to reach good reproduction scales in the close-up range (see also close-up photography with supplementary lenses, Part VIII). The 50mm, *f*1.0 is extremely fast for its focal length as is my own particular favourite; the 85mm, *f*1.2. Then there is the 135mm, *f*2.8 Softfocus lens; a slightly misleading name as this lens will focus sharply in the normal setting but it can also be set to two soft focus positions of varying degree, which, particularly with large apertures, introduce a delicate haze around the sharp outline of the subject.

Canon's long lenses are particularly fast, especially the 200mm, *f*1.8 and the 300mm, *f*2.8. Then there is the Canon 600mm, extremely fast at *f*4. The Fisheye 15mm, *f*2.8 occupies a special place amongst the fixed focal length lenses. This lens depicts the subject space as a flat representation of a semicircular area, the details at the centre appear disproportionally large, but relatively undistorted, while towards the edge of the picture the details become increasingly smaller and seem to be crowded together. Canon lenses with suffix U (USM) are lenses with an ultrasonic motor – a particularly fast and almost inaudible AF motor.

Lenses with suffix L are optically excellent, constructed of special glasses with outstanding reproduction qualities due to the characteristics of the glasses.

Fixed focal length AF lenses for the EOS by Canon

Lens mm	*Angle of view*	*Close-up limit/cm scale*	*Greatest repro*	*Smallest aperture*	*Filter size*
wide-angle					
EF 15mm ƒ2.8 (Fish-eye)	*180°*	*20*	*1:8.1*	*22*	*slot-in*
EF 24mm ƒ2.8	*84°*	*25*	*1:7*	*22*	*58*
EF 28mm ƒ2.8	*75°*	*30*	*1:7.7*	*22*	*52*
standard					
EF 50mm ƒ1 LU	*46°*	*60*	*1:9*	*16*	*72*
EF 50mm ƒ1.8	*46°*	*45*	*1:6.6*	*22*	*52*
EF 50mm ƒ2.5 (Compact macro)	*46°*	*22.8*	*1:2*	*32*	*52*
portrait lenses					
EF 85mm ƒ1.2LU	*28°30'*	*95*	*1:10*	*16*	*72*
EF 135mm ƒ2.8 (Soft focus)	*18°*	*130*	*1:8*	*32*	*52*
telephoto lenses					
EF 200mm ƒ1.8LU	*12°*	*250*	*1:12*	*22*	*48*
EF 300mm ƒ2.8LU	*8°15'*	*300*	*1:9*	*32*	*48*
EF 600mm ƒ4LU	*4°10'*	*600*	*1:10*	*32*	*48*

Lens weight in g: 330 (EF 15mm ƒ2.8), 270, 185, 985, 190, 280, 1025, 390, 3000, 2855, 6000 (EF 600mm ƒ4)

U = ultrasonic - especially quiet and fast AF motor
L = precisely corrected for outstanding reproduction quality

Extender:	**Exclusive to lens:**
EF x2	*EF 200 ƒ1.8L, EF 300 ƒ2.8L*
EF x1.4	*EF 200 ƒ1.8L, EF 300 ƒ2.8L, EF 600 ƒ4L*
and	
EF life-size converter for	*EF 50mm ƒ2.5 Compact macro*

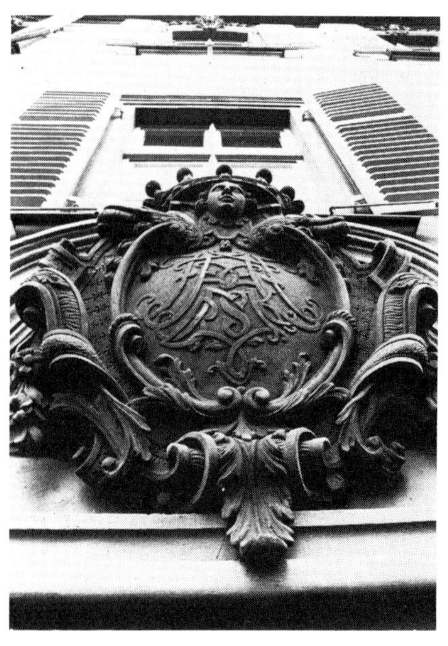

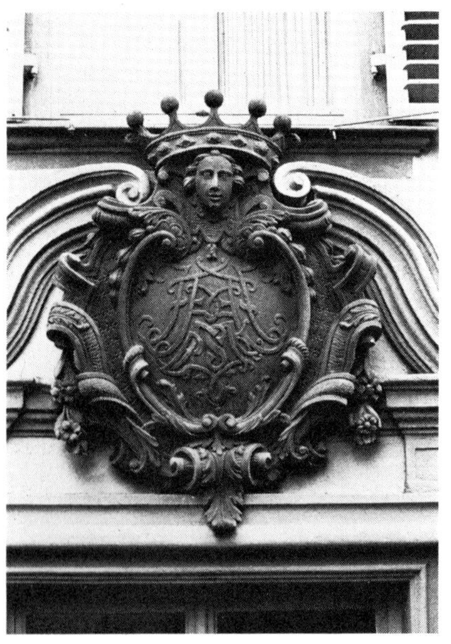

A heraldic emblem on a higher plane.
above left: seen at an effective angle with the 24mm lens
above: the same subject represented by a 50mm lens
left: the 100mm lens from further away shows the subject entirely without. converging lines.

Colour illustration,right:
a child in Bali try to sell a shell necklace to a European tourist. A subject like this can be taken with AF-lock or by M-focus.

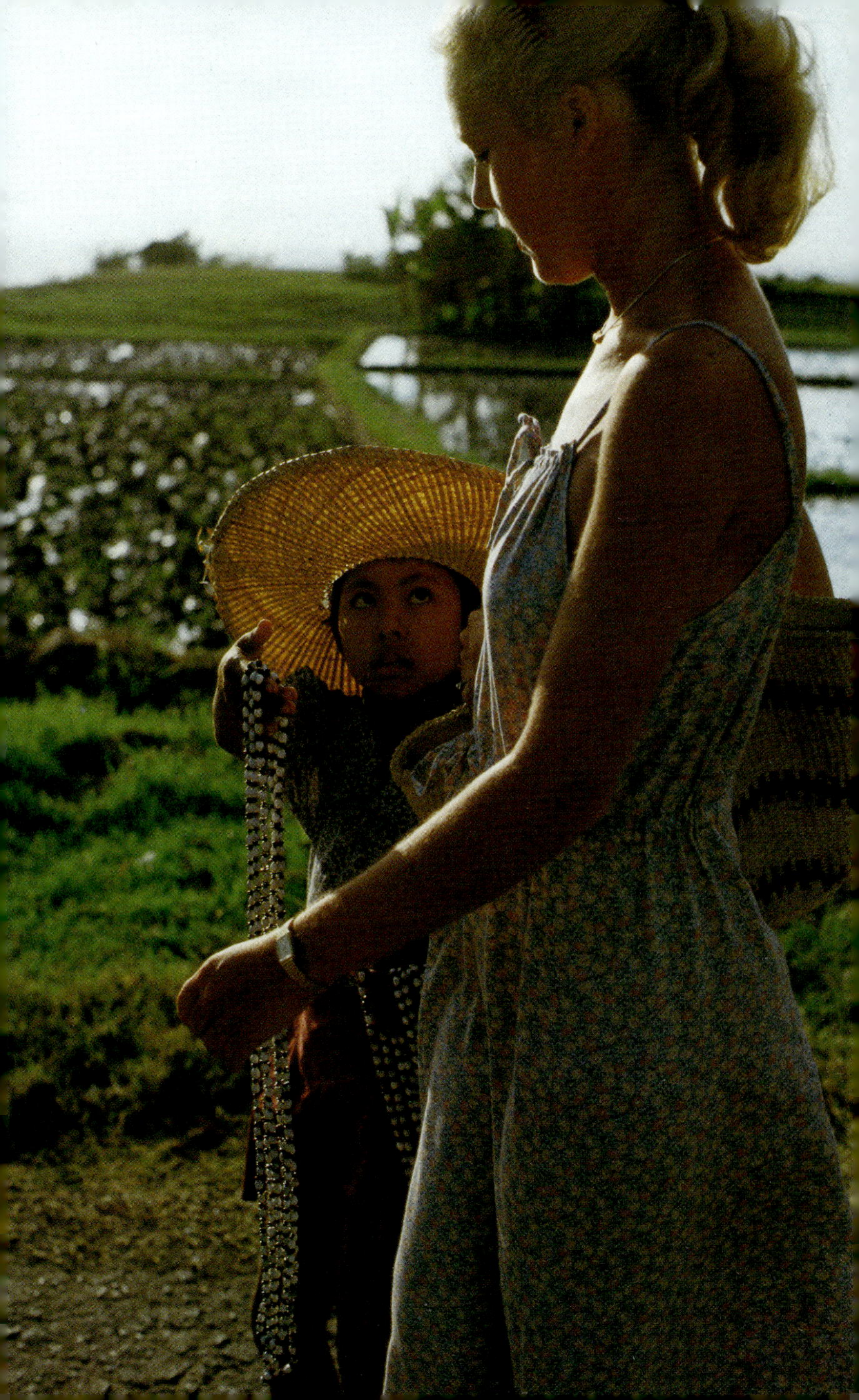

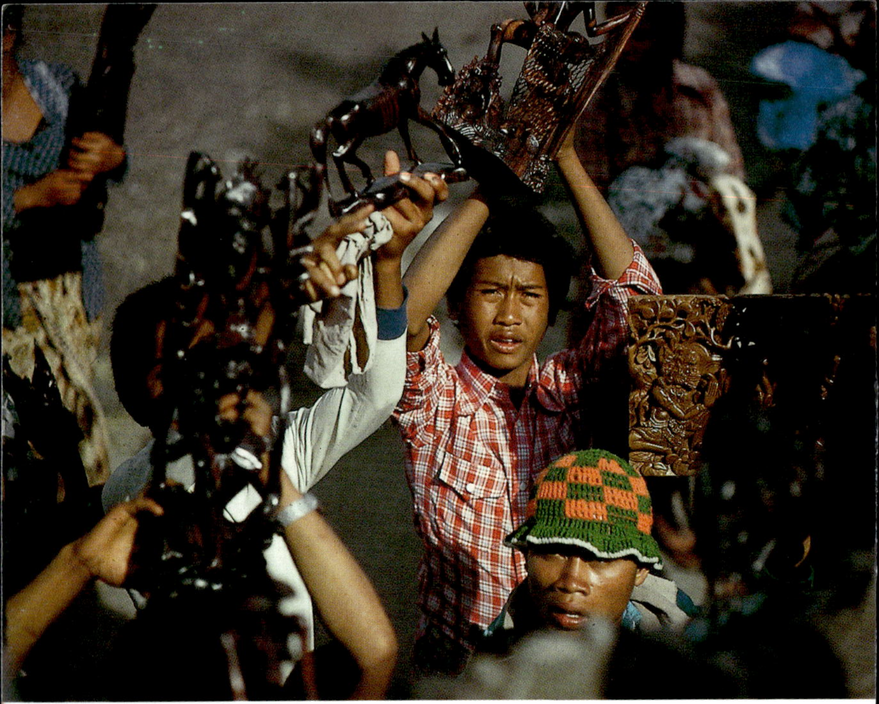

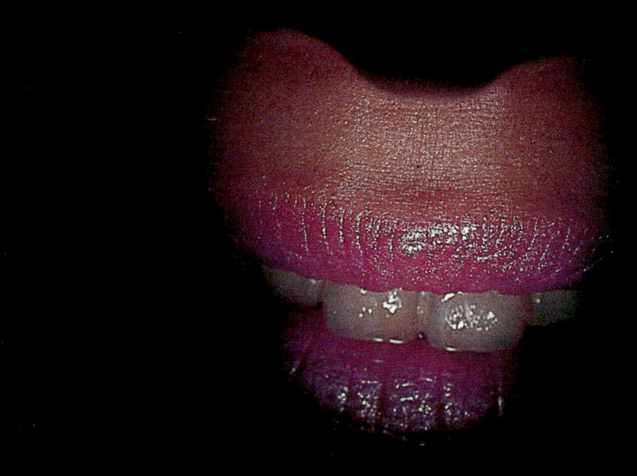

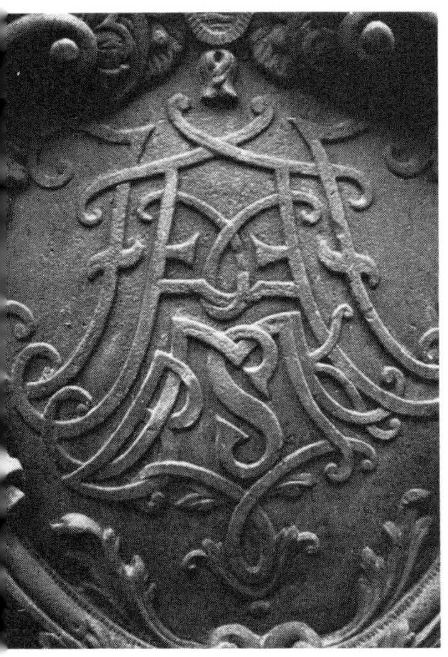

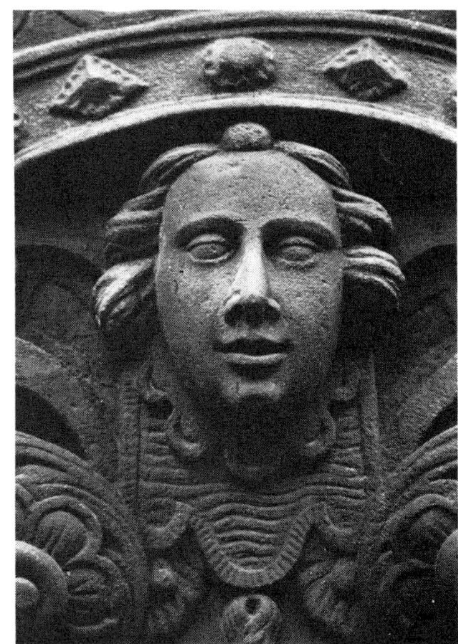

Black-and-white illustrations: two details brought closer with the 180mm lens.

Colour illustrations, top: Bali souvenir trader. In this case the subject is placed right at the centre of the frame and AF-SERVO with Tv mode to ensure fast enough shutter speeds, was the most suitable shooting mode to capture this subject.
Bottom: to produce the correct illumination use a projector with a mask attached to the front of it for a proper close-up light with snoot. To meter the subject you should change over to spot metering.

Lenses with continuously adjustable focal length

Lenses with variable focal length tend to be better the shorter the range in focal length. The purchase of a 2x zoom – i.e. a zoom where the longest focal length divided by the shortest equals 2, represents no risk. Should you be interested in a 3X or even a 4X zoom then you have to consider the matter carefully. Either decide on a less expensive type and use it only with the aperture slightly stopped down or decide to make a big dent in your savings and buy the best as far as lens correction is concerned. This means, if you are buying Canon, a lens type L. The new generation of zoom lenses with special correction are almost as good as fixed focal length lenses. For professional use I consider almost all fixed focal length lenses, specially corrected zooms and zoom lenses with short range in focal length (2X) as suitable.

Since I have used the newest types of zoom lenses I had to abandon my reservations about zoom lenses in general. So far I had the opportunity of trying out and assessing the following lenses:

Canon EF 35-70mm, *f*3.5-4.5 rotary zoom as well as the EF 35-105mm and the EF 70-210mm, *f*4 slide zooms. As I have already listed the arguments against zoom lenses, I shall now list their advantages:

- Zoom lenses combine a finely and continuously adjustable range of focal lengths in one compact, relatively light lens unit.
- A simple movement changes the focal length, making constant lens changing unnecessary – no need to carry a heavy and large supply of fixed focal length lenses.
- Close-ups are possible without additional accessories. Close-up distances down to 90cm are possible, even in automatic flash control – see table for reproduction scales and close-up limits.
- Zoom lenses allow some special effect and trick shots.
- The focus can be set very precisely by the following trick: choose the longest focal length setting on the lens, allow the autofocus to set the focus, keep release halfway pressed and change the focal length setting back to the required framing and release.

The various zoom lenses are offered either as rotating or as sliding.

Rotating zoom: the focal length setting is chosen by turning a ring on the lens tube. This is slower but generally better for shorter focal length lenses. With a slide mechanism the rather short range would be traversed too quickly and could not be controlled as easily.

Slide zoom: as the name suggests the focal lengths are traversed by sliding a sleeve along the lens tube. This is more suitable for bridging greater focal length ranges, which is generally the case with telephoto zooms. A further advantage is that the front element does not rotate, as with the rotating zoom. If the whole lens turns for focal length settings together with the filter thread, then there could be difficulties if a polarising filter is attached.

Zoom AF lenses for the EOS by Canon

Lens mm	*Angle of view*	*Close-up limit/cm*	*Greatest repro scale*	*Smallest aperture*	*Filter size*
Wide to mid-range					
20-35, *f*2.8LU	94-63°	50	1:12.5	22	72
28-70, *f*3.5-4.5	75-34°	39	1:4.5	22-29	52
28-80, *f*2.8-4LU	75-30°	50	1:5	22	72
35-70, *f*3.5-4.5	63-34°	39	1:5	22-29	52
35-70, *f*3.5-4.5 A	63-34°	39	1:5	22-29	52
35-105, *f*3.5-4.5	63-23°20'	95	1:1.75	22-29	58
35-135, *f*3.5-4.5	63-18°	95	1:5	22-29	52
standard to tele					
50-200, *f*3.5-4.5	46-12°	120	1:45	22-29	58
50-200, *f*3.5-4.5L	46-12°	120	1:45	22-29	58
telephoto					
70-210, *f*4	34-11°20'	120	1:4.1	32	58
80-200, *f*2.8L	30-12°	180	1:8	32	72
100-200, *f*4.5	24-12°	190	1:8.5	32	58
100-300, *f*5.6	24-8°15'	1500	1:3.85	32	58
100-300, *f*5.6L	24-8°15'	1500	1:3.85	32	58

Lens weight in g: 540 (20-35, f2.8 LU),285, 945, 245, 230, 400, 475, 690, 695, 605, 1330, 520, 685, 695 (100-300, f5.6L)

U = ultrasonic - especially quiet and fast AF motor
L = precisely corrected for outstanding reproduction quality
A = can be used Only as an AF lens

***Lens Hoods**:*

Some telephoto lenses have an integral hood as does the compact Macro 50 mm. If the lens hood is not integral then I generally use a rubber lens hood, available for tele and for wide-angle lenses (Kaiser, B+W, Hama, Rowi). The rubber hoods have an additional advantage that they present a certain protection to the front lens; it is also possible to use it as a cushion if you want to press the lens against a pane of glass or support it, hood folded back to provide a soft support, against some firm surface.

Rubber lens hoods are particularly suitable for zoom lenses. If the zoom lens is brought back to the wide-angle setting and the lens hood threatens to vignette the frame, then it is simply folded back.

Always use a lens hood with zoom lenses, particularly telephoto zooms, as these lenses are particularly prone to flare.

Converters – focal length extenders with certain limitations

Optical units that are inserted between camera and lens are called extenders or converters. They are used to extend the focal length of the lens but also to reach further into the macro range. To use one of these extenders makes sense only if they are suitable for both the far range and the close-up (macro) range. The description of a converter usually includes the factor by which the focal length is increased.

Extender (Converter) extension factors

Factor	*1.4*	*2*	*3*
Focal length extension (e.g. 200mm lens)	*x1.4 (280mm)*	*x2 (400mm)*	*x3 (600mm)*
reproduction scale, linear magnification	*x1.4*	*x2*	*x3*
reproduction scale, area magnification	*x2*	*x4*	*x9*
loss in lens speed	*:2*	*:4*	*:9*

As you might have expected nothing in life is free and the use of an extender is at the cost of lens speed. Moreover, one usually has to stop down to at least *f*4.

Canon offers three special extenders:

- Life-size converter EF (2x): for Compact Macro EF 50mm, *f*2.5. With this extender you can reach reproduction scales of up to 1:1.
- Extender EF 2x: for EF 200mm, *f*1.8L and EF 300mm, *f*2.8L.
- Extender EF 1.4x: for EF 200mm, *f*1.8L, EF 300mm, *f*2.8L and EF 600mm, *f*4L.

Novoflex offer a special bellows for extreme macro photography with the EOS.

The ideal lens combination

What lenses you buy will depend largely on what particular subjects you are interested in. In my case I am listing them in order of importance:

1. 85mm, *f*1.2
2. 35-70mm, *f*3.5-4.5 (or 100, 105, 135mm)
3. 400mm, *f*5.6 APO

and also

4. 70-210mm, *f*3.5-4.5 Apo

If the budget is limited, I would restrict myself to the first two lenses. The 400mm lens is a most useful addition to the set because it is so light and compact for its focal length. I find it particularly suitable for architectural details, statues and details in frescos on high ceilings.

Those of you who are interested in sports or animal photography will probably think of adding the fast 300mm, *f*2.8 or even the heavyweight 600mm, or perhaps a telephoto zoom.

Snapshot and available-light photographers pursue an expensive hobby; the fast lens implies high precision and expensive materials and these lenses are costly. You can choose from the 50mm, *f*1.0L, the 85mm, *f*1.2L, the 135mm, *f*2.8 and the 200mm, *f*1.8L.

For the lover of close-up and macro photography there is also a wide choice; the Compact Macro EF 50mm, *f*2.5 allows reproduction scales of 1:2 without any accessory. If the Life Size Converter EF 2x is attached, the reproduction scale is increased to 1:1 – true life size. The Macro Ring Lite ML3, specially designed for this lens, consists of a two-flash ring with battery-powered modelling light. This flash provides soft, uniform and automatically controlled lighting for the close-up subject and even for portrait photography. Close-up lenses are another possibility for macro photography – these achromatic supplementary lenses are particularly suitable for telephoto lenses with filter diameter 55mm. And then there is the bellows (Novoflex) for the professional set-up.

For portraits, shooting distances of between 1 and 2m are the most suitable. The choice is between the 85mm, *f*1.2, the 135mm, *f*2.8 softfocus (which has settings for both soft and sharp focus) and perhaps one of the zoom lenses.

Image Creation Through Different Focal Length Lenses

Large, pin-sharp depth of field versus contrast between sharpness and unsharpness

Characteristics of various focal length lenses with regard to the extent of depth of field can be classified as follows:

- Super wide-angle – 15-24mm – a large depth of field, the subjects within the picture are extremely small.
- Wide-angle – 28-35mm – a relatively large depth of field, subjects shown quite small.
- Normal/standard – 40-55mm – a reasonable depth of field, average reproduction of size.
- Portrait – 70-135mm – reproduction scale not excessively small.
- Telephoto – 135-1000mm – a small section of the subject is represented relatively large.

The sharply-depicted subject space in front of and behind the focusing plane – the depth-of-field – is greater for each focal length, the smaller the aperture and the greater the distance to the subject. The sharply-depicted subject space behind the focusing plane is twice as long as in front. Therefore you need to focus on a detail somewhere within the centre third of the total space that needs to be shown in sharp focus. Otherwise use Depth mode which will calculate the appropriate settings for you. The above rule applies to all lenses and settings with the exception of the close-up and macro range; in this case the depth of field extends equally in front and behind the focusing plane.

Pin-sharp representation of a large subject depth from close-up to infinity has a strong effect on us, because our own eye would not be able to observe everything at once in sharp focus. We may be under the impression, that we see the entire scene at any given time in sharp focus, but this is an illusion, a reconstruction in our mind of several images, our eyes re-focusing on each one in quick succession. Only in the photographic two-dimensional representation of a three-dimensional space are we able to show everything sharply at one given time.

To obtain large depth-of-field for a given lens the aperture has to be stopped down. Very small apertures, smaller than *f*11, reduce the general sharpness of the picture because of diffraction.

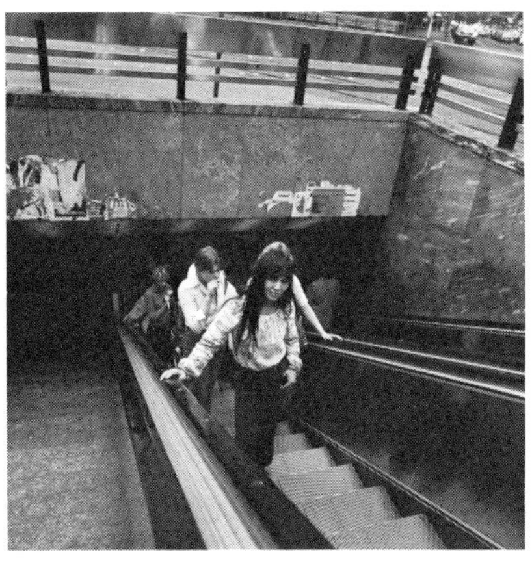

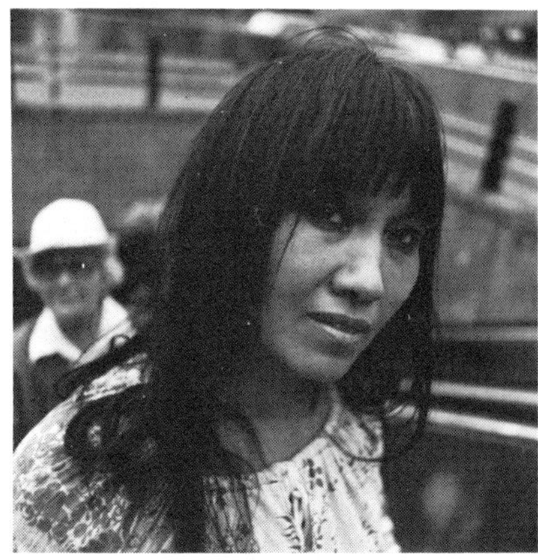

Comparisons:
Left: wide-angle picture from a great distance.
Right: wide-angle picture from close-up – about 40cm. The head seems close to the camera, divorced from the background. The face shows distortions due to the perspective of the near distance, characteristic for close shots with a wide-angle lens.

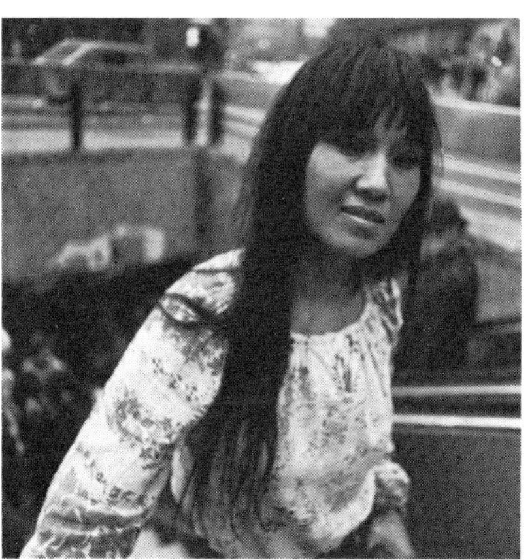

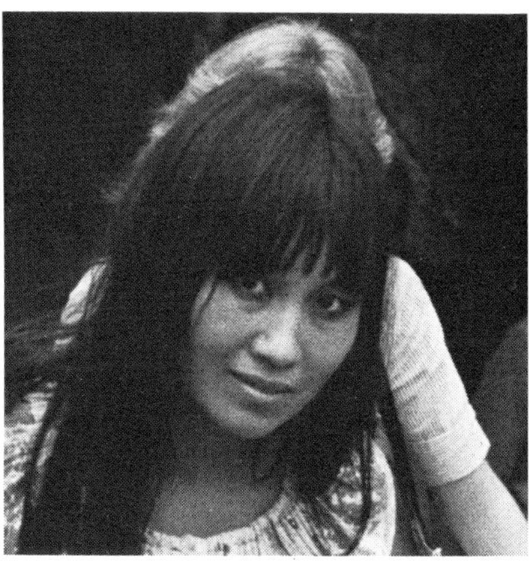

Left: picture taken with a long lens from a great distance – the same distance as the wide-angle shot in the picture, top left. The woman seems distanced despite the large reproduction scale, she seems to belong in the background.
Right: an enlargement of a detail from the wide-angle picture, top left. The perspective of this detail is exactly the same as the picture on the left, which was taken by the long lens. This proves that the perspective of a picture depends entirely on the viewpoint. The focal length of the lens plays a rôle only insofar as one can move closer to a subject with a shorter focal length and still show it in its entirety.

Even more impressive than total sharpness is "contrasting sharpness". In this case a narrow depth of field with a pin-sharp subject contrasted against a more or less blurred fore- and background. This impression cannot be reproduced by the human eye and our brain is also unable to create this impression for us. This effect can be maximised by using a long lens, aperture wide open, subject taken at very close range. With these settings only a very narrow depth from the subject space will be sharp, the immediate fore- and background very much out of focus. The greater the contrast between sharp main subject, within a blurred fore- and background, the more interesting and powerful is the effect.

Focal length and perspective

It should be made clear that the focal length of the lens has no effect whatsoever on the relative size of objects in a scene. Assume we take a wide-angle shot with a 24mm lens. The apparent distance between a hut in the foreground and a hill in the background appears to be about 70 metres. Now we take a picture from exactly the same viewpoint but this time with a 240mm lens. What will be the difference, if any, between the first and second shots? The only difference will be that everything in the long focus shot will be larger and less of the scene will be included in the picture but the relative sizes of objects and apparent distances will be exactly the same as in the picture taken with the wide-angle lens.

If the long focus negative is enlarged to make say an 8x10in. print and the wide-angle negative, or rather part of it, is enlarged so that the image in the print is exactly the same size as in the enlargement from the long focus negative, the two prints will be identical as regards the perspective they show. The much bigger degree of enlargement from the wide-angle negative is likely to be less sharp and more grainy than the other but that is all.

Differences in perspective associated with lenses of different focal lengths arise solely from differences in viewpoints. A long focus lens is usually employed for distant scenes and a wide-angle lens, with its short focal length, is often used simply because a close viewpoint is forced on the photographer by the situation of the subject. The stateroom in a ship is normally photographed with a wide-angle lens with a short focal length only because there is no room to use a more distant viewpoint and a longer focal length lens.

Close-ups of small creatures – lizards, frogs, butterflies, beetles – are best taken with longer focus lenses. These allow reasonable reproduction scales at larger shooting distances. The photographer does not have to get too close thereby scaring the little creature away. A useful combination is the AF mode with IR metering flash which ensures that the small creature is captured sharply.

With photographs of small, stationary objects such as plants the

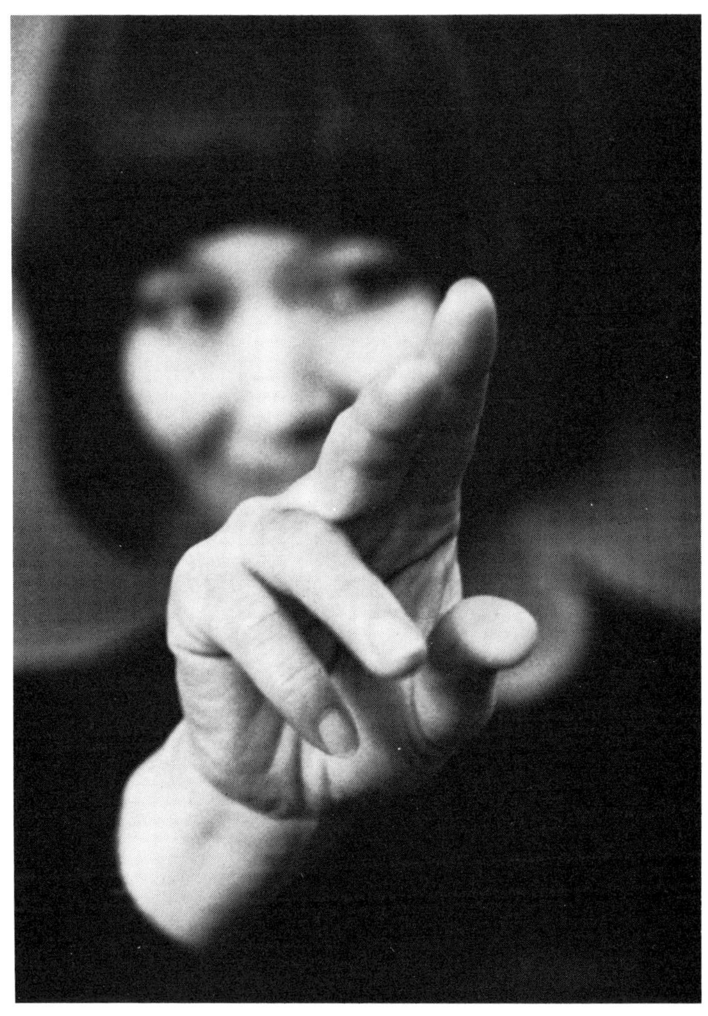

Very selective focus. Focal length set to 100mm, wide open aperture, set manually in Av mode.

situation can best be mastered with short focal lengths. With a 24mm lens one can get to within 20 to 18cm (reproduction scale 1:4). This shooting distance can be reduced with a supplementary lens and the reproduction scale is increased accordingly. With the exception of the 300 EZ Speedlite, all other EOS Speedlites can be adjusted to the angle of view of the 24mm lens to illuminate the entire field.

Natural perspective

There is a definite relationship between the focal length of the lens, the degree of enlargement used in making the final image seen by the viewer and the viewing distance that conveys the same impression as if the scene were perceived by the naked eye. For natural-looking perspective a contact print from a negative or a colour slide should be viewed from a distance equal to the focal length of the lens. Neither of the two, viewed with the unaided eye, can exhibit natural-looking perspective as the lens is likely to have a focal length of perhaps 50mm.

The normal eye can focus sharply on objects no nearer than about 10in. unless, of course, a magnifier is used.

If an enlargement is being viewed, the distance for natural perspective is equal to the focal length of the lens multiplied by the degree on enlargement used in making the print. If the whole of a 35mm negative is enlarged to make a print 10in. long the degree of enlargement has to be about 7.25x. Assuming that the negative was made with a 50mm lens, the distance for natural-looking perspective will be 7.25 x 50mm which equals about 14in., which would be a comfortable viewing distance for an 8x10in. print. A 5x enlargement from a 35mm negative taken with a 50mm lens would be about 7.5in. long and would have to be viewed from 10in., which is the closest distance which the normal eye can accommodate. Prints made at lower magnifications could never be seen with natural perspective because of the inability of the eye to focus closer than 10in.

How about a colour slide taken with a 50mm lens and projected on a screen to give a picture 5ft wide (60in.). This ought to be viewed from a distance of about equal to 60x2 or 120in. This means standing at 10 feet from the screen at which distance the picture would show a realism that would be missing at distances differing greatly from this. The effect of using the correct viewing distances when looking at photographic images can be quite dramatic as experiments will show.

Uniform flash illumination

Distance between light source and subject, for a subject depth of 1m	*Reflected illumination intensity between foreground and background*
1m	*4:1*
2m	*2.25:1*
3m	*1.77:1*
4m	*1.56:1*
5m	*1.44:1*
6m	*1.36:1*
7m	*1.29:1*
8m	*1.25:1*
9m	*1.23:1*
10m	*1.21:1*

Sometimes one has to illuminate a subject with a larger spatial depth, perhaps a group of people several rows deep. How this is done can be read off the above table. The calculation is based on the law of the propagation of light, i.e. the intensity of light decreases as the square of the distance from its source.

Let's take the situation of a subject one distance unit away from the light source and one unit deep. In this case the front edge of a subject receives four times as much light as the background. If the distance to the light source is increased to ten units, then the relative loss in illumination level between front and back is only 1/5, which makes little difference to the picture.

Conclusion: if it is important to illuminate a certain spatial depth uniformly then we have to move the light source further away from the subject. If the flashgun is in the camera's hotshoe then the following applies; with a longer focal length the shooting distance to the subject will also be greater and the result will be a reasonably well-lit picture. If we are using a short focal length, which forces us to go closer to the subject, then the foreground will be brightly-lit against a background that is lost in darkness.

Using a tele-light to shoot in interiors with light walls and ceilings is particularly good, as the light reflected from the bright surfaces fills-in shadows and thus improves the situation even further.

Effective filling-in of shadows in interiors with bright walls and ceiling:

- *arrange the light source – halogen lamp or flash – as far away from the subject as possible,*
- *set flash reflector to wide-angle setting (if possible, 24mm),*
- *indirect illumination provides the most uniform light in depth.*

If I have to make copies, say a map, a drawing, etc., then I usually use just one light, perhaps a high-power halogen lamp. I arrange this laterally, at an angle of 30 to 45° from as far away as possible.

The "Gabelmo" – the baroque Neptune fountain by Kaspar Metzner (1698) in Bamberg.

Top row:
left and centre: two different views, taken with a 24mm lens
right: taken with a 50mm lens.

Centre row:
left: view, without foreground, with a 50mm lens.
centre: the whole figure shown at a greater distance with s 135mm lens.
right: a close-up taken from below with the 180mm lens

Bottom row:
three "portraits" taken with a 210mm focal length lens.

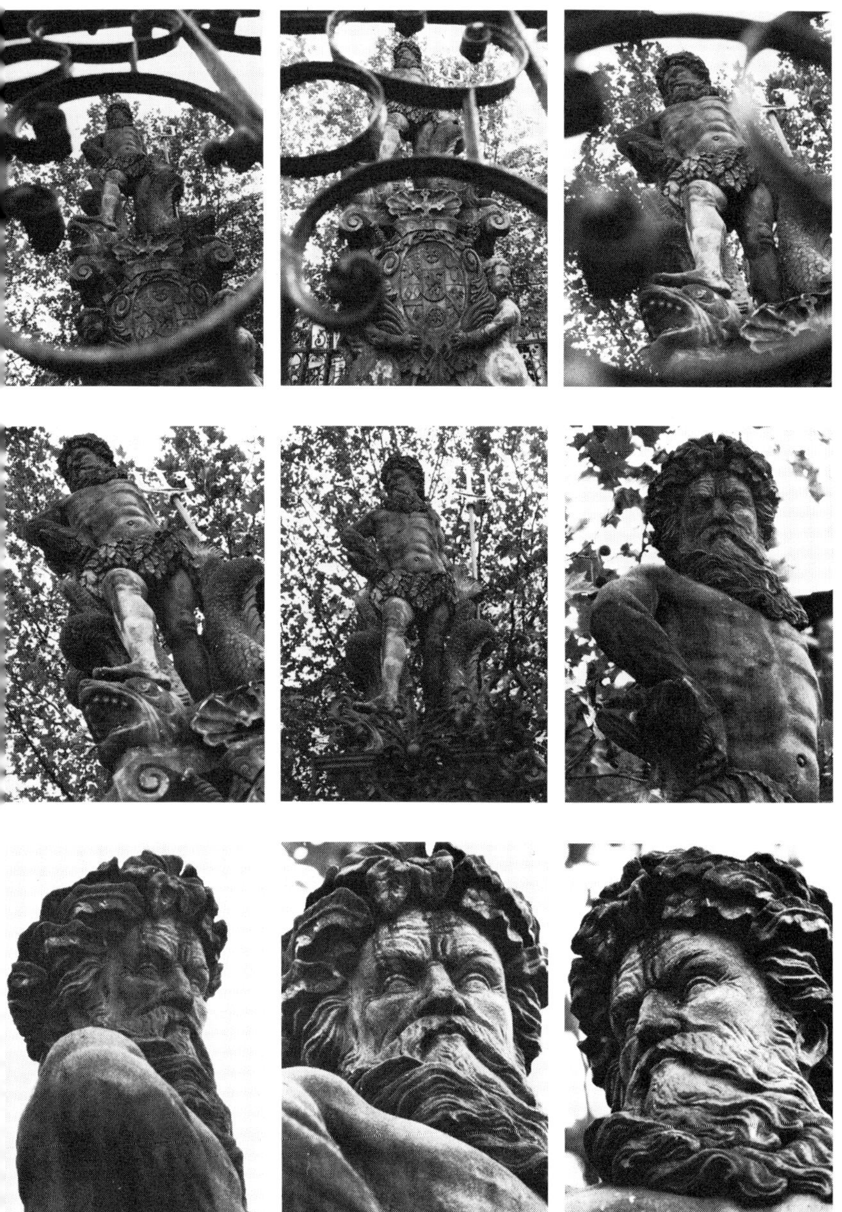

From the complimentary to the grotesque picture – just a small step...

One important principle in photography says; move as close to the subject as possible – and after you have taken the picture, move one step even closer and take another. Although this rule applies also to standard and to telephoto lenses, it is of particular importance for wide-angle lenses. The task here is to contrast the relatively large foreground object against a strongly diminished background. Such pictures are effective because they contradict our usual perception of the world around us. We generally keep a certain distance from the subject we look at – usually about 1.2 to 1.5m. (Naturally, this does not apply to smaller objects, for example a text that we are reading or another small object that we handle.) A wide-angle lens allows us to depict a foreground object from as close as 1m against a distant background. This leads to changes in the apparent shape of the foreground object due to the extreme perspective, which is unusual, because we generally do not adopt such a close and oblique viewpoint.

The smooth outlines of a boat or a racing car, the elegant lines of an antique vase, are further enhanced by this treatment. This effect is further increased by adopting a low shooting position from as close as possible. The façade of a house or a tower, taken from street level with the camera pointing up at a steep angle, can produce interesting results. The strongly converging lines have to be carefully arranged within the rectangle of the frame to lend the high structure extra height.

On the other hand, some subjects are quite unsuitable for this treatment. The result is a caricature, a distortion of reality. Faces become ugly masks. Have you ever tried to shoot a head with a 24mm lens; try to move to within 35cm of the head, camera at a steep angle from the top – the cranium swollen to a huge bulbous shape, the mouth shrunk to a small orifice, the chin totally withered. If you change the angle and look at the person from below then even the meekest character assumes a threatening aspect with the chin jutting out menacingly. If the light is arranged directly from below then the whole face turns into a grotesque mask.

Part VIII

Small and Large Accessories

Front Lens Attachments

Close-up and magnifying lenses for macro photography

The close-up range begins with reproduction scales of 1:10 and ends with reproduction at actual size, i.e. the picture produced on the slide or negative is the same size as the original. If we reach beyond the reproduction scale of 1:1 we are talking of magnified pictures. Close-ups from about 1:6 and magnified pictures are often referred to as macro photography. Apart from the previously-mentioned 50mm macro lens there are various extenders and three more devices which are quite important:

- the magnifier S is attached to the eyepiece for exact focusing of the subject.
- two types of angle viewfinders (A2 and B). As the name implies, this is also attached to the eyepiece and allows focusing from right angles to the eyepiece, for example, if the camera is placed on the floor. This is also useful for candid shots "around the corner".

Simple close-up lenses allow us to advance further into the close-up range. For short focal length lenses you should use stronger lenses (perhaps 2 or more dioptres), for longer lenses 0.5 to 1.0 dioptres should be suitable. The use of a close-up lens has one disadvantage, the sharpness declines towards the edge of the picture. However, if you are taking flowers, leaves, small insects, etc. then this makes no difference. For copying, however, this is quite unsuitable. Otherwise they present quite a reasonable solution to achieve larger reproduction scales without loss of lens speed. The lens should be stopped well down to minimise loss of image quality and to achieve maximum depth of field.

Especially worth considering are the excellent achromatic supplementary lenses from Minolta and Leitz (Elpro).

The following also applies to supplementary lenses:

1. The greater the power (more dioptres), the closer you can move to the subject and the larger the reproduction scale.
2. The longer the focal length of the lens, the greater the effect of the supplementary lens of a given power (which explains why a longer lens produces larger reproduction scales).

If you are using the EF 35-105mm, *f*3.5-4.5 lens and a 2 dioptre supplementary lens, you can achieve reproduction scales of 1:2. With the EF 50mm, *f*2.5 macro the reproduction scale is 1:1.5.

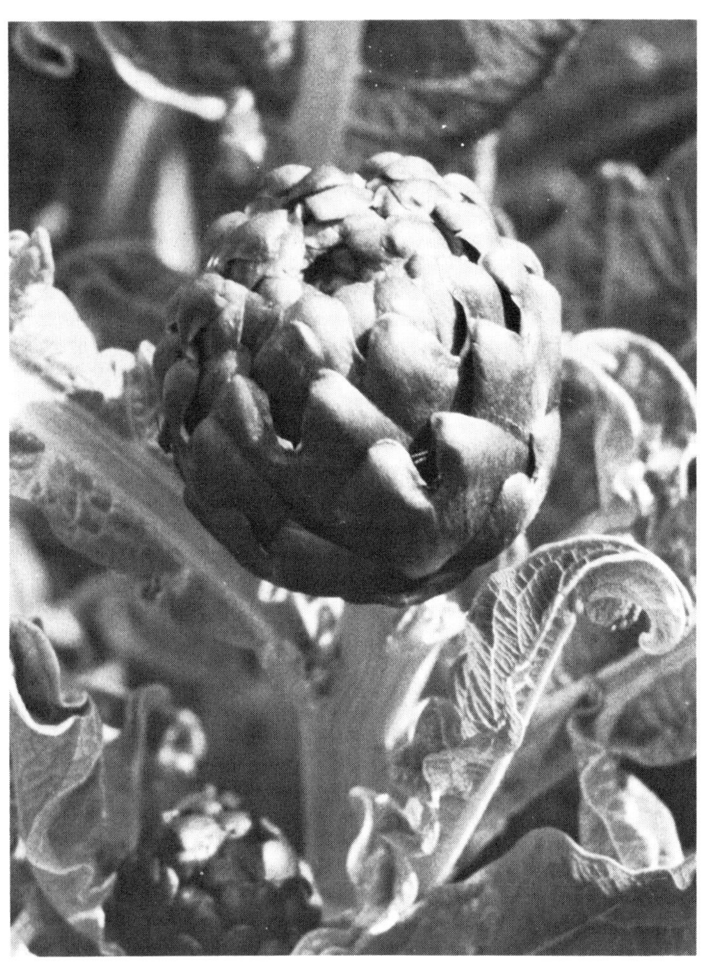

Close-up, taken with an achromatic supplementary lens and wide open aperture.

One accessory manufacturer with a wide range of products (Hama) supplies so-called coupling rings 52+52 and 52+58. These allow lenses to be combined via their filter thread, front lens facing front lens. If a longer focal length lens is attached to the camera with a shorter focal length inversely fixed via a coupling ring and thus used as a supplementary lens, the result will be pictures with reproduction scales in excess of 1:1. When using this arrangement make sure the lens is set to M-Focus. Vignetting will be a problem that is difficult to overcome. I therefore recommend the special Novoflex bellows if you are really interested in macro photography. With the bellows all automatic functions, apart from autofocus, are active. The additional use of a supplementary lens, which I personally prefer to the extension rings, extends the range of the bellows even further.

Filters

There is a wide range of filters on the market but most of them are needed only for particular effects. Only six are really important, and if we include colour IR photography, the total is 7.

Filters

My 7 most important filters:

for colour photography

UV Skylight filter (almost colourless)
circular polarising filter
R(KR)12 (brown-orange)
yellow-orange (colour infrared)

for black-and-white

UV Skylight filter (colourless)
circular polarising filter
red filter (deep)
orange filter
green filter (deep)

to this list you may wish to add the KR1.5 (Skylight 1A) and 80B (daylight film in tungsten light) for colour and the 2X Yellow for black and white

Filters for black-and-white film:
- UV filter – to protect the front element against dust, fingermarks, grit, rain, etc.
- deep red filter to enhance contrast in architectural photography in sunlight – the brickwork and stones remain light, the sky nearly black, shadows deep, also for landscapes with dramatic skies. The blue of the sky and sea turns nearly black. The contrast is even further enhanced in bright sunshine.
- orange filter: to be used when the deep-red filter absorbs too much light.
- green or yellow-green filter: for landscapes, the blue of the sky is darkened, green foliage is lightened.
- circular polarising filter: effect as below, under "filters for colour slides".

> *Regardless of what filter is attached to the lens, the exposure metering is through the lens and the effect of the filter is automatically taken into consideration. However, I would recommend an extra frame with an exposure compensation of +1 for pictures taken with a deep red filter.*

Filters for colour print film:
- UV skylight filter
- circular polarising filter (see "filters for colour slides")

If you wish to make black-and-white prints from colour negatives then you can use the appropriate filter during printing.

Filters for Colour Slide Film:
- UV filter – to protect the front element against dust, fingermarks, grit, rain, etc. and to prevent a blue bias in the presence of strong UV radiation, such as in the mountains, near the sea and whenever the sun is high in the sky.
- brown-orange filter R (or KR) 12 for colour correction to enable the use of tungsten slide film in daylight.
- polarising filter: whenever the sky is pale blue in bright sunshine the use of this filter will turn it a darker blue, especially if the sun is at right angles to the shooting direction. The colour of flowers, foliage, brick walls, painted walls, etc. is also enhanced. Shots taken on dull or wet days may benefit by the use of polarising filters, the specularly reflected light on wet surfaces is reduced, increasing the intensity of the colours. A polarising filter can subdue reflections from non-metallic surfaces.

Guide to the use of polarising filters

1. *Use only a circular polarising filter, which is the only suitable type for the EOS-1. The cheaper linear polarising filter may deceive the exposure metering system, resulting in incorrect exposures.*

2. *On clear days, the increase in colour intensity is most noticeable whenever the sun is at right angles to the shooting position.*

3. *The effect depends on the position of the filter – it may be turned in its mount. Turn it and observe the effect in the viewfinder. Between the strongest and the weakest effect is a turning angle of 90°. Some front elements turn during focusing and you therefore have to adjust the polarising filter after the lens has been focused.*

4. *If you turn your EOS-1 from cross- to upright format, or the other way round, then the filter has to be adjusted.*

5. *On very sunny days the effect of the polarising filter is further increased by entering an exposure compensation of between –1/3rd to –2/3rd.*

Filter adapter rings

The various lenses have different filter sizes. You can get adapters which allow larger diameter filters to be used for lenses with smaller filter diameters.

B + W supply, amongst others, the following adapters:

- from 72 to 58 mm
- from 58 to 52 mm
- from 55 to 52 mm
- and also from 55 to 58 mm.

Please note: do not use a larger filter than a 52mm for the popular EF 35-70mm, *f*3.5-4.5 zoom as the front element of this lens moves in and out of the tube. Filters with larger diameters would therefore restrict the movement of the front element, both in automatic and manual focusing. The EF 35-105mm, *f*3.5-4.5 zoom does not suffer from this problem.

It is possible to get adapters to use smaller filters in larger filter diameters. However, this can cause vignetting, particularly with the shorter focal length lenses. Make sure this does not happen and carefully check the image in the viewfinder.

The Multi-Function Databack and other useful accessories

The Databacks

To change the standard back for the data back:
- open the camera;
- push down the locking mechanism on the top of the hinge with your fingernail and tilt the back at an angle;
- lift the back out of the lower hinge;
- fit the data back in the lower hinge;
- push down locking lever with your fingernail and align back panel with top hinge;
- release the locking lever to engage.

Once fitted the Command Back can stay on the camera. Nothing can happen if it is set to OFF. The advantage is that you now also have a clock to check the time. It is not necessary, however, to expose the time on the film.

Balu Bolong; a holy Hindu Bali temple on the west coast of Lombok. The blurred blooms in the foreground add some colour to the subject. This through-view with a lot of unsharp foreground is no problem in AF-lock.

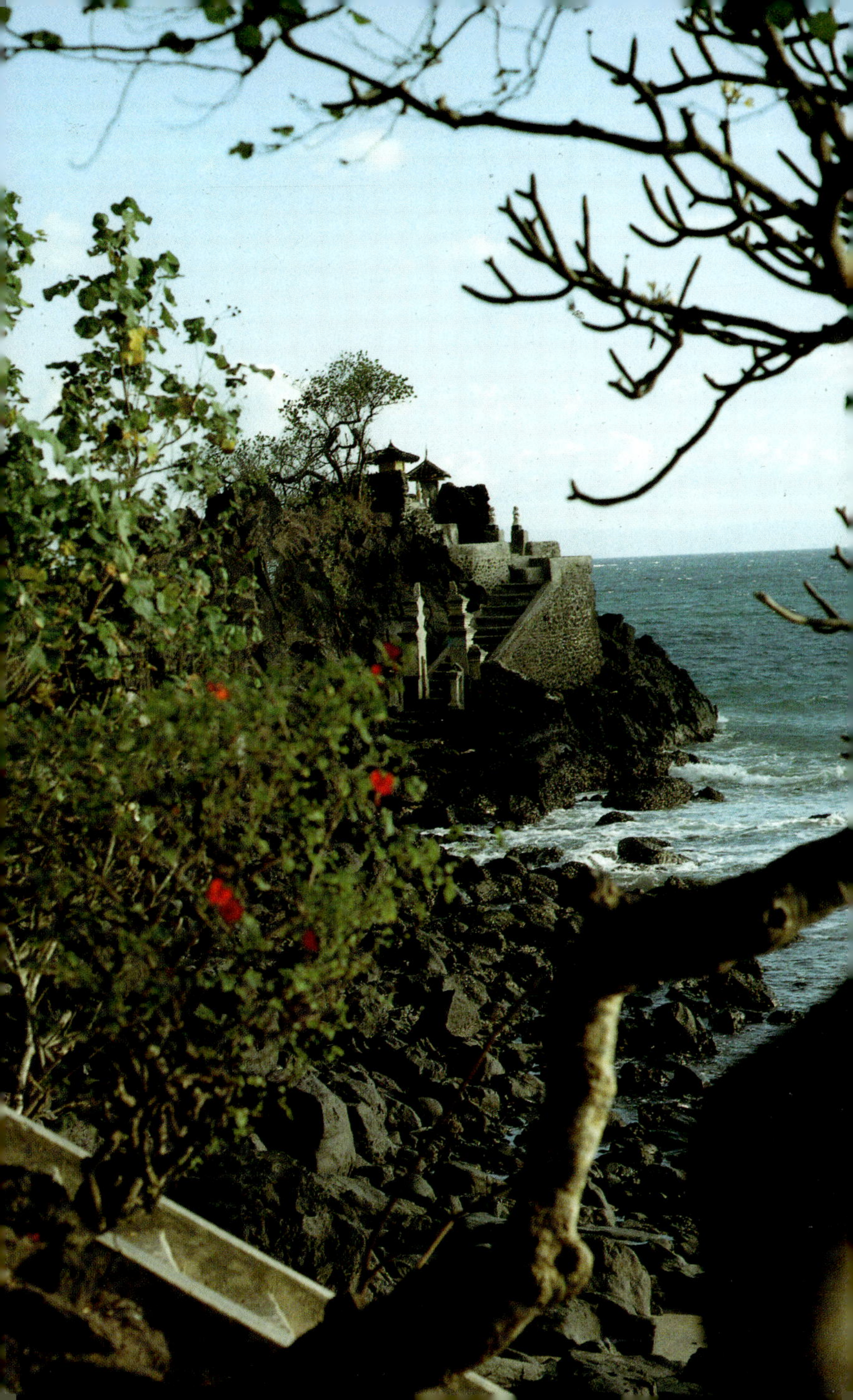

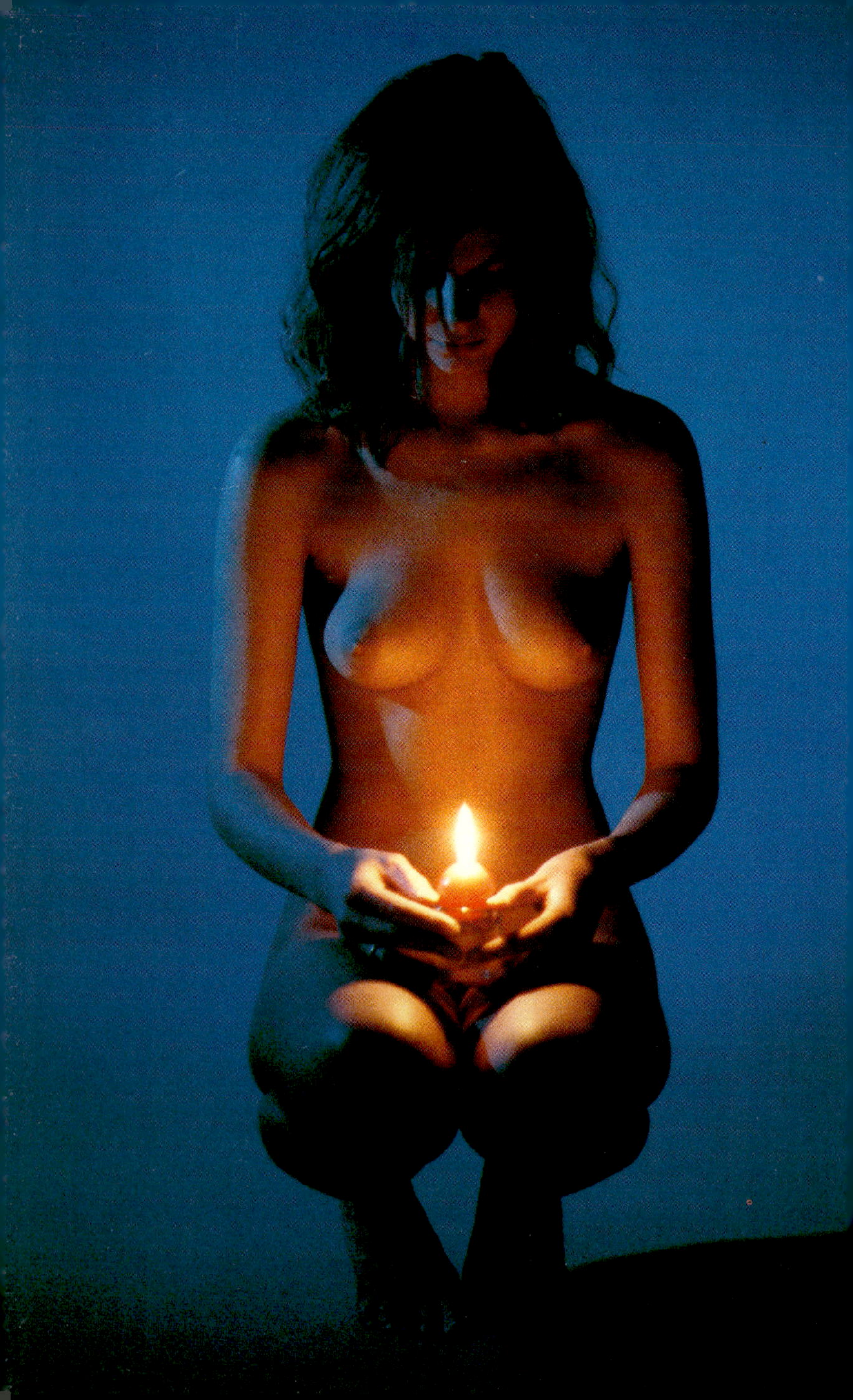

Command Back E1 for EOS-1

This camera back, made for the EOS-1 imprints the date, time of day, frame counter number, and an arbitrary 6-digit number, plus the letters A to F. But, as its name implies, its prime function is as a time control for the camera which makes unattended time-lapse photography possible. The interval timer can be set to release the shutter at fixed intervals, which can be from one second to almost a day (23 hours and 59 minutes to be precise). The possibilities are endless, from recording the opening of a flower bud, to the growth of a plant over a month, from changing weather patterns to astronomical studies. The frame counter setting can be used to stop the camera after a set number of exposures. The Comand Back E1 can also act as a self-timer to release the shutter after a predetermined time, or as a long-exposure timer to hold the shutter open for a pre-determined time on 'bulb'.

Power Drive Booster E1 for EOS-1

The built-in motor drive of the Canon EOS-1 can advance the film and fire the shutter at a rate of 2.5 frames per second. This is fast enough for most ordinary purposes, but if you need to capture the right moment in a rapidly changing scene, or a fleeting facial expression, then the Power Drive Booster E1 comes into its own, with a speed of 5.5 fps. For anyone engaged in sports photography, some types of wildlife photography, news reporting – particularly "doorstepping" celebrities – it is an essential tool. But beware! It is not the lazy man's way of getting the perfect picture – press the button and hope that one of the shots will be IT. It goes through film so fast that you could well find that the vital moment was lost because the 36 exposures were already used. Using a motor drive of this speed needs the fine judgement and split-second timing in pressing the release that only comes from experience.

This picture was taken with a very fast tungsten film. The subject was illuminated only by the glow of flame, the background was illuminated by two blue shop-window spotlights. Exposure should be by spot metering for the light skin tones. The candle light has to be slightly overexposed otherwise the rest of the subject would be lost in total darkness.

Besides these exciting, heat-of-the-moment applications, the Power Drive Booster E1 is also used in careful scientific and technical work. Examples might be the study of machinery in motion or the gait of an animal.

The Power Drive Booster E1 adds a lot of weight and bulk to the camera, but the combination improves balance and provides a better grip than the camera alone. It also has a shutter release button and an AE-lock on the base. This unique feature makes the camera equally easy to operate in both the vertical and the horizontal formats because these two controls always fall in the same position for the fingers whichever way the camera is held. When it is attached to the camera, it powers the camera as well from its eight size AA cells. Three film wind modes are available with the Booster: S (single frame); CH (continuous at up to 5.5 fps); and CL (continuous at up to 3 fps).

Remote release

The remote release socket is on the right side of the E1. Connect the remote cable 60T3 (60cm) to this socket. A 10m extension, the 1000T3, is also available. If the two are connected, by cable adapter T3, the total length is 1060cm.

Cableless release is possible by infrared remote release LC.2. This works in a similar manner as an infrared remote release for a slide projector.

Further interesting small accessories

If your eyesight lies outside the dioptric adjustment range of +1 to -3 that is provided as standard in the viewfinder, you can change the eyepiece for a special frame that holds eyesight correction lenses E.

Canon offer seven interchangeable viewfinder screens with different focusing aids. These screens are supplied with a special little tool which you will need to perform the task. The different types are described in the manual.
Of particular interest are:

Type D: laser full matte screen with grid. This is useful for exact alignment of the camera for copying and also for architectural photography;

Type H: matte screen with vertical and horizontal scale for close-up and macro photography. Useful to measure subjects and for architecture.

Part IX

EOS Lenses and Camera Reference

FIXED FOCUS LENSES

EF 15mm *f*2.8 Fisheye

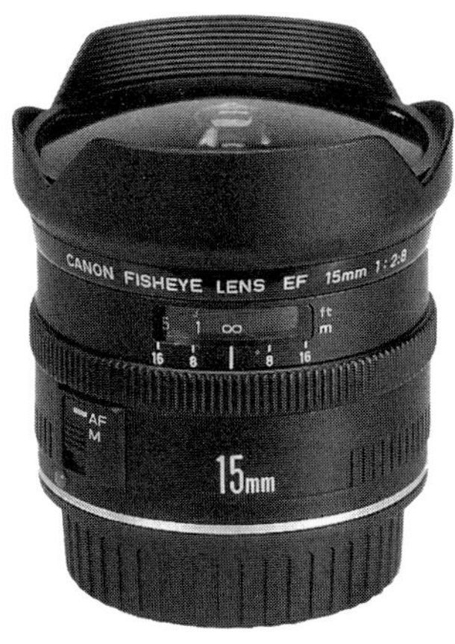

This lens is a new design for the EOS system; the previous 15mm *f*2.8 for the FD mount had nine elements in eight groups, whereas this lens has eight elements in seven groups giving improved optical quality compared to its predecessor. This is a full frame fisheye covering 180°, so to avoid vignetting, filters are fitted at the rear of the lens. Rather than the fixed set of dial-in filters used on the older design, Canon have provided a slot at the rear of their new fisheye lens into which gelatin filters can be slotted.

EF 24mm *f*2.8

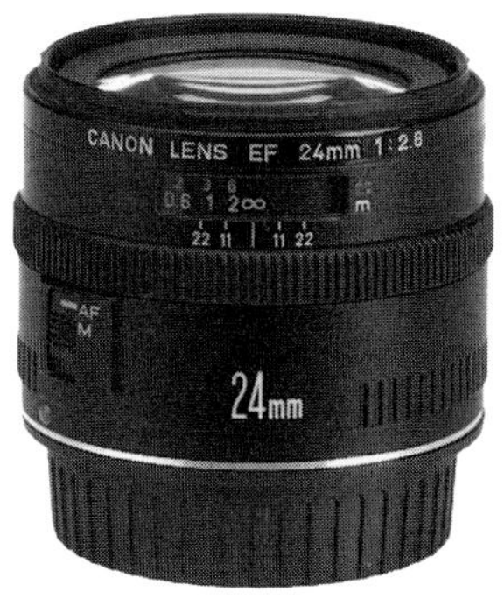

This popular universal wide-angle lens has been redesigned for the EF mount version. The new design is claimed to be free from rectlinear distortion, and uses internal focusing through a cam system rather than a helicoid drive.

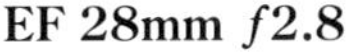

EF 28mm *f*2.8

A budget-priced compact wide-angle, the 28mm *f*2.8 uses aspheric elements to perform superbly with a mere 5 elements. A standard choice for quality-conscious photographers – a distortion-free general wide-angle.

EF 50mm *f*1.0

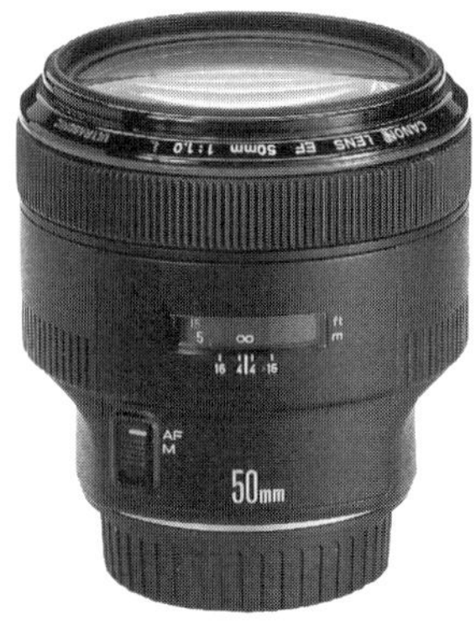

The fastest 35mm standard lens currently made, this very unusual design incorporates two aspheric elements and 9 spheric elements. Some of these elements are 'floating' – move independently – to maintain sharpness throughout the focusing range

Such unique features do make the lens quite large but for low-light press work the advantages far outweight this disadvantage.

The use of aspheric elements and low dispersion types of glass have resulted in a lens with excellent colour correction and absence of optical aberrations.

EF 50mm *f*1.8

The standard 50mm lens for the EOS system, closely related to the FD range 50mm *f*1.8. This lens is a tried and tested performer, ideal as the basis for a larger system.

EF 50mm *f*2.5 Macro

Macro lenses are specially designed to focus on very close subjects without requiring any accessories. The 50mm *f*2.5 is one of the fastest such lenses made, ensuring bright viewing as well as rapid autofocus performance at higher magnifications. Used alone, it covers the range from infinity to half life size (1:2). An optional Life Size Converter gives even closer focusing.

EF 100mm *f*2.8 Macro

A newly-introduced 100mm macro lens which focuses down to life-size without extension tubes, the 100mm uses a mount design which allows a very compact overall size despite a focusing extension of 100mm from infinity.

EF 85mm *f*1.2L

One of the fastest 85mm portrait and sports photography lenses made, the *f*1.2L uses the USM motor and both aspheric elements and floating groups for unequalled low-light performance from 8 elements in 7 groups.

EF 135mm *f*2.8 Soft Focus Lens

This lens has been designed specially for portrait photography, incorporating a variable soft-focus effect which is frequently used to improve skin tone and add halation to backlit hair. When, however, the soft focus control ring is set to "0", this lens is just as sharp as any other 135mm. Relatively low cost, a fast maximum aperture and good all-round performance make the 135mm a practical alternative to zoom lenses for outdoor travel and landscape work.

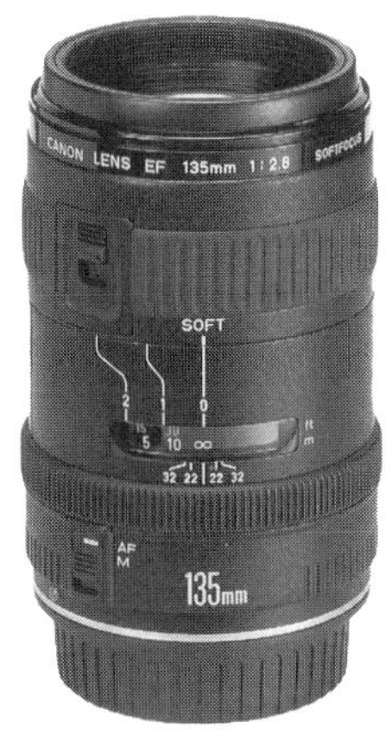

EF 200mm *f*1.8L

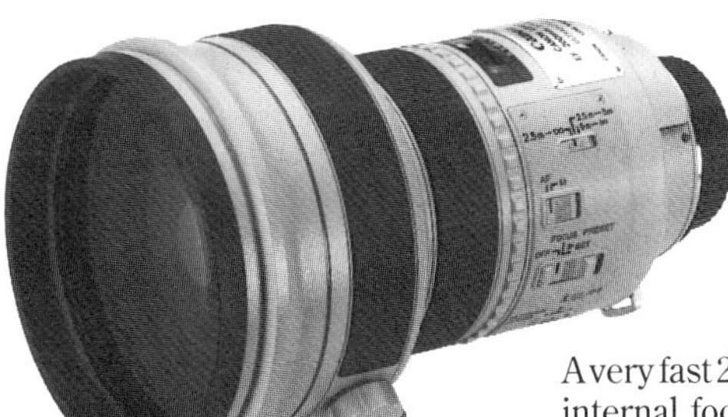

A very fast 200mm lens which uses internal focus driven by Canon's UltraSonic Motor, which not only finds sharp focus very rapidly but also does it very quietly. The combination of length, speed and quiet focusing make this an ideal lens for the nature photographer.

EF 300mm *f*2.8L

A longer lens which is also ideal for nature photography, as well as sports, news and fashion work. It too combines long focal length with speed. It is powered by the USM motor which enables it to focus from infinity down to three metres in just over half a second.

This lens also has the new feature 'focus memory' – a distance entered into the lens memory can be recalled rapidly, and the lens will give an audible bleep when the pre-set distance is in focus. This feature can be very useful when photographing track events, where you want to catch the intermittent action on the circuit and fill in the time in between with candids of the crowd.

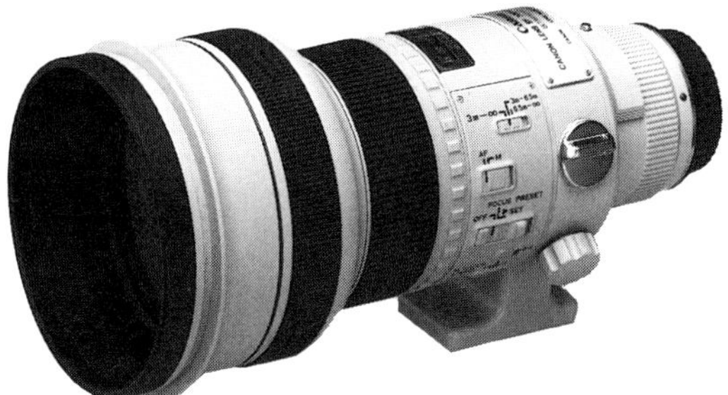

EF 600mm *f*4L

Essentially a larger brother to the 300mm, the 600mm offers one stop more in maximum aperture than can be achieved when using a converter on the 300mm. It features focus memory and all the primary functions of the 300mm, together with three pre-settable focus zones to prevent hunting over a wide range, and three speeds for electronic manual focusing. Its performance is considered equal to the 300mm, and exceptional for a 600mm.

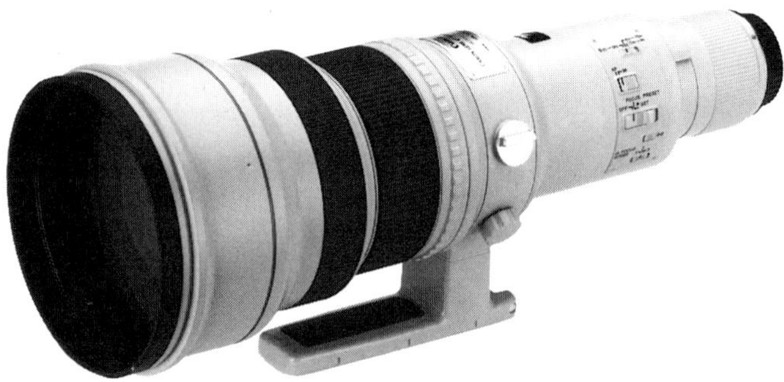

Canon Extender EF 2x
Canon Extender EF 1.4x

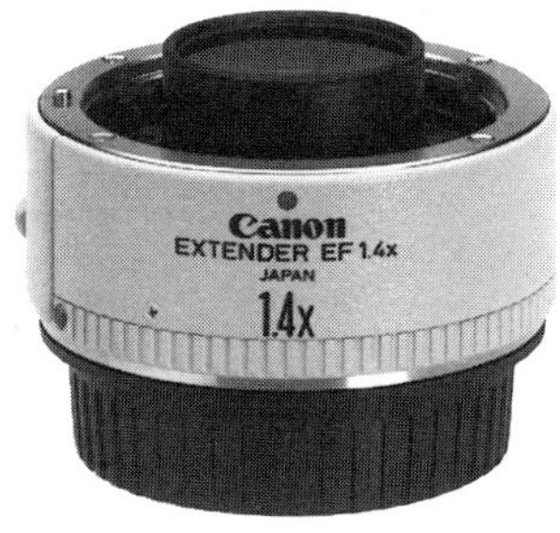

These lens converters (tele-converter or multiplier) either double the focal length of whichever compatible lens it is fitted *behind*, or mulitply it by 1.4x. Extenders fit between the camera body and the lens.

A 7-element 5-group design, the 2x is very small and light. Both the optical construction and the mount contacts are matched to a limited set of fast telephoto EF lenses – the EF 200mm *f*1.8L, EF 300mm *f*2.8L, and EF 600mm *f*4L designs. It produces (with these lenses respectively) working combinations of 400mm *f*3.5, 600mm *f*5.6 and 1200mm *f*8.

The 1.4x has the advantage of losing just one *f*-stop in maximum working aperture. It also benefits from a simpler 5-element, 4-group design which helps maintain maximum contrast, and is very small indeed.

The combinations provided with the 200, 300 and 600mm lenses are:

280mm *f*2.5
420mm *f*4
840mm *f*5.6

The EF Extenders can *not* be used with any other EF lenses.

ZOOM LENSES

EF 20-35mm *f*2.8L

Few zoom lenses cover this range, and the Canon 20-35mm is unmatched in any other system. It has a non-rotating front element and internal focusing, with an aspheric element and floating groups. The result is an extreme wide-angle 1.5:1 ratio zoom with very well corrected geometry, flatness of field, and close focusing ability.

The 20-35mm uses 15 elements in 11 groups and takes 72mm filters; it covers a true angular field range of 94° – 63°. The entire normal w/a range in one lens.

EF 28-70mm *f*3.5-4.5II

A glass molded aspherical element helps keep the design of this new lens very compact, while a moving internal baffle limits veiling glare. Zooming is internal, with focusing by the front group, which rotates.. A good general-purpose standard zoom, the 28-70mm is often sold with the EOS-1 as an alternative to the standard 50mm lens.

The lens focuses down to 39m at all focal lengths, which enables it to be used for close-ups at larger than one-tenth life-size.

EF 28-80mm *f*2.8-4L

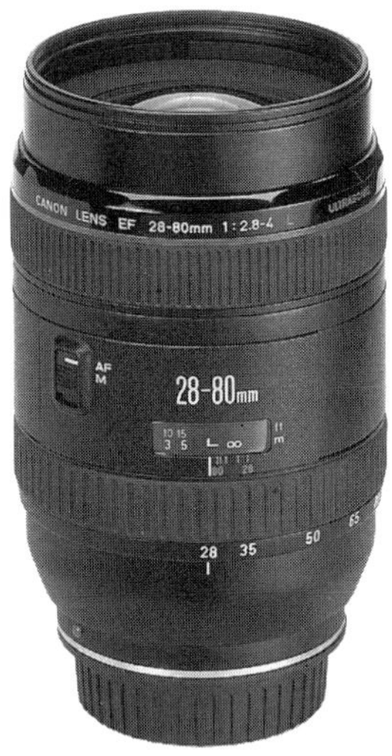

The difference between this lens and the 28-70mm II is not simply one of focal length range and aperture. It is an ultra-high performance 'L' series lens which uses two aspheric elements, low dispersion glass and a complex mechanical design. It also features the ultrasonic focusing motor rather than the AFD used in the 28-70mm, and the 80mm length is achieved without any loss of close focusing ability.

The L-series lens is however far larger and heavier than the ordinary lens, taking 72mm filters as opposed to 52mm. It is a choice made principally by those requiring the ultimate in image-quality.

EF 35-70mm *f*3.5-4.5

A budget-priced alternative to the 28-70mm in place of a standard 50mm lens, the 35-70mm is both small and light. Although it is not an L-series lens, the optical performance is very good.

EF 35-70mm A

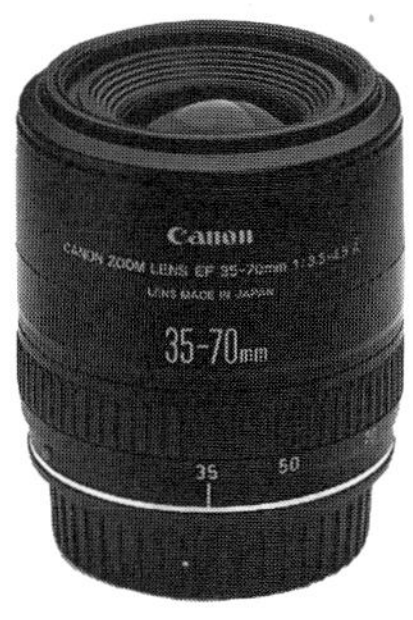

An entry-level lens for simpler EOS cameras – has no manual focusing. The A-series lenses (see also the 100-200mm, overleaf) are not optically inferior to the normal EF lenses of the same specification, but the absence of the focusing ring reduces the versatility of a camera like the EOS-1. If you already own an A-series lens from another EOS, and trade up to ownership of the EOS-1, there is certainly no need to change the lens as well.

EF 35-80mm *f*4-5.6 Power Zoom

A simple but attractive idea – push-button power zooming on a still SLR AF lens, recently introduced (mainly for basic EOS models).

EF 35-105mm *f*3.5-4.5

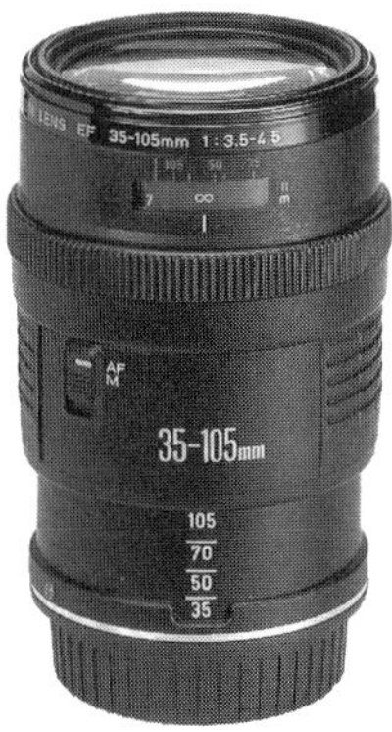

For those wanting an extended range in a single lens, the 35-105mm is still small enough to be considered a replacement for the standard 50mm. The zoom action is push-pull rather than rotary, and some barrel distortion is evident (as is the case with all zooms of this range).

EF 35-135mm *f*3.5-4.5

The ultimate all-round lens encompassing wide-angle to telephoto, the 35-135mm nevertheless had the same maximum aperture range as its 35-70 and 35-105mm brethren. This lens is both larger and more expensive than the 35-105mm.

EF 35-135mm *f*4-5.6 USM

A new EF 35-135mm *f*4-5.6 USM lens has been made available as a low-priced, silent focusing option. and new grip styling. The penalty is a smaller maximum aperture, but the price-tag is well below the 'pro' 35-135mm.

EF 50-200mm *f*3.5-4.5
EF 50-200mm *f*3.5-4.5L

With a fast maximum aperture for its 4:1 ratio, this lens is nevertheless fairly small and is very quick to use. The 'L' design is almost identical in appearance but features an expensive optical configuration for professional performance.

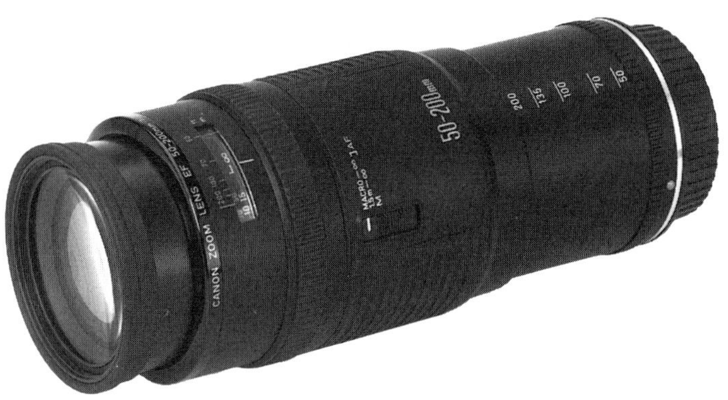

EF 70-210mm *f*4

The most popular tele zoom, both compact and light, with a range exceeding the 'prime' lens collection between 85mm and 200mm. Forms a complete outfit when twinned with a 28-70mm. This lens uses molded glass aspheric elements and is a state-of-the-art design.

EF 70-210mm *f*3.5-4.5 USM

A new design with the silent USM motor for focusing, new rubber grip focusing ring, similar in price to the *f*4 design, with a variable maximum aperture rather than a constant *f*4 during zooming.

EF 100-200mm *f*4.5

This is a budget lens with a very simple 10 element design and a focusing range restricted to 1.9 metres. Canon has always offered a lens of this type for those who want a light 'alpine' tele-zoom, and it does reduce the weight of an all round outfit at just 520g.

EF 100-200mm *f*4.5 A

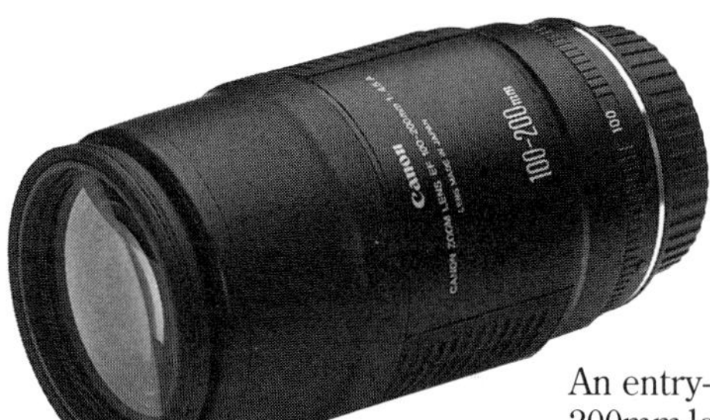

An entry-level version of the 100-200mm lens, cutting the cost even more, and omitting the manual focusing ring. Intended for owners of basic EOS models as the second lens in an outfit starting with 35-70mm A lens.

EF 80-200mm *f*2.8L

Rear focusing for high speed combines with no less than three ultra-low dispersion elements in this very fast tele zoom design. The lens is nearly apochromatic in correction, and it used by fashion and portrait photographers as well as sports, wilderness and natural history specialists. The penalty is weight, at just under 1500g.

EF 100-300mm *f*5.6
EF 100-300mm *f*5.6L

The ideal focal length range for outdoor telephotography in good light, the 100-300 is an alternative to the 70-210mm for those who need the extra focal length, but can not justify the cost of a separate 300mm lens.

The only limitation of the 100-300mm is the aperture – a constant *f*5.6, which means that good light fast film or flash will be needed for action shots. It focuses down to 2 metres, which actually means it will take a 'bigger' close-up than, for example, the 28-70mm..

The type L lens is otherwise identical in specification to the ordinary 100-300mm zoom, the 100-300mm L uses ultra-low dispersion glasses and a single crystal fluorite element. It is a near-apochromat and gives substantially better distant views at 300mm. The cost of this version is far higher than the normal 100-300mm.

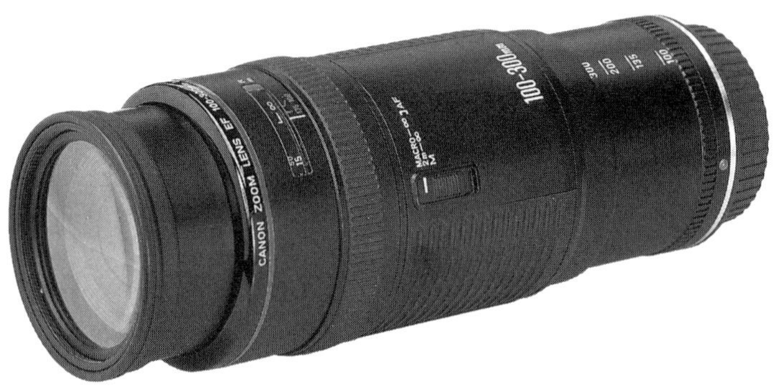

EF 100-300mm *f*4.5-5.6 USM

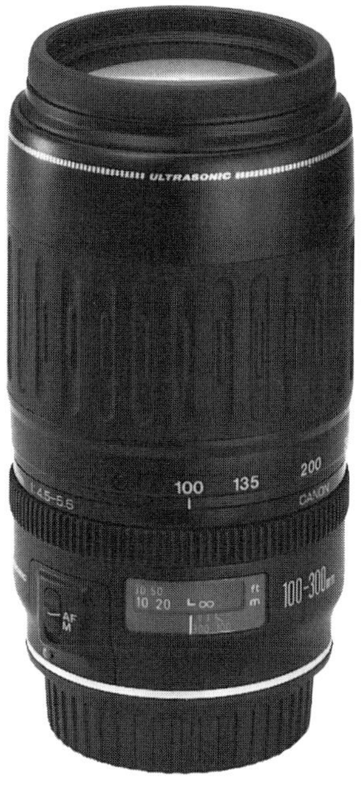

A new design of EF lens, with a faster maximum aperture at its shortest focal length, and the rapid USM focusing motor. The zoom grip has a new rubber ribbed styling which is being introduced for most EOS system lenses.

The styling of the other newer USM lenses – which are a result of Canon's developing the USM module to fit smaller lens barrels – is shown clearly in this photograph.

Future Canon lenses will probably follow this style, rather than the cosmetic finish of the existing lenses shown in this section.

You should not however feel that it is necessary to 'upgrade' lenses purely because of their cosmetic appearance. All the Canon EF series lenses are matched in performance and quality to the EOS-1 body, and in the case of the newer low-cost USM designs the optical unit may have been 'updated' to reduce weight and size rather than improve the image itself.

New Canon EF series lenses are being introduced at frequent intervals, and you should keep in touch with your dealer or photographic publications to update the information given here.

EOS-1 at-a-glance

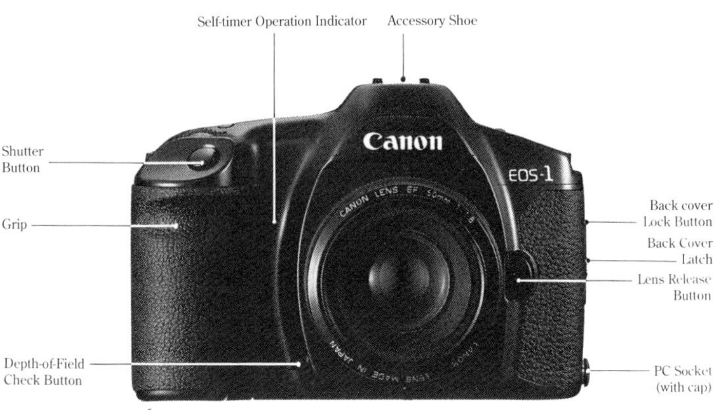

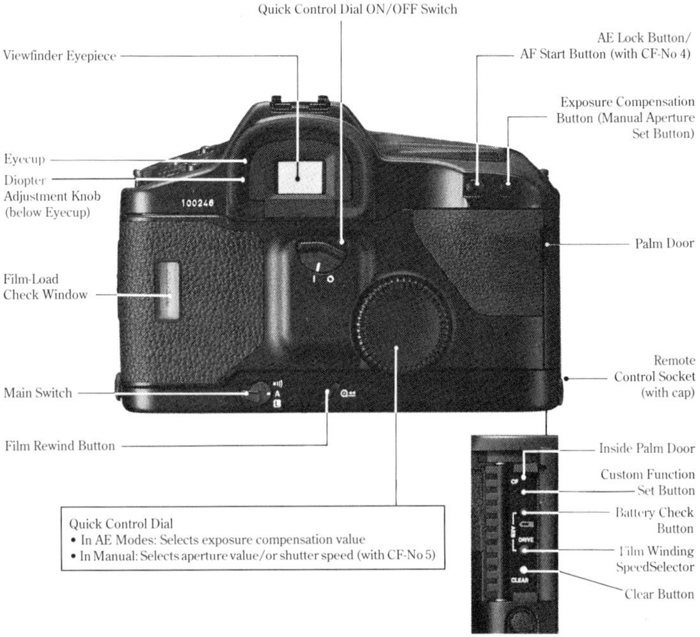

Quick Control Dial ON/OFF Switch

Viewfinder Eyepiece

AE Lock Button/ AF Start Button (with CF-No 4)

Exposure Compensation Button (Manual Aperture Set Button)

Eyecup

Diopter Adjustment Knob (below Eyecup)

Palm Door

Film-Load Check Window

Remote Control Socket (with cap)

Main Switch

Film Rewind Button

Inside Palm Door

Custom Function Set Button

Battery Check Button

Film Winding SpeedSelector

Clear Button

Quick Control Dial
- In AE Modes: Selects exposure compensation value
- In Manual: Selects aperture value/or shutter speed (with CF-No 5)

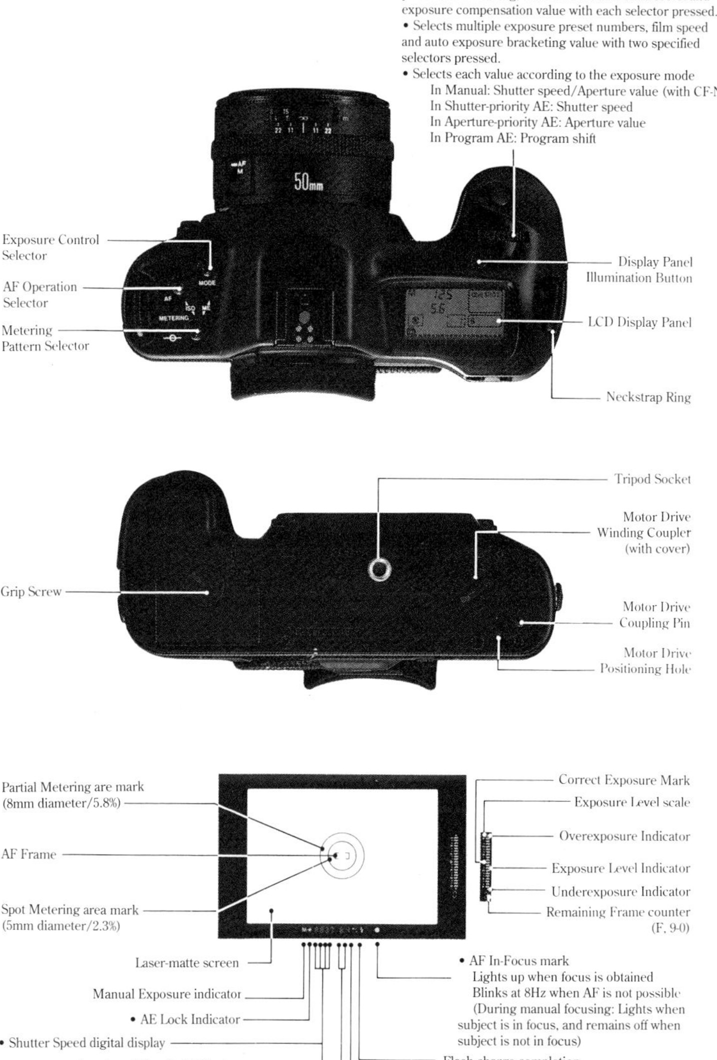

No mark – Lights Up. • Mark – lights up or blinks depending on condition. Out of exposure range – blinks at 2 Hz.

Index